BARRINGTON FAMILY LETTERS

1628–1632

BARRINGTON
FAMILY LETTERS
1628–1632

edited by
ARTHUR SEARLE

CAMDEN FOURTH SERIES
VOLUME 28

LONDON
OFFICES OF THE ROYAL HISTORICAL SOCIETY
UNIVERSITY COLLEGE LONDON,
GOWER STREET, WC1
1983

British Library Cataloguing in Publication Data

Barrington family letters, 1628–1632.—
(Camden fourth series; v.28)
1. Barrington (*Family*)
I. Searle, Arthur   II. Series
929′.2′0942   DA306.B/

ISBN 0-86193-098-3

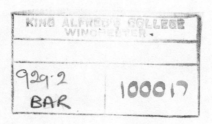

Printed and bound in Great Britain by
Butler & Tanner Ltd, Frome and London

CONTENTS

PREFACE

The letters of the Barrington family in the British Library (Egerton 2643-2651) range from c.1490 to 1713, but unequal survival within those years means that some periods are represented by far greater numbers than others. The letters for the years 1628-32 include the large group addressed to Lady Joan Barrington after the death of her husband, Sir Francis. He died in July 1628, and although she lived on until 1641 the last dated letters to her to survive (apart from two isolated examples from 1640) are from 1632; a change in her servants and so in record-keeping procedures within her household seems the most likely explanation. Most of the undated letters to her (in Eg. 2650) seem also to belong to these years; wherever possible dates have been assigned to them (with certainty or strong probability) from internal evidence, and the letters inserted in the appropriate order. Revised dates have been assigned to a small number of letters already placed in sequence in the British Library. Otherwise this edition comprises all letters in the collection from Eg. 2644, f. 275 to Eg. 2646, f. 46, together with those letters from Eg. 2650 which can be shown to belong to the years 1628-32.

The quantity of letters to Lady Joan Barrington at this period, as well as their content, indicate that she was the focal point of the extended family, the dowager and respected matriarch on a recognisable early seventeenth-century pattern.[1] As a result, the principal significance of the letters lies in what they to have to show of the nature of the family at that time, its structure and, more remarkably, the quality of the relationships it contained. Letters can be particularly revealing in this respect. Although by their nature they relate principally to the wider kin structure, not to the nuclear family, on which they usually have little light to shed, they often embody the continuation of a relationship, between parent and child (the most frequent in this case) or between servant and master, once the household has in some respect been broken up.

Among the qualifications on the use of letters as evidence for the increasingly important question of the quality of family life in seventeenth-century England are such restrictive features as class and position. For this reason in particular the introduction seeks briefly to indicate the position of the Barringtons in economic, political and religious terms at this period, as well as to summarise their earlier

[1] Cf. The Private Correspondence of Jane, Lady Cornwallis, ed. Richard Griffin, Lord Braybrooke (1842), selections from letters now E.R.O., D/DBy C11-26.

history. The survival of Lady Joan's personal account book has made possible the attempt to reconstruct something of her daily life during these years. Lastly, attention is given to the creation and history of the archive. Though the letters have unifying themes they are from diverse writers and make references to the ramifications of the Barrington and allied families. Brief biographies of the principal correspondents are appended.

I gratefully acknowledge the help in this work of Austin Woolrych, Gordon Forster and Ian Roy, of my former colleagues at the Essex Record Office (particularly Nancy Briggs) and my present colleagues at the British Library, and of the many whom I first met when they were researching seventeenth century subjects in the archives at Chelmsford, among them Brian Quintrell, Christopher Thompson, Alan Macfarlane, Clive Holmes, Jim Sharpe and especially Richard Dunn, whose continued encouragement, advice and sharing of ideas I value most of all. All errors are entirely my responsibility.

ARTHUR SEARLE

ABBREVIATIONS

Place of publication London unless otherwise stated

A.P.C.	*Acts of the Privy Council*
B.L.	British Library
Birch	T. Birch, *The Court and Times of Charles I*, 1848.
Bodl.	Bodleian Library, Oxford
C.S.P.D.	*Calendar of State Papers, Domestic*
C.S.P.Col.	*Calendar of State Papers, Colonial*
Colvin	R. B. Colvin, *Lieutenants and Keepers of the Rolls of the County of Essex*, 1934
D.N.B.	*Dictionary of National Biography*
Dahl	F. Dahl, *A Bibliography of English Corantos and Periodical Newsbooks*, 1925. References are to item numbers
Eg.	British Library, Egerton MS.
E.R.O.	Essex Record Office
Foster	J. Foster, *Alumni Oxonienses*, Oxford, 1891
Gardiner	S. R. Gardiner, *History of England from the accession of James I to the outbreak of the Civil War*, 1883-4.
G.E.C., *Baronetage*	*Complete Baronetage*, 1901-1909
G.E.C., *Peerage*	G.E.C., ed. V. Gibbs and others, *The Complete Peerage*, 1910-1955
Hunts. R.O.	Huntingdonshire Record Office
I.O.W.R.O.	Isle of Wight Record Office
Keeler	M. F. Keeler, *The Long Parliament*, Philadelphia, 1954
M. of P.	*Return of the names of every member returned to serve in each parliament*, 1878
Morant	P. Morant, *The History and Antiquities of the County of Essex*, 1768
n.d.	not dated
Noble	M. Noble, *Memoires of the Protectoral-House of Cromwell*, Birmingham, 1787
P.R.O.	Public Record Office
Roberts	M. Roberts, *Gustavus Adolphus*, 1953, 1958
Smith	H. Smith, *The Ecclesiastical History of Essex*, Colchester, [1933]

T.E.A.S.,
n.s., i, ii

William Clayton, ed. G. A. Lowndes, 'The History of the Barrington Family', *Transactions of the Essex Archaeological Society*, new series, i. 251–275 and ii. 3–54, Colchester, 1878, 1884.

V.C.H.

Victoria County History (with county and volume number)

Venn

J. and J. A. Venn, *Alumni Cantabrigienses*, Cambridge, 1922

Visitations of Essex

W. C. Metcalfe, *Visitations of Essex*, Harleian Society, xiii, 1878

INTRODUCTION

Much has been made of the fluctuating fortunes of gentry families in the sixteenth century.[1] Some would say too much, since the gentry as a class is recognisable but not clearly definable. Amid the flurry of speculation about the factors which might be responsible, geographical location was by all accounts important, so that the Barringtons, who were undoubted gentry, were lucky to find themselves firmly rooted in south-east England. But that was an ancient piece of luck; when Robert, Lord Rich supported Sir Francis Barrington in the parliamentary election of 1604 he wrote of 'the aunciente name of Barrington ... whose auncestors I canne averre to be knightes before Englishe was in England, or anie name of knightes that I knowe were in the countrye, that nowe make greate shew and are newe comers in amonge us ...'[2] The Barrington ancestry can indeed be traced back before the conquest. Then, from at least the time of Henry I, they held the hereditary office of woodward or forester of Hatfield Forest and lived at Barrington Hall, on the edge of the forest in the north of the parish of Hatfield Broad Oak in north west Essex.[3]

A later stroke of fortune—and though few details are known, 'luck' can hardly be the right term this time—was the marriage between Thomas Barrington and Winifred Hastings in 1559.[4] By this one alliance wealth and status were secured to nourish the ancient gentry of the Barringtons. Winifred, the widow of Sir Thomas Hastings, was born Winifred Pole, one of the two daughters and co-heiresses of Henry Pole, Lord Montagu; therefore, as well as the niece of Cardinal Pole, she was the granddaughter of Margaret Plantagenet, Countess of Salisbury, and the great-granddaughter of George, Duke of Clarence, brother of Edward IV. Through her the Barringtons were able to elaborate the quarterings of their arms to include the royal arms of England.[5] Her elder sister Katharine had married Francis, second

[1] This introduction is a shortened version of that which appears in the present writer's 'Letters of the Barrington Family, 1628–32' (M.Phil. thesis, University of Leeds, 1982). A more detailed and more fully annotated account, in particular of the growth and value of the family estate, will be found there.

[2] Eg. 2644, f. 151.

[3] *T.E.A.S.*, n.s., i. 252, 253.

[4] *T.E.A.S.*, n.s., ii. 8.

[5] E.R.O., D/DQs 45. Francis Quarles, who was godson to Sir Francis Barrington, considered descent from the Barringtons to be enough to fill even 'Th'insatiate vastnesse of an Heraults tongue'. Quarles, *Hosanna and Threnodes*, ed. J. Horden, (Liverpool, 1960), 27.

Earl of Huntingdon, so Winifred brought to her marriage not only
the Pole tradition of loyalty to the old faith, which was hardly in
accord with the religious temper of the Barringtons, but also a
connection with the active puritanism of the second and third earls
of Huntingdon. More important by far, her first marriage had
been childless, so that she also brought to the Barringtons her share
of her grandmother's estates, granted to the two sisters when first
Mary and then Elizabeth effectively reversed the attainder on the
Countess.

How the Barringtons rationalised their vastly increased landholdings is explained below; essentially, however, they remained an Essex
family. They gave up the medieval office of forester and in its place
gradually assumed the various duties of county government which
formed the new route to power in the land: sheriff, justice of the peace,
deputy lieutenant, member of parliament. Sir Thomas achieved all of
these positions except deputy lieutenant. The eldest of his and Winifred's sons, Francis, occupied this position as well, and was able to
miss out the more onerous first stage of sheriff. Francis was knighted
by James I in 1603 and created baronet in the second patent of 1611.
It was also Sir Francis and his children who, by their marriages, built
up the Barrington 'connection', that alliance of puritan and politically
like-minded families which has been held typical of the parliamentary
gentry of England on the eve of the civil war.[1] It is largely the domestic
affections of this group of kin which are illuminated by the section of
the Barrington correspondence presented here.

Lady Joan Barrington, the recipient of most of these letters, entered
the family in 1579, when, as Joan Cromwell, she married Francis
Barrington.[2] She was one of the eleven children of Sir Henry Cromwell
of Hinchinbrook, so that in time she had among her nephews Oliver
Cromwell, John Hampden, Oliver St. John and the regicide Edward
Whalley. The children of Francis and Joan and the ramifications of
the alliances they made are set out in Table 3. Besides their political
significance, almost without exception they reflect and reinforce the
general religious puritanism which Francis and Joan, prompted no
doubt by upbringing as well as inclination, erected into an unshake-
able family principle.

---

[1] J. H. Hexter, *The Reign of King Pym* (Cambridge, Mass., 1961), 78.
[2] E.R.O., D/DHt T126/23. This is the marriage settlement. Only a single fragment
of the early parish register of Hatfield Broad Oak survives, so that precise dates of
marriage, baptism and burial of members of the family are often in doubt.

The Barringtons in the seventeenth century

(a) *Estates*

Because of the lack of a surviving coherent series of estate surveys and
accounts, details of the Barrington family's landholdings have to be
pieced together from an incomplete set of deeds and from fragments
of steward's rough papers. Even so, the main pattern for the sixteenth
and early seventeenth centuries is clear: a loosely-knit estate accumulated over a long period of local marriage alliances in south-east
England was transformed by the addition of the Countess of Salisbury's estates, brought into the family by the marriage of Thomas
Barrington with Lady Winifred Hastings.

In the middle of the fifteenth century the family held their ancient
seat of Barrington Hall together with three other manors in Essex, two
in Hertfordshire and one each in Cambridgeshire and Suffolk.[1] Lady
Winifred was able to add all of the estates granted to her in 1554 at
the reversal of the attainder on her grandmother: four manors (and
two advowsons) in Yorkshire, two manors in the Isle of Wight, two in
Buckinghamshire, the manor and half-hundred jurisdiction of Clavering in Essex, and one manor each in Hertfordshire, Lincolnshire
and Monmouthshire.[2]

Sir Thomas Hastings died in 1558. Thomas Barrington and Lady
Winifred were married the following year. Soon afterwards the con-
solidation of the estate began. Distant isolated (and unprofitable)
property was sold off; in 1566 Thomas Barrington purchased the site
and manor of the priory of Hatfield Broad Oak.[3] This moved the
family's interests from the periphery to the centre of their large home
parish. With the priory came the lease, from Trinity College, Cambridge, of the major part of the tithes of Hatfield Broad Oak; the
importance of the lease to the family shows up in the protracted
negotiations for its renewal in 1606.[4] The purchase of the priory
together with the ownership of Clavering (very close to Hatfield)
made a valuable group of holdings. From this fact stems the
seventeenth-century pattern of a consolidated holding in Essex—the
half-hundred being a real basis for political power in addition to the
influence by patronage that ordinary landownership could give—with
the other estates derived from the Countess of Salisbury pared away
to the two main elements in Yorkshire and the Isle of Wight.

Nonetheless, the principal properties in Hatfield, the manor and
the forest, still belonged to Lord Rich, the chief beneficiary in Essex

[1] E.R.O., D/DBa F7.
[2] *Calendar of Patent Rolls, 1553-4*, 147-8
[3] B.L., Add. Ch. 28634, 28635.
[4] Eg. 2644, ff. 157-165.

from the post-Reformation changes in landownership. The forest in particular was a constant source of dispute—between Rich, Barrington, lesser landowners and the commoners—especially after an arbitration of 1576 gave the Barringtons the right to make enclosures in the forest in return for the surrender of their office of forester. The presence of Lady Winifred, an aristocratic outsider, did not help, and the new social and economic pretensions of the Barringtons were attributed directly to her.[1] Those pretensions suffered a blow in 1592 when Rich sold the forest to Lord Morley, whose manor of Great Hallingbury lay close by. Tensions with the Morley family were only eased by a further arbitration of 1615 which enabled the Barringtons to lease the soil of their enclosures within the forest, an arrangement which suited the major landowners although it prejudiced the commoners by effectively reducing their legal rights.[2] But by this time good relations between Rich and Barrington had been established. In 1608 Lord Rich leased the manor house (Hatfield Bury) and a large part of the demesne lands to Sir Francis Barrington's kinsman and servant, Richard Hildersham.[3] In 1611, besides taking the commoners to the court of Chancery over the forest, Sir Francis seems to have moved from Barrington Hall to the Priory House in the centre of the parish, making this henceforth the principal family residence. That same year the entire Barrington estate was subject to re-settlement on the first marriage of Sir Thomas Barrington, then in 1612 Sir Francis purchased the manor of Hatfield outright from Lord Rich for £8,000.[4] The basis of the Essex estate was complete.

The estates retained in the Isle of Wight and in Yorkshire were substantial. The Isle of Wight property included land in six parishes, rights over wrecks cast up on the shores of the manors, royalties on hunting in Elmsworth Park and for most of the period ensured election to at least one of the parliamentary seats for the borough of Newtown. Writing in the 1630s Sir John Oglander thought Swainston the best manor in the island. He resented Sir Thomas Barrington as an absentee landlord: 'He liveth in Essex, doth no service here and skimmeth away the cream of our country'.[5] Another islander, Sir John Dingley, had urged Sir Thomas Barrington to take up residence in the island when he was contemplating the purchase of Carisbrooke Park in 1629. Dingley held out the prospect that the ownership of the park as well as Swainston would make Sir Thomas a strong candidate for the office

[1] E.R.O., D/DB T16/2,3; D. Shorrocks, 'Hatfield Forest, 1547-1857', *Essex Review*, lxiv (1955), 57; P.R.O., C2. Jas. I, B9.2(1).

[2] E.R.O., D/DBa T8/16.

[3] E.R.O., D/DU 472/7; Northumberland R.O., Alnwick MSS. XII.7. Box 2b.

[4] E.R.O., D/DB L1/3/7.

[5] F. Bamford, *A Royalist's Notebook* (1936), 137.

of Captain of the island. Sir Thomas purchased the park in March 1631, principally persuaded by the reported value of the standing timber.[1] In August Lord Treasurer Weston, the newly appointed Captain, arrived and ordered a stop on the felling and sale of timber from the park so that it could be available to repair the defences of the island. He was enthusiastically supported in carrying out the order by the deputy lieutenants, Sir John Oglander and Sir Edward Dennys. Sir Thomas found it necessary to visit the island himself in September, and he and his wife spent anxious months in the early summer of 1632 politicking in London to secure the park's re-purchase by the crown. He finally escaped from the venture in December 1632 when the timber sales he had contracted were allowed and the park was re-purchased.[2]

Cottingham, in the East Riding, was the most valuable of the Yorkshire manors, with Wintringham Park and a rent from the town of Hull for water supply among its assets.[3] This was retained. Lesser manors were sold off in the seventeenth century, but the advowsons were important to a family of the Barrington's religious persuasion and allowed them to protect, at least temporarily, Ezekiel Rogers and Thomas Shepard.

The circumstances of Sir Thomas Barrington's two marriages meant that two more elements were administered with these three main parts of the estate during most of the period covered by the correspondence. As a result of the early death of his first wife, Gobert lands in Leicestershire and property in St. Anne, Blackfriars, London, came to the family while John Barrington was a minor. In a similar way Sir Thomas and Lady Judith, his second wife, had control of the wardship of her two sons by her first marriage and so of the Smith estates in Hertfordshire and Lincolnshire.[4] Lady Judith was an assiduous business-woman, increasingly taking over the administration of the entire Barrington estate in the 1630s as Sir Thomas became more involved in political affairs. She lavished great care on the Hertfordshire property. She turned to the matter before her second marriage and had soon paid off most of the debts incurred by her first husband. Both of her sons, for whom it must be assumed all this effort was undertaken, died before her so that in the 1640s she received the entire income from her Smith jointure lands. In 1621 Lady Judith had estimated the Hertfordshire and Lincolnshire property to be worth £685 p.a.; a fragment of an account of her 'private estate' drawn up

[1] I.O.W.R.O., SW 227, 241, 242, 244, 247, 248.
[2] I.O.W.R.O., OG 16/4, 50; letters 246-248.
[3] E.R.O., D/DBa E10; V.C.H., *Yorks.*, East Riding, i (Hull), 371-72.
[4] E.R.O., D/DBa E60, L18, Z11 and D/DK T111; V.C.H., *Herts.*, ii. 199-200.

by the steward John Kendal shows the extraordinary figure of £3,498 as income for the period from November 1641 to July 1642, though this apparently included return on money invested in a merchant venture.[1]

The vexed question of the value of the three basic elements of the estate would be far from simple even if complete accounts survived. One very rough account, which simply totals income as four items each year for the years 1636–41 without identifying the source of the sums, produces an annual average of £2,895.[2] With all due allowance made, other fragmentary sources point to a remarkably similar figure, so that it seems safe, even conservative, to say that the basic family estate produced something like £3,000 annually in the 1630s.

Jointures, wardships, dowagers, not to mention the constant stream of law-suits, could increase or decrease the total. During the years covered by the letters, and beyond, Lady Joan was plagued by a long-running dispute with George Fenn, the tenant of Clavering Bury Farm and her bailiff in Clavering. Clavering was part of Lady Joan's jointure. The complicated series of trust deeds which accomplished the settlement on Sir Thomas Barrington's first marriage in 1611 renewed that jointure and also gave her a life interest in the main Hatfield manors; Sir Thomas's wife, who brought a portion of £3,000, had Barrington Hall and the lesser Hatfield manors as her jointure. Despite this, the effect of the trust deeds was to settle the whole estate on the family and its main line of descent as securely as was legally possible at that time. The trust was apparently renewed when Sir Thomas married again in 1624, though direct evidence is lacking. However, there do survive deeds of a further complex series of trusts created by Sir Thomas from 1636 onwards, as part of which transaction the ageing Lady Joan surrendered to the trustees her life interest in most of her jointure and in the Hatfield manors. The initial trustees included Oliver St. John's servant John Thurloe (later to be the Commonwealth and Protectorate Secretary of State), and it is easy to see St. John as the adviser in the legal processes. What appears to be the final trust in the series, broken and re-made on the marriage of Sir John Barrington in 1640, had among its trustees St. John himself, John Pym and Lord Mandeville (Earl of Manchester from 1642): here was the Barrington political connection at work socially.[3]

Trusts and law suits together protected the Barrington estates in the long and the short run. But even after Lady Joan had made over her principal jointure properties to Sir Thomas's use under the trust, her

[1] E.R.O., D/DBa A41/3.
[2] E.R.O., D/DBa A41/4.
[3] E.R.O., D/DHt T126/36, 37, 39, 40, 43, 59, D/DU 472/14 and D/DA T177.

income must have been the largest variable affecting the yearly sum at the disposal of the head of the family. Right up to her death in 1641 she retained the lease of the tithes of Hatfield Broad Oak, bequeathed to her by Sir Francis. Her annual income for 1628–38 averaged £1,237, a sum which included rent for tithes from the Hatfield properties of her sons Sir Thomas and Robert, payments from the estate which would not have been made under other circumstances.[1]

(b) *Politics*

In Elizabeth's reign the first Sir Thomas Barrington established a clear role for his family in local administration, very much as he established its social and financial position. He was twice sheriff of Essex (1562 and 1580), a justice of the peace, if not a particularly regular attender at quarter sessions, from 1564 until his death in 1580, and was elected as second knight of the shire to the parliament of 1572.[2] He died before parliament was summoned again; the fruits of the family's political status, as of their wealth, were left for his son Sir Francis Barrington to enjoy.

Francis joined the commission of the peace in 1586, becoming one of the county's more active magistrates as well as a member of the bench for the borough sessions at Saffron Walden. In 1601, on being appointed one of the muster commissioners for Essex, he was 'a gentleman that her Majestie doth favorably regarde both for being of honnorable bloud and for the sondry good services which he doth her in the contry where he resideth . . .' That same year Francis was elected to parliament as a knight of the shire for Essex, in the second place which his father had occupied. At his accession James I ended the muster commission for Essex by appointing the Earl of Sussex as Lord Lieutenant of the county; as one of Sussex's deputies, Barrington was securely placed among the élite at the head of the county's administrative structure.[3]

The election of 1604 demonstrates the extent to which Sir Francis had developed a political commitment in opposition to the court and to which a political consciousness had grown up within county society. From at least this time forward Barrington clearly represented a party, for so it was termed. He occupied the second place as knight of the shire once more, precedence going to the court candidate only on the

[1] E.R.O., D/DBa A15, ff. 1–7 (end reversed).
[2] Colvin, 181–182; J. Samaha, *Law and Order in Historical Perspective* (1974), 151; *T.E.A.S.*, n.s., ii. 7.
[3] E.R.O., T/A 401/2, D/DBa 013A; Colvin, 55–56; *A.P.C., 1601–4*, 264; B.W. Quintrell, 'The Government of the County of Essex, 1603–1642' (Ph.D. thesis, University of London, 1965).

throw of a dice; the first place was his in every subsequent parliament in his lifetime except that of 1614.[1] The importance of the alliance between Lord Rich and Sir Francis emerges clearly from this election. The association between the two families (the Riches becoming Earls of Warwick in 1618) was to govern the course of county politics, without any serious rupture, until the middle 1640s.

The keystone to Francis Barrington's reputation as a champion of faith and freedom was set in place by his opposition to the crown in the parliament of 1626 and in the succeeding matter of the forced loan. With this he earned near martyrdom and eulogistic praise after his death. In the wake of the rupture in parliament between Buckingham and the puritan party the Earl of Warwick was relieved of his position as Lord Lieutenant and struck out of the commission of the peace in September 1626; at the same time Sir Francis was deprived of his positions as deputy and J.P.[2] The stage was set for strong action by the crown. A proclamation for a new loan was issued on 8 October. Essex was to be included, despite heavy military expenditure borne in 1625. The detailed commission for the county issued on 20 October revealed just how swiftly and widely the council intended the loan to be collected; the commissioners were chosen from a broad section of county society and as well as the deprived justices and ex-M.P.s it included the recusant Lord Petre.[3] The commissioners met at Romford on Tuesday 25 October where all except Sir Francis Barrington and Sir William Masham complied. They were brought before the Council on Wednesday 26th, where they refused the oath to be examined as to their reasons for not subscribing; that same evening Sir Francis was committed to the Marshalsea prison and his son-in-law to the Fleet.[4]

The government continued to meet opposition. Another Essex commissioner, Sir Harbottle Grimston, was imprisoned in February 1627. On 5 March it was ordered that a hundred men should be pressed into the army from the county and that fifty of them should be drawn from a named group of loan resisters. The frightened deputies appealed for help to their absent Lord Lieutenant, but in the mean time summoned the listed resisters from the county town of Chelmsford to appear before them during the assize sitting there on 13 March. Seven men appeared, no longer from the governing community of the county but prosperous townsmen, and all seven refused to take the press

---

[1] Eg. 2644, ff.130–153; M. E. Bohannon, 'The Essex Election of 1604', *English Historical Review*, xlviii (1933), 395–413; C. Thompson, 'The Third Lord Rich and the Essex Election of 1604', *Essex Journal*, xiv (1979), 2–6.

[2] B.L., Harl. 390, f. 123; Bodl., Firth C4, p. 247.

[3] *Ibid*. pp. 249–66.

[4] *A.P.C., June–Dec. 1626*, 328; *C.S.P.D., 1625–6*, 469.

money. They were arrested on 14 March. The Council even considered executing them under martial law, but eventually their case was referred to Star Chamber and they were retained in custody.[1]

Clearly the government had gone too far. In the summer the prisoners were removed from London to restricted liberty in counties other than their own. Sir Francis had lived in the Marshalsea in conditions which would also allow the presence of his wife and of his daughter Lady Ruth Lamplugh; nevertheless his petition of June 1627 for release had blamed close imprisonment for his weak physical state. The physician's certificate accompanying the petition claimed that prison endangered his life, and this was the general report: he was said to be 'in so deep a consumption (having sucked a woman's breast these five weeks) that he is not likely to ... live long'. He was granted liberty for the county of Surrey, but was only well enough to move to 'a garden house' in Southwark.[2]

The king finally extended clemency as a 'new year's gift' for all the loan prisoners, the Council ordering their release on 2 January 1628. Rumour of an impending election followed swiftly. The strength of feeling in Essex in favour of the released men, which can only have been increased by the renewed billeting of soldiers in the county, can be judged from the report that 12,000 freeholders hurried to Stratford in support of Barrington and Grimston on a rumour that the sheriff was attempting to hold a secret election there. This was in February, before even the election writs had been issued. The knights of the shire were eventually chosen on 3 March, at 'our famous election in Essex, where Sir Francis Barrington and Sir Harbottle Grimston had all the voices of 15,000 men, those who say least, and were there 10,000 freeholders'. Masham was elected at Colchester by the ordinary burgesses against the wishes of the bailiffs, aldermen and common council. This disputed election was upheld by the commons when Sir Francis, in one of his first actions as an M.P., presented his son-in-law's case to the Committee of Privileges.[3]

Sir Francis Barrington lived only until July 1628. It is in the context of the events of his last years that he was described as one who 'haith shutt upp his dayes with honor and reputacion', 'the comfort of his country', 'one of the mirrors of our tyme', and was still 'renouned' forty years after his death.[4]

[1] Bodl., Firth C4, pp. 298–300; *A.P.C.*, *Jan–Aug, 1627*, 130 *et seq.*; Birch, i. 206–208. I am grateful to Miss H. E. P. Grieve for allowing me access to her research on the history of Chelmsford.

[2] *T.E.A.S.*, n.s., ii. 23; B.L., Harl. 390, f. 273; *A.P.C. Jan–Aug, 1627*, 346–47.

[3] Birch, i. 323; B.L., Harl. 390, f. 361 and Harl. 6799, ff. 228, 324; *Journals of the House of Commons*, i. 876–77.

[4] Letters 3, 7; Giles Firmin, *The Real Christian* (1670), epistle dedicatory.

Both Sir Thomas Barrington and his younger brother Robert sat in the parliament of 1628 with their father, as the members for the borough of Newtown in the Isle of Wight. Sir Thomas was already an experienced parliamentarian, having represented the borough on four previous occasions. As a sitting member in 1628 he was unable to take his father's seat for Essex, which went to Robert, Lord Rich, Warwick's son. It was not until 1640 and the Short Parliament that Sir Thomas was able to take his rightful place as the first knight of the shire. Locally too, he was slow to fill the role expected of him. He was first put into the commission of the peace in 1624 and appears scarcely to have acted at all before being excluded from office over the loan question. He was a justice of the peace for the county once more by the end of 1628, but was in London during the first part of 1629 so again can hardly have been active. In the summer of 1629 Sir William Masham observed that 'My brother ... begines now to affect our countrye business', urging Lady Joan to encourage her son's new involvement in local affairs.[1] By the autumn of 1630 the demands of estate management and a natural melancholy were finally set aside and Sir Thomas became properly active at quarter sessions and in the divisional meetings of justices.

His action followed hard on the heels of the issue of the printed 'Book of Orders', and the Privy Council's strongest appeal for more strictness in local government, in September 1630. Sir Thomas's involvement is apparent from his correspondence with his wife's kinsman, Lord Dorchester, the Secretary of State. There Barrington professed 'an honest hart to devote my selfe to serve his Majesty, the State and perticularly my owne County that I reside in'.[2] There may in fact have been some criticism of Sir Thomas's earlier neglect of county business. After illness had kept him at home during the summer of 1631, Lady Judith was prompted to approach Dorchester once more, expressing fears that her husband's period of forced inactivity might lead 'some unfrendly neighbours to take advantage in nominating him Sheriff, before itt be longe. His father was considered of in this kinde all his time to be free, spending much yearly in the countie's service, and his time taken up in being Deputy Lieftenant; the same reasons may be for his sonne.' But, she added, 'as longe as we are under your Lordship's protection, wee shall take the presumption to be the more secure'; that protection was effective, for the onerous office was indeed avoided.[3]

Sir Thomas Barrington's character was markedly different from

[1] P.R.O., Index 4211, f. 168v; E.R.O., Q/SR 263/93; letters 29, 44.
[2] P.R.O., S.P. 16/168/50.
[3] P.R.O., S.P. 16/205/83; letters 213, 215.

that of his father, more hesitant, introspective, artistic – conceited too, in his later days of pre-eminence in the county, if Lionel Cranfield's business associate is to be believed[1] – nor was he able to make so strong an impact. But gradually after the death of Sir Francis he extended the scope of his activities outside the county as well as within it. In January 1631 he was admitted to the Providence Island company of which he was deputy governor from May 1631 (with Warwick's brother, the Earl of Holland, as governor); his letter from London in June, where he writes that he is 'solicited so much as that I hardly know my owne strength' marks his (perhaps rather surprised) entry into the political puritanism of his generation, deeply contrasted to his father's more heroic brand, which was a remnant of the era of his kinsmen Huntingdon and Hastings.[2]

How much Sir Thomas was expected to play a leading part in local administration is shown by Masham's relieved comment when this finally took place. His involvement gave him the vital experience and the indispensable trust of all parties within the county which allowed him successfully to assume the leadership of the community and its committee in the early years of the civil war. Personal temperament and the general change in political circumstances brought Sir Thomas Barrington less into conflict with the court than his father until the meeting of the Long Parliament. His confident assumption of leadership and his able assertion of the county's independence after the outbreak of war are all the more remarkable.

(c) *Religion*

The marriage between Francis Barrington and Joan Cromwell was a union of Godly spirits, a cornerstone of the puritan connection in parliament in the 1620s. In the Barrington family puritanism went back at least one generation further, to the first Sir Thomas; he possessed the 'precious pearle of love of God's word ... so that the heat thereof flameth out, to the benefit of many dwelling ... in those partes of Essex, by reason of that godly exercise of preaching ...'[3] His wife, Lady Winifred, was thought to have had other opinions. Her husband's death came at precisely the time when increased action was being taken against catholics in the localities, and she was among the first recusants to be presented at quarter sessions in Essex in July 1581, for not attending church. However, the process was not pursued and

---

[1] Kent County Archives, Sackville MSS (U).

[2] *C.S.P.Col.*, *1547–1660*, 147; letter 186.

[3] Moses Wilton, *The Sermons of Master Ralfe Gualter upon the Prophet Zaphaniah* (1580), epistle dedicatory. Wilton, rector of Fleet in Lincolnshire from 1582, was the son-in-law of William Josselin, a substantial yeoman landowner of Hatfield Broad Oak. E.R.O., D/ABW 21/177 and D/DBa F13/1.

after October 1582 she ceased to be presented. Sir Thomas Barrington passed on his religious opinions and fervour to his son Francis. He is supposed to have converted his mother, who lived on until 1602, celebrating the achievement by having her gold crucifix melted down and made into rings, each engraved with an inscription appropriately contrasting 'false Devotion' with 'true Religion'.[1]

Whatever Lady Winifred's own religious affiliations may have been, she brought the Barrington's other connections which could only strengthen their growing puritanism. At the end of his life, Sir Francis Hastings showed considerable respect for his cousin, Sir Francis Barrington. By that time the younger man had proved his opinions and beliefs in the commons in 1604 as well as in the petitioning of the king out of parliament, events in which Hastings was himself very much involved. A petition to the king from west Essex, in 1604, led to the appearance before the Privy Council of Richard Hildersham, who was Sir Francis Barrington's steward, and kinsman to both Hastings and Barrington.[2]

The parliament of 1626, the loan and imprisonment were the ultimate public demonstrations of Sir Francis Barrington's commitment. The private background can be drawn only from fragments of information. During his imprisonment in the Marshalsea he heard two sermons each Sunday. He regarded Archbishop Ussher, the adviser and support within the church of two generations of moderate puritans, as his 'most noble friend'. Both Ussher and his chaplain Nicholas Bernard preached sermons at Hatfield.[3] A number of puritan divines dedicated works to Sir Francis. Some linked him with other members of the family. Robert Yarrow dedicated a work jointly to Sir Francis and Lady Joan, John Wing chose Sir Francis, Sir Thomas, and Sir William Masham.[4] Thomas Barnes indicated a more inclusive puritan community: within his collection of sermons *Needful Helpes: against Desperate Perplexitie* of 1624 one is dedicated to Sir Francis, Sir Thomas Eliot and Sir Nathaniel Barnardiston, another to their wives, and to Mrs Joanna Mildmay of Terling Hall, 'the joy of the justified, in Christ the justifier, wished'. Adam Harsnett chose Lady Joan and her widowed kinswoman, Lady Mary Eden, as dedicatees of his *Cordiall for the Afflicted* in 1632.

Although the Barringtons did not own the living of Hatfield Broad Oak, they were able to exercise some patronage in their own parish:

[1] E.R.O., Q/SR 78/46, 79/89, 82/53; *T.E.A.S.*, n.s., ii. 10.

[2] Eg. 2644, f. 172; B.L., Add. 38492; Smith, 19, 20.

[3] B.L., Harl. 390, f. 192; Eg. 2644, ff. 236, 250; E.R.O., D/DBa F5/1.

[4] Robert Yarrow, *Soveraigne Comforts for a Troubled Conscience* (1619); John Wing, *The Saints Advantage* (1624).

for over thirty years before the beginning of the civil war there was a town lecturer supported by the family, and at various times they also had a chaplain in their household. The first lecturer we know of was John Huckle. He was in Hatfield before 1600 and in 1605 he was licensed to preach as lecturer there without subscription, as the result of a letter from unnamed patrons, carried to London by the vicar. When he died in Hatfield in 1625 he was a minor landowner with £300 to dispose of.[1] James Harrison was appointed lecturer, in succession to Huckle, in 1626, and it was as 'lecturer in Sir Thomas Barrington's parish' that he was in trouble with the ecclesiastical authorities in 1636–7, for curtailing the set form of prayers in favour of a sermon four hours long.[2] For some years Harrison also filled the role of domestic chaplain, with responsibilities to the family as well as the town, although he did not live at the Priory. It was during Huckle's time as lecturer, in 1610, that the redoubtable Ezekiel Rogers entered the Barrington household as chaplain. He was the son of Richard Rogers, the lecturer at Wethersfield, and a cousin of John Rogers the Dedham lecturer. Rogers was only twenty years old when he went to live with the Barringtons at Hatfield. There he was able 'not only to *do good* by his profitable preaching, but also to *get good* by his conversation with persons of honor . . . , and he *knew* and *used* his opportunity to the utmost'. His early letters to Lady Joan from Yorkshire are touchingly imploring, written with 'faithfullest affections' and with spiritual epistolary contact depicted in physical imagery: 'I shoulde then know how to apply my selfe to your estate if I had but your hand to feele your pulse . . .' He was clearly much affected by her, 'the first with whom I had any so serious and solemne converse about matters tending to the worke of grace . . .'[3]

The Barringtons' direct patronage was limited to their two Yorkshire livings. When Rogers left Hatfield it was to accept Sir Francis's gift of the living of Rowley 'in hopes that his more lively ministry might be particularly successful in awakening those drowsy corners of the north'.[4] He held the living until 1638, when he left for New England. Rogers had been welcomed in Yorkshire as a 'carfull and faithfull . . . pastor'; the words are those of William Chantrell, rector of Walkington, the other living in the gift of the Barringtons. He too may have been a chaplain in the Barrington household, though this can only have been for a short time. His faithful service at Walkington

---

[1] Greater London R.O., D/LC 338, ff. 203b, 217b; P.R.O., Prob. 11/45; P. Collinson, *The Elizabethan Puritan Movement* (1967), 379; E.R.O., D/ABW 21/177.

[2] Eg. 2644, f. 230; Smith, 49, 55.

[3] Cotton Mather, *Magnalia Christi Americana* (Hertford, Connecticut, 1858), i. 408–413; Eg. 2644, ff. 196, 203.

[4] Mather, i. 409.

lasted from 1616 to 1643, with only occasional brushes with the
authorities over his religious views.[1]

Two letters indicate the respect which Lady Joan Barrington commanded in the puritan establishment in Essex as well as the continuing
strength of the connection between the Rich and Barrington families.
In 1631 Sir Gilbert Gerard suggested that she might be able to
influence the way in which the Earl of Warwick disposed of one of the
livings in his patronage. On another occasion Warwick assured her 'I
had sooner taken your recommendation then all the bishops in this
kingdom'.[2] Lady Joan's account book reveals regular support for
James Harrison, frequent presents to George Wilson, the vicar of
Elsenham (near enough for him to assist at Hatfield Broad Oak),
occasional gifts to other local clergymen, such as Jeremiah Dyke at
Epping and Stephen Marshall at Finchingfield, and gifts to puritan
writers like Adam Harsnett and Arthur Hildersham. In addition she
made gifts in time of trouble to some notable puritan clergy in the
county: in 1629 she gave money to Richard Blackerby, the father-in-
law and teacher of Samuel Fairclough, Thomas Hooker received help
when he was being hounded from the county in 1630, and Nathaniel
Ward was given £5 in 1634, after he had been deprived of his living
at Stondon Massey and shortly before he left for Massachusetts.[3]

However, by far the largest single gift made by Lady Joan to any
clergyman went to the very un-puritan Leonard Mawe, bishop of
Bath and Wells and master of Trinity College, Cambridge. The occasion was the renewal after Sir Francis Barrington's death of the lease
from the college of the tithes of Hatfield. Tension was bound to arise
from a position whereby the controlling family supported their own
clergy, could not influence appointments to the living, and yet had a
financial interest in it. In a dispute with a neighbour in 1626 Sir
Francis defended the disparity between the low value of the vicarage
and the income from his own tithes as lessee of the parsonage: 'Yow
must give the colledge and their farmors leave to dispose of their owne
and not take upon you to determine that which is not yours to
dispose'.[4] He added that he would willingly contribute to the maintenance of the vicar, but as a parishioner only. Others were expected
to do the same. When in June 1629 Harrison was visiting Lady Joan
in Harrow, a number of parishioners went to High Laver to hear a
more puritan sermon than Francis Parker, the vicar of Hatfield, could

[1] Eg. 2644, f. 201; R. A. Marchant, *The Puritans and the Church Courts, 1560–1640* (1960),
63, 238.
[2] Letter 219.
[3] E.R.O., D/DBa A15 *passim*.
[4] Eg. 2644, f. 24.

provide. As Harrison wrote, 'Mr Parker vowed ... that, were it not for the love he did beare me, I should not preach in Hatfield till they were willing to come to heare him in the afternoones'.[1]

In their letters the clergy strive, with varying degrees of tact, to remind their patrons of their duties. Roger Williams, at this time chaplain to the Masham family, was among the most outspoken. He quoted Luke's gospel to support the point that high birth, fortune and spiritual firmness brought with them equally great obligations. When Sir Francis Barrington was in prison James Harrison reflected both the nature of patronage and its two spheres of influence, for he saw himself as carrying out in Hatfield the work of his absent patrons, both in public and in their family: 'I find none unwilling to submit to the course undertaken by your worship's appointment for their good ...' Harrison, indeed, saw Hatfield as the extended family of the Barringtons: after his first visit, when considering the post of lecturer there, he thanked for their good opinions first Lady Joan, then her family, then the town.[2] He recognised the encouragement that Sir Francis and Lady Joan could give simply by their presence, but was most elaborate in his pleas during Lady Joan's absence at Harrow in 1629–30. Were she to come back to Hatfield '... I would not doubt to see the auncient honor of your family revyved and flourishe againe in constant and setled course of all good and religious exercise with blessing from the lord, both outward and inward ...'; without her 'I have just cause to feare the stay and continuance of these we now have with us, being ... doubtfull without the comfort of your society.'[3]

The letters provide evidence of the reaction of family and clergy (where it was naturally strongest) to the prolonged crisis of faith which Lady Joan appears to have suffered after the death of her husband. It was in terms of the family that Roger Williams saw her troubles:

> Call to mind what a cut ... it will be ... if ever you cast up your eye toward heaven and see so many blessed branches in the bosome of Christ, and your stock rejected.[4]

Others couched their criticism more tactfully and the presumption of the much younger Williams, who had already presumed to love her niece, led Lady Joan to refuse to see him.[5]

It was in the aftermath of this dispute and still with religious doubts that Lady Joan withdrew from Hatfield, her family and community,

[1] Letter 41.
[2] E.R.O., D/DBa F43; Eg. 2644, f. 230.
[3] Letter 57.
[4] Letter 38.
[5] A. Searle, 'Overmuch Liberty: Roger Williams in Essex', *Essex Journal*, iii (1968), 85–92.

to live for more than a year with her daughter and son-in-law at Harrow. It is tempting to see an outburst in one of Sir Thomas Barrington's letters (the immediate occasion of which is unclear) as his reaction to constant clerical scrutiny:

> I thanke God I can and doe desyre my freinds advices, but thare is an envyous aspect and an indevor to deprave that nothing but reproch can satisfye; I desire to heear of any fault, but doe not desyre to live where people search and hunt after faults ...[1]

Lady Joan Barrington at Hatfield Broad Oak

Sir Francis Barrington left careful instructions for his own burial:

> ... as it is the commaundement of God that his saincts should be decently laid into the earth when they are dead it is my desire that when my dayes shall bee finished my dead corpse may be accompanied to the grave by my Christian and religious freinds and neighbours without any pompe or solemnitie and layde in my chappell in Hatfeild Broadok church, being the place where most of my predecessors, my parents and children deceased weare formerly buryed ...[2]

Sir Francis was 68 or 69 when he died in the summer of 1628; Lady Joan was then apparently already 70 years old.[3] Most of these letters are addressed to her during the succeeding four years. Very few letters written by Lady Joan herself survive, all but one later in date than those she received presented here.[4] Each is a short and practical expression of her concern and affection for her children and grandchildren, so that, few as they are, they bear out the mixture of respect and affection which appears in almost all of the letters written to her. Something of her strength of character is evident in the support she gave to Sir Francis by staying with him during his imprisonment over the forced loan. Another provision of Sir Francis's will (drawn up on the day he entered prison) names her his executrix 'for the good of our Children and many more', assuring both his children and servants that they would have her 'love and true affection' and exhorting them 'to be dutifull and respective to her.'

At the time of his death Sir Francis and Lady Joan occupied the

---

[1] Letter 206.
[2] P.R.O., P.C.C. wills, 70 Barrington.
[3] G.E.C., *Baronetage;* E.R.O., D/DBa L20.
[4] Eg. 2646, ff. 50, 62, 102. Each of them, like the letter printed with letter 168, is written in the hand of Toby Bridge and signed rather shakily by Lady Joan.

Priory House, next to the church in the small market town of Hatfield. Their eldest son, Sir Thomas, and his wife Lady Judith, were living in the old ancestral home, Barrington Hall, which had been settled on them at their marriage. Barrington Hall was situated rather remotely, away to the north of Hatfield. The other substantial house the family owned in the parish, Hatfield Bury, occupied by the second son, Robert, stood opposite the church.

For a while after Sir Francis died Lady Joan continued to live at the Priory and Sir Thomas and Lady Judith at Barrington Hall. In the autumn of 1628 Lady Joan's steward Tobias Bridge began to keep 'my Ladie's Booke'.[1] This one source illuminates the circumstances of her daily life and shows how she adjusted to her new position as dowager. In the front of the account book Toby entered weekly expenditure on behalf of his mistress, lumping the week's ordinary household costs together, but listing exceptional payments separately; at the end he entered her income from her jointure lands and the property left her by Sir Francis in his will. Besides forming a basis for assessing the gradual reorganisation of Lady Joan's household circumstances after her husband's death, the book also provides a means of measuring her spheres of influence and an index of the importance she attached to those members of her circle whose circumstances provided the possibility and the need for her to support them either financially or in kind.

Lady Joan left the Priory for between two and three weeks at Christmas 1628-9 to stay with the Mashams at Otes in High Laver, about four miles from Hatfield. She returned to stay at Hatfield until 17 June 1629, when she undertook the more arduous journey to Harrow-on-the-Hill in Middlesex, for a prolonged stay with her son-in-law and daughter Gerard. Letters from Sir Thomas Barrington show the inevitable strain in relations between widowed mother and eldest son in the period when the estate was being taken over by the new heir. Lady Joan's absence provided the opportunity for Sir Thomas and Lady Judith to move into the Priory, but it may also have been thought wise in order to ease the course of these negotiations. Sir Gilbert Gerard began to act as Lady Joan's representative, and from at least this time onwards there was an especially strong bond of affection between son-in-law and mother-in-law. Her return to Hatfield was expected and apparently planned in October of 1629, but she stayed on into the summer of the following year, at least partly to see the safe delivery of her daughter Lady Mary Gerard's child.

While Lady Joan was away alterations and rearrangements were carried out to the rambling timber structure of the Priory House, to

[1] E.R.O., D/DBa A15.

suit Sir Thomas and Lady Judith.[1] New bedchambers were provided to accommodate the increased numbers of the family and their servants and a new dairy was built and equipped. Inside, minor alterations reflected new tastes: a portrait of Theodore Beza, the sixteenth-century Calvinist scholar, was removed from the upper gallery and twenty-six new pictures, landscapes as well as portraits, were hung in the larger Lower Gallery. In the Great Parlour the additions included a chest of viols and maps of Essex, Germany and the world.

While at Harrow, Lady Joan paid £5 each week to her daughter, Lady Gerard; when she finally left, in mid-July 1630, she returned to Hatfield on a similar basis, paying £5 weekly to Sir Thomas as 'rent for the Priorie'. Her weekly payments to Lady Gerard suggest something more than a temporary arrangement, giving point as her stay lengthened to the worried pleas of those who wanted her back in Essex. The weekly payments which she made to Lady Judith after her return made it clear that hers then became a distinct household within a household, a separate beneficent presence in the town of Hatfield.

The chief member of this subsidiary household was Toby Bridge, the keeper of the account book. He was Lady Joan's own steward, having previously kept accounts for Sir Francis. Sir Thomas employed his own clerk and steward, John Kendal. Bridge, who received £5 each Michaelmas and Lady Day from Lady Joan, was married and occupied a house of his own near to the Priory. Next in line was Lady Joan's 'man', Isaac Ewers, who was in her service from the time the account book was begun until shortly after his marriage (to another of her servants), in August 1632.[2] Isaac received £3 each half year and his duties included undertaking journeys (on estate business or to make contact with other branches of the family) at considerable distances. The footboy Robin was in Lady Joan's service until the end of 1631, receiving £2.10s wages each half year. Female attendants included three girls from one middle-ranking Hatfield family, who served for short overlapping periods. It was the eldest, Joan (or Jug) Smith, who married Isaac Ewers. They continued to work together in the household until August and Lady Joan's generosity was considerable when their child, also Joan, was born the following February. At a higher level Lady Joan at times had her own grandchildren as well as the children of close relatives, and neighbouring familes of standing, to live as part of her household. There was of course ample precedent

---

[1] *T.E.A.S.*, n.s., iii. 155–176 and E.R.O., D/DBa E3, inventories of Hatfield Priory in 1629 and 1632. The 1629 inventory 'of all such goods in Hatfeilde Priorie as weare delivered to Sir Thomas Barrington' was taken on 26 June, ten days after Lady Joan left the house. The original is now lost.

[2] He can be identified as the regicide Isaac Ewers, 'at first but a serving man'. *D.N.B.*; Eg. 2647, f. 31.

in England for bringing up girls in particular in another family, that 'familiar nursery'.[1] The impoverished Richard Whalley saw an additional advantage in the system. When he could no longer afford the half-yearly £20 he normally sent to keep his daughter in Lady Joan's household he suggested that she should stay and work for her living, the most important consideration being the increased chance of making a good match which life in a big house would bring to any girl.[2] When Jane contracted a romantic interest in Roger Williams, who was wthout money or prospects, it is easy to understand why it had to be crushed.

During the period covered by both the account book and the letters, three girls from Lady Joan's family were with her; there were her granddaughters Joan Meux and Joan Gerard as well as her niece Jane Whalley. Jane, the eldest, who had been with Lady Joan since 1622, received £5 each half year and very few incidental payments were made on her behalf. But when in May 1630 she was finally married (to William Hook, then incumbent of Upper Clatford in Hampshire, later chaplain to Cromwell) she was given the unprecedented sum of £100 and two gowns costing £15. 15s. Joan Meux stayed with Lady Joan until 1634; her allowance was £10 each half year up to Michaelmas 1630, £15 thereafter. Joan Gerard was the youngest and most favoured. She was too young to receive a substantial regular sum until Lady Day 1634, but from then until 1636 she received £15 each half year. Before 1634 the incidental sums laid out on her behalf grew as she did, even when she was still with Lady Joan but in her own parents' house at Harrow.

One more member of the family must be counted as part of Lady Joan's inner circle, her daughter Ruth, Lady Lamplugh. She separated from her husband in 1626 and re-entered her parent's household, with ties so close that she accompanied them to the Marshalsea in 1628. She was with her mother at Harrow in 1629–30 and is remembered by others in postscripts to letters written to Lady Joan, with obvious regard for the position she occupied in the old lady's feelings. From 1628–1634 she was receiving £20 each half year from her mother. Of the other children, only John Barrington, the youngest son, needed financial assistance. This was given unstintingly, despite the hesistant requests in his letters. (He had already received his portion from his father when he took up his chosen military career.) From December 1628 to September 1630, the period during which he was recovering from a broken leg and waiting in London to obtain a place as a soldier, his mother paid out a total of £120 either to him or

[1] Richard Brathwait, *The English Gentlewoman* (1631), 205.
[2] Eg. 2644, f. 205.

on his behalf. At Michaelmas 1630, a very few months before his death, he received the first payment of what was intended to be a regular half-yearly allowance of £12. 10s.

Little of significance emerges from payments to the rest of Lady Joan's children, but a pattern is sometimes discernible in gifts to grandchildren. Sir Thomas's eldest son, John, and his eldest stepson, Rowland Smith, were at Trinity College, Cambridge, together from Easter 1633. Lady Joan's gifts to John were of either 20s. or 10s.; on each occasion that they were given Rowland received either 10s. or 5s. With these two at Cambridge was Jack Burles, a son of another Barrington client family in Hatfield; a gift to him was never omitted, but his scale was 2s. 6d. Lady Joan celebrated the marriage of her granddaughter Joan Altham with Oliver St. John (a candidate of whom she approved more strongly than did some members of her family) with the gift of a silver basin, ewer and livery pots costing £66. 14s. and the birth of their first child with a further £10 expenditure on plate. Two more people received recurring financial assistance from Lady Joan; a goddaughter, Lady Mary Eliot, who received a total of £12, given on five separate occasions in two and a half years, and her nephew Sir Francis Harris, who was given 20s. each year.

Lady Joan's dependants in Hatfield Broad Oak included one distant relative of the Barrington family, Margaret Hildersham, who received £3 each half year, variously described as an annuity or as quarterage.[1] Outside the family the principal beneficiary was James Harrison, the lecturer and chaplain, who received £10 a year. There are also frequent entries for small gifts to his wife, who took care of the young John Gerard when Lady Joan was at Otes in 1628-29. Other payments, less regular and of less obvious purpose, demonstrate the extent of Lady Joan's patronage in Hatfield. Apart from the payments to her family and servants mentioned, more than 140 names are listed in fifteen years, and this in a parish of some 700 people, scattered in subsidiary hamlets as well as in the 'town' where the Priory was situated.[2]

Outside of Hatfield two carriers were frequently paid for bringing goods from London, where tradesmen regularly patronised included Mr Adcocke the dressmaker and Mr Cooke the apothecary. The physicians Lady Joan called on were Thomas Burnett from Braintree (fifteen payments were made to him or his apothecary in five years) or John Remington of Great Dunmow (ten payments). Finally, as

---

[1] She was the sister-in-law of Sir Francis Barrington's steward Richard Hildersham. Her will indicates that she had been in the service of Lady Winifred Hastings. E.R.O., D/ABW 53/100.

[2] Population estimated from E.R.O., T/A 420 and Q/RTh 5.

steward of her manors, Lady Joan paid £4 each year to George Scott, a man well connected with the minor gentry families of the locality.[1] A different kind of benevolence exercised by Lady Joan, which certainly ranged far and which may have been quite frequent, is suggested by the cure for a child's illness sought from her by a man who had travelled from Harrow just for her advice.[2] On acts of this kind the account book is, of course, silent.

It was at Hatfield that Lady Joan Barrington 'willingly bid adue to all the seeming greatnes and glory of this world' in December 1641. She died in the hope of resurrection and eternal life 'with all the Elect Angells and Saintes'.[3] The will in which she expressed these sentiments also expressed, in a detailed list of bequests, a confidence that the hierarchy of family and community which she had fostered would continue. She was able to leave money to two granddaughters and four great-granddaughters named Joan. The rest of her widespread family were remembered with the same mixture of favouritism and regard for position that the account book shows. £3,000 was ready in her iron chest for the executors to use in paying out the bequests. Secure in her status as well as her society, Lady Joan was able to choose as her executors four baronets: her son and three sons-in-law.

At well over eighty years old Lady Joan had outlived most of her generation and some of the next. Shortly before the old lady died Francis Quarles dedicated to her his *Threnodes* on the death of her daughter Lady Elizabeth Masham. In the dedication he observed: 'Your Ladiship hath been an old Scholler in Gods Schoole, and knowes well, when, how, and for what, to mourne'.[4]

The Barrington Letters

More good fortune than foresight is responsible for the preservation of the records of the Barrington family. Surviving material is dispersed among a number of different repositories and collections, so that it is only on paper that it can now be assembled as a single unit.[5] Its assembly and history before the present century are also complicated. The greater part of the collection dates from before the failure of the direct line of the family with the death in 1715 of Sir Charles Barring-

---

[1] Scott was the brother-in-law of Lady Joan's protégé Lady Mary Eliot. Letter 3.
[2] Letter 188.
[3] P.R.O., P.C.C. wills, 151 Evelyn.
[4] Quarles, 25. More detail of Quarles's connections with the Essex gentry is to be found in K. J. Höltgen, *Francis Quarles, 1592–1644* (Tübingen, 1978).
[5] A partial reconstruction of the components of the original archive is given by F. G. Emmison in *Archives*, viii (1968), 130–132 and in *Guide to the Essex Record Office* (Chelmsford, 1969), 124–126. The modern movement of the archive is succinctly traced by N. Briggs in *Bulletin of the National Register of Archives*, 14 (1967), 19–21.

ton. The earliest of the letters were received before the family moved their residence from Barrington Hall to Hatfield Priory, and rather more than half of the medieval deeds relate to the family and their own holdings up to that time. These two elements must have comprised a muniment collected at the first Barrington Hall; to them were added the medieval deeds of Hatfield Priory. Such court rolls and other manorial documents as survive would have been added similarly, piecemeal with the acquisition of manors.

During the seventeenth century, while the family lived at the Priory with Barrington Hall leased out, the main collection of correspondence, account books and estate records was formed. The whole archive can be assumed to have accumulated undisturbed at the Priory until the wayward demolition of the building early in the eighteenth century. The new house, which was later Victorianised into the present Barrington Hall, was not begun until after 1734, when John Shales Barrington inherited the Hatfield estate, and then he chose a site well to the north of the church and of the old Priory house. William Holman, writing c.1720, recorded the position between times: the Priory house 'has been for some time demolished and its Scite converted into Gardens ... on the north side of the chancel of the parish church is a vestry room where the ancient writings of the Barrington family are kept.' This room, immediately to the east of the Barrington family chapel in the church, still housed records in 1771 and only ceased to be used as a store room in 1881, when it was converted into an organ chamber.[1]

The new Barrington Hall was largely uninhabited until it was put in order by G. A. Lowndes, on whom the estate devolved, in the 1860s. The Barrington family muniments were in his possession and at the house when they were the subject of a Historical Manuscripts Commission *Report* by A. J. Horwood, published in 1879.[2] The manuscripts acquired by the British Museum by purchase from Lowndes in 1886 were basically those which had been described in detail in that report, including virtually all the letters. Those left behind were at risk again when the house was put up for sale in 1908. Fortunately the vicar at the time, Canon F. W. Galpin, was a distinguished antiquary as well as musical historian; he removed all he could back to the safety of the church library. There they were freely available to scholars, as both Professor Wallace Notestein and Miss M. E. Bohannon, the chief among those working on them, attested. These documents from the

---

[1] E.R.O., T/P 195/16; Trinity College MSS., Box 9, III. g; *T.E.A.S.*, n.s., ix. 113.

[2] Lowndes (Barrington) MSS., H.M.C., 7th *Report*, Appendix, 537–589. Horwood had reported briefly on the manuscripts to the annual general meeting of the Essex Archaeological Society at Hatfield Broad Oak in 1874; *T.E.A.S.*, n.s., i. 127.

church were deposited in the Essex Record Office in 1939, 1940, 1946 and 1955, with a final group of deeds which had earlier been overlooked added in 1965.

As has already been indicated, the pattern of survival of the correspondence now in the British Library suggests that the letters as they accrued may have been kept by servants rather than by members of the family. Steward's papers deposited in the Essex Record Office in 1969 included notes and calculations scribbled on blank or almost blank sheets torn from letters, and a few complete family letters had found their way into these bundles of rough papers. Some of the letters bear endorsements, apparently written in the seventeenth century, which imply that they were then arranged in bundles by correspondent.

The uneven survival within the correspondence as a whole is presumably the result of this haphazard method of original preservation and of the subsequent complications of the archive's history. There are a few important sixteenth century letters, a fascinating small group relating to the Essex county parliamentary election of 1604, and an increasing but erratic survival thereafter, within which are three large and more concentrated groups where the survival rate is clearly exceptionally high: the family letters of 1628-32, Sir Thomas Barrington's correspondence for the early years of the civil war until his death in 1644 (the largest group of all), and estate correspondence of the later 1660s and early 1670s.

It is the group of letters for 1628-32 which is printed in the following pages, in chronological order, as nearly as that can now be reconstructed. Those were the years when Lady Joan Barrington's eldest son, Sir Thomas, was beginning to occupy a leading position in county affairs. He and his brother Robert were M.P.s, so also were her sons-in-law Sir Gilbert Gerard and Sir William Masham. They all had frequent occasion to be away, and so to write. Lady Joan's daughter Winifred, and her husband Sir William Meux, lived in the Isle of Wight. The Mashams and another daughter, Joan, married to Sir Richard Everard, lived elsewhere in Essex. The Gerards lived at Harrow in Middlesex. Lady Joan's stay with them there for a year in 1629-30 was perhaps the most important factor of all in generating letters to her from her family and friends.

But beyond this there is a pattern of distinct groups within the letters from this period, just as there is within the correspondence as a whole. Some are letters from a single correspondent, for example John Barrington, or from a distinct group such as the clergy. Most, though, are subject groups, such as the letters of condolence written following the death of Sir Francis Barrington in July 1628, and the letters written to Lady Joan at various times when members of her family were in

London, that 'perpetuall mapp of our times ... the center where all affaires of importance disclose and discover them selves'.[1] Three short periods of these London letters stand out: 30 November 1628–2 March 1629, for most of which time parliament was in session, October–November 1631 when Masham and Sir Thomas Barrington were in London trying to escape selection as sheriff of Essex, and April–May 1632 when Sir Thomas and his wife were negotiating the re-sale of Carisbrooke Park. The writers were eager to pass on details of the successes of the Protestant cause in Europe as well as the news of the town. Printed newsbooks were often enclosed with the letters – on one occasion the suggestible William Masham became caught up in their phraseology, offering Lady Joan 'advisoes' – but many of the writers in the Barrington circle were better and sooner informed than either the contemporary corantos or the other manuscript newsletters of the time which have subsequently been published.[2]

The few estate letters within our period of 1628–32 are scattered throughout the chronological arrangement. They deal with affairs after Sir Francis Barrington's death, with Lady Joan's jointure lands, and, in the case of a very few 'strays', with Lady Judith Barrington's Hertfordshire estate. One other subject of greater note is similarly scattered. During these years Lady Joan's granddaughters Joan Meux and Joan Altham reached marriageable age; the search for husbands, in which their grandmother's opinion was of paramount importance, crops up repeatedly.

[1] Letter 12.
[2] Letter 214. In the notes to the letters reference has been made to Dahl and Birch to supply or confirm a date, or to reveal a significant time difference between the letter and the printed source.

GENEALOGICAL TABLES

Letter writers in CAPITALS

TABLE 1 — BARRINGTON ANCESTRY AND CONNECTIONS

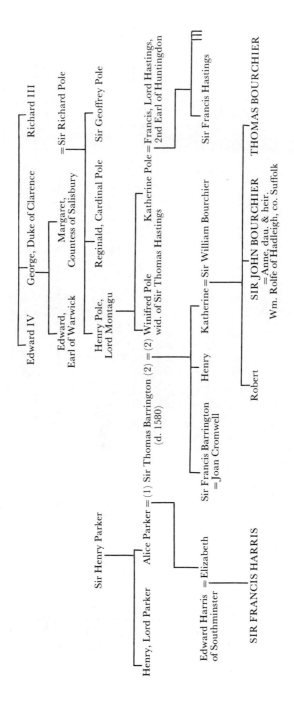

TABLE 2 — CROMWELL

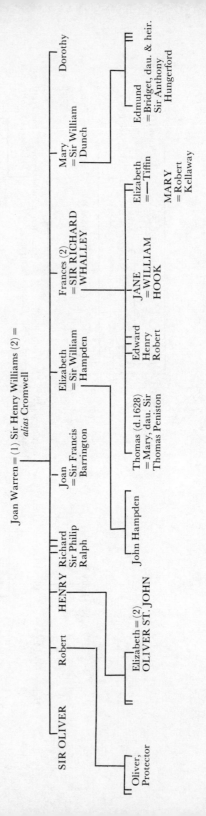

TABLE 3 — DESCENDANTS OF LADY JOAN AND SIR FRANCIS BARRINGTON

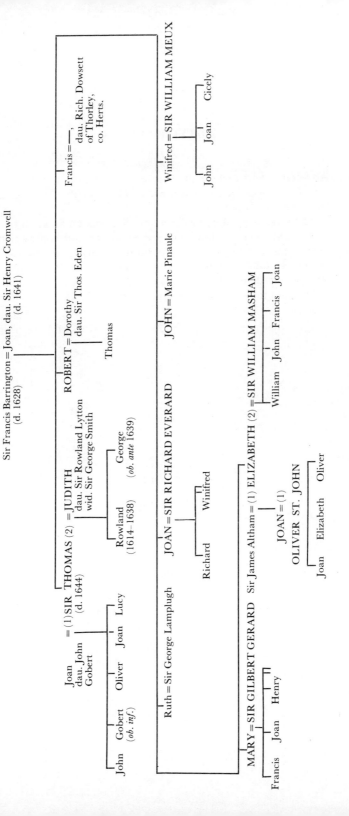

EDITORIAL NOTE

All letters, except where stated, are addressed to Lady Joan Barrington. The references given at the head of each letter are B. L. Egerton MS. and folio numbers.

The original spelling has been retained; punctuation and capitalisation have been modernised. Abbreviations and contractions have been expanded throughout. Doubtful readings and editorial matter in the text, including the suggested reconstruction of missing passages, are indicated in square brackets. All but a few of the letters are holograph; the exceptions are indicated.

BARRINGTON FAMILY LETTERS

1   *Richard Whalley,*[1] *22 July 1628*   (*2644, f. 275*)

My honourable and most worthy lady sister   The flyinge report
of the death of your truly noble, perfectly religious and most well
merittinge common wealth's husband, Sir Frances Barrington, rightly
remembreth unto mee that godly and true sayinge of the prophet
Isaiah, cap. 57,1: *the righteous perisheth, and no man considereth it in heart,
and mercifull men are taken away, and no man understandeth that the righteous
is taken away from the evill to come.* Give mee leave even thoroughly to
grieve with yow, both for myselfe, the whole common wealth and my
children's trust reposed in him; yet to rejoyce and to comfort my selfe
with you for him by these words in the next vearse: *peace shall come, they
shall rest in their bedds, evryone that walketh before him,* as most assuredly
hee dooth; and therefore in great thanksgivinge say yow, with all that
knew him, *beatus est ille, qui mortuus est in domino, quia opera ejus sequuntur
illum.* Hee lived in honour, dyed in peace, forewent God's heavy
judgement – most like to befall us – and shall rise in glory eternall. Oh
sister, rejoyce; good maddam rejoyce, rejoyce, even contrary to flesh
and blood, rejoyce for his departure, show your humble thanckfullnes
to almighty God that hath these many yeares yoke fellow in your

---

[1] The salutation and signature only are written by Whalley, the rest in the hand of an
amanuensis. Richard Whalley inherited estates in Nottinghamshire from his grandfather, a supporter of the protector Somerset and receiver for the Court of Augmenta-
tions in Yorkshire. Whalley was sheriff of Nottinghamshire in 1595-6, and an M.P. in
1597 and 1601. His second wife, the mother of his children, was Frances Cromwell,
Lady Joan Barrington's sister. She died in 1623; by the time of this letter Whalley, who
over-indulged in law suits even by the standards of the day, was in severely reduced
financial circumstances. This must have been due in large part to the furious dispute
with his eldest son Thomas which he mentions in this letter. Whalley had re-married in
1626, at the height of that dispute and perhaps as part of it, although he claimed at the
time that he was 'enforced to marry to get a nurse to look to me'. He nonetheless
outlived Thomas, so that the estates once more passed to a grandson, the royalist
Peniston Whalley. Richard Whalley's surviving sons were of quite the contrary political
persuasion: his second son was Edward Whalley, major-general and regicide, the third
Henry, judge-advocate to the English and Scottish armies in 1655. This letter is the last
of a series in which Whalley bewails in colourful terms his financial plight and the
ungrateful behaviour of his eldest son. Table 2; K. S. S. Train, *Nottinghamshire Visitation,
1662-4* (Thoroton Soc., xiii. 1950), 64; John Thoresby, *Thoroton's History of Nottinghamshire,* i. (1797), 248-9; *D.N.B.*; *M. of P.,* i. 390, 394; Noble, ii. 135, 140, 141; Eg. 2644,
ff. 202, 205, 207, 234, 243.

bosome one more then an angell: and for your selfe rejoyce that you have beene as a fruitfull vine unto your husband's house, and have received most plentifully children, the especiall blessinge about your table. And why? Because you both have lived in the feare of the lord; and therein dooe I holde myselfe happy that you please to vouchsafe the educacion of my poore daughter, your niece whom, good maddam, let continue with you, and God graunt her grace either to please you or never to accounte mee her father; and whom I likewise beseech you to bestow in marriage, and her porcion, I hope shall surely in convenient tyme bee provided with advantage.[1] I have sent her by this bearer the third and last volume of Mr Parkins' workes which were her mother's,[2] and further will remember her if I may understand her dutifull care to please you. But, good maddam, keepe her from overmuch liberty and fantasticke new fashions.

Dolefull remembrance makes it troublesome to your ladyshippe I know to reade, and paine and weakenes in mee – for I am greatly troubled with the strangury[3] and soddainly growne very weake, that I must now prepare for my end – also makes it unpleasant to mee to write, especially on this subject, onely God hath not forsaken mee, but in my aged years hath blessed mee with a good wife who is both religious, patient for my infirmityes, cherishinge my weakenes and neither desireth to hinder, neither shall, any my children one obulus. But their eldest brother, without God's especiall proteccion and your worthy sonne's godly care over them, will devoure them all I seealready. Therefore, with my and my wive's due remembrances to your ladyshipp and all my noble cosens, beseecheth the almighty to comfort you and them.

Your ladyshipp's ever oblyged weake brother

Richard Whalley

My sonne Henry, who I thancke God dooth well in London and is married there, I expect very speedyly will bringe his wife downe to see mee ere I dy, which cannot bee longe to. Were it that your ladyshipp would bee pleased to spare her service to dooe her duty to mee in company with her sister, if her sister dooe come downe, else not – that I might once see all my children ere I dy – it would be some comfort to mee, and I were much bound to your ladyshipp, but thus, that you will assuredly receive her within one moneth after into your service

---

[1] See Introduction, 19.

[2] Three-volume editions of the works of William Perkins, a favourite author of Whalley's, were issued in Cambridge in 1608, 1609 and 1612 and in London in 1606, 1612 and 1616.

[3] A urinary disease.

againe, else in no condicion would I have her, for alas here is no preferment for her.
Screaveton, 22° July, 1628

Endorsed (f. 276b): To his honourable and most vertuous lady the Lady Joane Barrington barronettess at her house, Hatfeild in Essex, present theise

2 *Sir Gilbert Gerard, 29 July 1628* (*2644, f. 277*)

Good madam   I have according to your direction sent unto my ant Hampden for another [deer] for you, which wilbe readie to come to you by the next bearer, and I have taken order for the paying for them both.

I had some speech with you about my brother Barrington's wrighting unto Mr Goodwin, but there was nothing resolved on. I thinke it were very fitt it were done spedily lest he suppose the busines be at an end, and it were pittie my neece should loose so honest a gentleman.[1] This vacation it's likelie he wilbe solicited by others, therefore you shall doe very well to procuer my brother to wright, and they say that Mr Perkins can conveigh the letter.

My wife is willing to entertaine your cooke maid if you part with her and shee be willing to come unto us. I pray lett mee heere from you about her by this bearer because I am offered another. If you have any occation to imploy mee I am readie to wait on you when you shall please to apoint. And so wishing you all hapines I rest
        Your dutifull sone   G. Gerard
Fl[ambards], 29 July, 1628

Endorsed (f. 278b): To my honourable good mother the Lady Johan Barrington these be given

[1] The proposed marriage was for Joan Meux. See letter 5.

3 *Sir Thomas and Lady Mary Eliot,*[1] *n.d., [late July 1628]* (*2644, f. 279*)

Good maddam   Albeit in true judgment ther be more cause of joy then sorow upon the departure of God's children out of this vale of misery into that kingdome of glory that is prepared for them, yet such is man's fraylty as wherby the best are subject to this infirmity. Herein, therfore, my wife and I professe ourselves partners with your ladiship in bewayling the decease of your most loveing and beloved housband, the comfort of his country and the joy of all that ever knew him, which is a better nam then Duke Barrington left behind him. But being now no remedy, lett us intreat your ladiship that we may joyne alsoe togeather in that rejoyceing which is left us, namely that his joyes are unspeakable albeit our losse is incompareable. Nor is he yet altogeather dead according to the condition of the most that goe hence, but in his virtues he still lives and shall outlast the longest man alive. Industrious he was and diligent in his service and attendance, both of God and his country, faythfull and firme to his frend and acquaintance, loveing and beloved of all; but to expresse his virtues to the full exceedeth any man's utterance. Lett us not therfore morne as men without hoope, but rather lett us shew forth our fayth on his behalfe by rejoycing more at his salvation the[n] over much to greive at his remove accompanied with such graces as he had.

We presume that upon this occasion your ladiship hath much resorte of frends that seeke to refresh you; we doe therfore the lesse hasten to come to you, intending yet erre longe to make bould to visite you, in the meane time presenting our continuall prayers unto the throne of the heavenly grace that, as on the one side God hath humbled you, soe on the other side he will comfort you in the remembrance of his mercies which endure for ever, wherof your ladiship hath from time to time received plentifull testimony. Soe prayeth

          Your continuall orators to the throne of grace

                                        Thomas Eliot, Mary Eliot

Endorsed (*f. 280b*): To the honourable good lady the Lady Jone Barrington thes be given at Hatfield

---

[1] Mary Eliot was the daughter of William Towse, serjeant at law, of Takeley in Essex, a parish adjoining Hatfield Broad Oak, and so related to such diverse members of Lady Joan's circle as the Suffolk Barnardistons and her steward George Scott. That she calls Lady Joan mother (see letter 4), suggests she was her goddaughter and may well have spent some time in her household. Her husband, Sir Thomas Eliot, inherited the central Essex estates of his father Edward (an active J.P. from 1586 to his death in 1595) but soon ran into financial trouble and had lost them all by 1635. *Visitations of Essex,* 191–2, 705; Bodl., MS. Rawl. Essex 6, ff. 125, 128; Morant, i. 133 and ii. 33, 74, 182; Samaha, 152.

4 *Lady Mary Eliot, n.d., [early August 1628]*   *(2644, f. 281)*

Dear ladye mother   Yett haeth pleased the lord by his devine providens to put a bitter cupe into your hand off which manye drinke, for 'tis not onlye your most loveinge indeared husband is taken awaye but our Jousa, our Jethore,[1] faithfull, painfull, resolutt capptaine genrall that gave the first onsett and bravelye stood outt not for the libbertyes betix mane and man but bewix God and man. Genracions to come shall bless God for such a nobell peare as he was, fewe in this kinddome left like him, if anye such. Whoss eyes gush not taeres for such a loss? Heilderberge maye tell us what this singn iss: the worthyes of our kinddome ar swept awaye, the blowe is not fare off and happie and bleseed is he, honnorabell in his life, being hid in Chirst in his death, beinge taekeing awaye when he was excuttinge his owne plase of honnor, the mouth of the contrye in assemblye of parlementt which God had decred. And all the witt of man could not but bye conclud, [as] we must, he is happie, and for ever of blessed memorye shall he continue. Yett now remains that we doe not morne as without hoope, excesiflye, but arther [rather], deare ladye, honnor him bye a wise cherefull submison to his will and grace preffeson by a pacientt imbracing the bitters pile he can put into our hand by faith. Elijah is gon but his mantell shall devid the watters. This God be the man of your councell, turne your watter most bitter to sewett wine and inabell you with corrage and holye zeell to stand forth for the maintenans of God's honnor as ever you have done, that the loss of a Joshua in all affaires to your power maye be cantervailed with a Deborah. Thus prayeth
        Your obediantt loveinge daughter   Marye Eliot

My man left this letter behind him. Pardon me, deare ladye, that I come not over to you. Soe sonne as posibell I will see you.

Endorsed (f. 282b): To the honnorabell my much respetted mother the Ladye Johana Barrington att hir howse give [these]

5 *Sir William Meux, 8 August 1628*   *(2644, f. 283)*

Madam   Itt may seeme strange yow have not herd all this while from mee, and were itt not but neglect of soe worthy a freinde would light uppon, scarcely should yow heare from mee these many dayes, itt may bee weekes, for the loss of soe deere a freinde, soe good a man, where spoken of brings sadness, much more written. But, good lady, lett this be our comfort, that as hee lived, soe dyed, happily chalking out a way for us to walke in, leaving behinde him a good name, much honored of all men.

[1] For Joshua and Jethroe?

Now madam, concerning yowr moneys heere behinde unpaide and the two fines contracted for, I will take the best course I can, but am afraide that parte of Elmsore rent not paide is somewhat desperate.¹ Concerning Jugg,² I am providing for her what I can; God bless our indevors. I have written to Sir Thomas Barrington to bring Mr Goodwin with him when hee comes downe, when God willing, itt shall appeare I will doe what is fitt. Thus, leaving yowr ladyship to the protection of our saviour, I rest yowr very loving son,
                William Meux

Kingston, the 8th of August, 1628
I thanck yowr ladyship for the blacks sent to mee and Jack and for our men. Jack,³ I thanck Christe, is well and remembers his duty unto yow.

Endorsed (*f. 284b*): To my much honored mother the Lady Barrington att Hattfeild give these

6   *Lady Mary Eden,*⁴ *13 [August] 1628*   (*2644, f. 285*)

Good madam and loving sister   I think to see yow ere sumer goeth, and if it would please yow to come to me and to staye a weake yow should be mad kindly wellcom as to your owne sister. And agane it would doe yow good and sumwhat to forget the great lose yow have had of so woorthy a frind. But let this be our comfort: he is now happye and he is gone but afore us, we doe not know how sone we shall follow after him. I have made bould to send yow a token, a payer of gloves to dress yow in. I wish I had a better token. I thanke yow for your ladyship's kindnes to my dawghter and that your love towards her do so contynue. And so, praying God to send yow health here and blised happynes hereafter, I doe comit yow to God, and so I rest
                Your loving sister   Mary Eden

¹ Elmesore in the parish of Calbourne, Isle of Wight. V.C.H., *Hampshire*, v. 218
² His daughter Joan, of marriageable age and living in Lady Joan's household.
³ His son.
⁴ Lady Eden, daughter of Brian Darcy of Tiptree in Essex, was the widow of Sir Thomas Eden of Ballingdon hamlet on the Essex-Suffolk border. Their daughter Dorothy was married to Robert Barrington. Walker described Lady Eden as 'a devout woman who much frequented lectures'. Augustine Page, *Supplement to the Suffolk Traveller* (1844), 971, 974; J. J. Howard, *Visitation of Suffolk* (1866), i. 11, 19; Smith, 174.

From Ballington Hall this xiii 1628[1]

Endorsed (*f. 286b*): To the right worshipfull her lovinge sister the Lady Barrington at Hatfield give thes

7   *Sir John Bourchier, 16 August 1628*   (*2644, f. 287*)

Good madame   Since the deathe of my worthye uncle I had noe oportunitye of writeing to your ladyship, neither have I now, but that I caused this messenger to goe somewhat out of his waye purposedlye to visit yow with theis lynes which are testimoneys of my true love and respect which I shall ever owe yow. The deathe of hym I hope will not be too much lamented by yow because yow are wise and have had longe experience of his true goodness, and theirfore he now possesseth that which we doe but live in hope of, which is happiness inexpressible. We shall goe to hym, but he can not come unto us; blessed are those that dye in the lorde, for they shall rest from theire labours and theire good workes shall followe them. The lorde gave hym life to bee one of the mirrors of our tyme, especiallye now of late, soe as he haith shutt upp his dayes with honor and reputacion, according to the psalmist such honor shall his saints have. The lord blesse yow and sende his spirritt to bee your comforter, which will I doubt not but aboundantly comforte yow. With my wife's and my service to yow and yours I will ever rest

         Your firmely loving nephew   John Bourchier

Beningbrough this 16th August, 1628

Endorsed [*in another hand*] (*f. 288b*): To the honourable his much esteemed ant the Lady Barrington att Hatfield Broad Oake, these be given, Essex

8   *Sir Gilbert Gerard, 18 August 1628*   (*2644, f. 289*)

Good madam   This bearer being to come unto you I can not lett him passe with out a few lines to lett your ladyship know that there is notheing that I more desire than to heare of your hapines, and according to your promise I shall expect a letter at London. I hope by

---

[1] No month is written.

this time you have resceived an answere of my brother Barrington his letter out of Sussex that so you may lett my brother Meux know by this bearer what is like to be the issue of that busines, which if I be not mistaken is worth the looking after, therfore I pray you not to be unmindfull of it. I shalbe gladd to heare how you have disposed of your harvest, and for your inventory there is noe hast, but when I next see you I will doe what service I can therein.

My wife remembers her duty unto you and seith shee hath not received all her bookes from you of phisicke, there being an old torne one left behind. And so desiering unto your ladyship all hapiness I rest

    Your dutifull sone   G. Gerard

18 August, 1628

Endorsed (*f. 290b*): To my honourable mother the Lady Johan Barrington these be given at Hattfield

9   *Sir Gilbert Gerard, 26 August 1628*   (*2644, f. 291*)

Good madam   This bearer being to goe unto Hatfield and letting me know so much I could not neglect this duty that I owe unto you, the rather because I know it wilbe pleasing unto you to heare of all our wellfare heare and that I did not shrink in the wetting when I last came from you. I know you will expect noe newes now, for the talke of the Duke of Buckingham's death doth take up all men's mindes and tounges so that nothing else is spoken of.[1] God grant it may not breed securitie in any of us, if it doe he that hath delivered us from him can bring upon us a worse scourge. You must pardon the fault of my paper. And when our harvest is done I purpose God willing to waite on you, in the meane time I rest

    Your dutifull sone   G. Gerard

26 August, 1628

Endorsed (*f. 292b*): To my honerd mother the Lady Johan Barrington these be given

---

[1] Buckingham had been assassinated on 23 Aug.

10   *William Chantrell, 18 September 1628*   (*2644, f. 293*)

Honorable ladie   Your sad hart (I hope) the sweet comforter,
even the spirit of grace and faith, hath cheered with the due consideration of that wise disposinge hand of God, who worketh all thinges
according to the good pleasure of his will. And I make no question but
that the resolution which your ladishipe hath of the compleat happiness your late worthy knight doth now injoy swallows up all worldly
sorrow for that uncomparable loss.

It is noe small comfort to thinke how in all those storms, both
boysterous and turbulent, he was brought to his sweet bed of rest in a
good old age, with much peace, much honor and great admiration of
all men. Wher he was not known for person, his memorie is honorable
and will ever live. He is gonne before us; wee remayne to follow in
that due tyme when our maister pleaseth to call.

If ever any age afforded fittness to say 'come lett us goe die with
him', it is even now, for if wee looke about us wee shall see the
foundations of the earth out of order. As the psalmist speakes: and
what hath the rightuous don? Out of your Christian readinge, hearing
and experience yow can draw fountaynes of sweet comfort to sollace
your selfe amidest these trialls, and non greater than this: your heavenly husbande will never leave nor forsake but lead yow through his
garden of spicknard and cynamon till he bringe yow to his mother
house to drinke spiced wine and wine of pomegranetes for ever.*

I need not increase your greife by tellinge yow what a loss the
church of God hath by his fall. But my prayer is that your goodly
ishew may daylie make up those breaches, that theire be a perpetuated
generation of the Barrington to the upholding of Gode's arke and the
glorie theirof.

Thus hoping that he who wipeth away all teares will establish your
noble hart in faith and pacience, that yow will say God is just in all his
sayings and holy in all his workes, I rest
       Your old servant   William Chantrell

Walkington, 18 September, 1628

Endorsed (*f. 294b*): To the noble and virtuous ladie, Ladie Johana
Barrington at Hatfeild Priorie in Essex

* [*In margin:*] Cant. 4.14, Cant. 8.2.

11   *William Chantrell, 18 November 1628*   *(2644, f. 295)*

Worthy ladie   I shall not neede to increase your greife by the
remembering your unvalewable losse; to him must wee goe, he can
not come to us. Our safest is to make sure and sounde preparation for
our selves against the like stroke. How speedely it will come, who
knowes when as all flesh is grass and the benignitie of it as is the flowre
of the feilde?

The longe distance of place enforces me to entreat your ladishipe to
accept the tender of these rude lines for the presentation of my humble
service, which I would doe in person when so ever I am there-unto
called. Truly madam, my domesticke and ministeriall imploymentes
will not give me leave to looke over Humber, but did any business fall
out wherin my service might speed yow or yours I should thinke my
selfe unhappie if I did not endevour the utmost to testifie my inmost
affection and dutie to yow and that familie from whom, under God,
I reseave my beinge in these partes. My prayers to the Lord is that
yow would still have a watchfull eye over the plantes of your owne
loynes, that they by your good encurragmentes may insist in the
steepes of theire worthy father of blessed memorie, that an holy steeme
may be directed from that holy root, a generation of the Barringtons
continewed that may still prayse the Lord. The God of grace and
glorie fill your hart with the sweet comfortes of his holy spirrit to all
eternitie. Thus humbly taking my leave,

I rest your ladiship servant   William Chantrell

Walkington, 18 November, 1628

Endorsed (*f. 296b*): To the honorable ladie the Ladie Johana Barrington
at Hatfeild Priorie in Essex, give [these]

12   *Sir Thomas Barrington, 30 November 1628*   *(2644, f. 297)*

Madame   Being kept in London by my occasions I am inabled
to be themore serviceable to you in relation of the occurents from this
place, whare is a perpetuall mapp of our times, being the center where
all affaires of importance disclose and discover them selves. We have
a committee of privy counsellors, 4 of the upper house and as many of
the house of commons, to whom the king hath committed the debate
and settling of somm good course for matter of religion; thus doe wee
heear that are at a distance, yet the newes is not verye vulgar. What
other greivances are in agitation I heear not. Diverse of the counsell
have spoken well in the cause of religion; I pray God the effects and

issu may croune the worke. The barrons in the Eschequer on Fryday last have resolved that what goods soever be ceazed by the king's officers for any pretended debt to the king, the cause must only be tryed in the Eschequer, the proper place for the king's revenew, and this must be donn by petition. This was the judgment concerning this part of tunage and poundage, which was argued then in the merchants' behalfe. Felton was executed yesterday at Tiborne, whare and when he condemned and bewayled his fact, dyed penitently and disavoued all justification of the deed, desyred all the people to pray for him and so ended his dayes, which closes this last scene of a straunge tragedye.[1] I pray God owr next innovation be more successfully happye.

The lord Keeper did yesterday express the king's pleasuer to the judges and bishops and all justices. [f. 297b] The first thing he spake unto was that the lawes showld be exactly executed by all the king's ministers against preists and Jesuites, the next that all justices showld give an account of non conformitant Papists and prosecute the lawe for their parts allso, then that the king would have an exact cataloge of all the recusants in or aboute London and proceed against them accordinge to statute of 3° Jac. and that of confinement. Then the bishopps had a charge to maintaine the trew religion of owr church and to suffer no innovation contrary to the booke of common prayer and the articles of owr church. Then my lord spake to the cyvill government to the kingdom and in generall of diverss abuses to be reformed, particularly only of the clarke of the markett, which the judges had strictly in charge to reforme. Then gave he a charge to all gentlemen to repaire into the countrye, to keepe up hospitallytie, and so concluded, but left us not satisfyed in any measuer proportionable to that expectation which was emong us concerning none of these points.

Madam, I heear both by my brother and others that (though Mr Collins[2] tould me this last weeke Oliver is verie well) yet he lookes ill. I beseich you comaund Wiltshier to fetch him, or any other, by somm meanes; I hope I am so well befreinded in Hatfield that more then one will take so short a journye for me. I will pay for a horss if that be

---

[1] The three points raised here also feature in the letter of Joseph Mead to Sir Martin Stuteville of 28 Nov. They are 1). the proposal for a new session of parliament and the likelihood of its dealing with religion, reported by Mead as having been raised by the king at the council board on 27 Nov.; 2). the case of the five merchants in the Exchequer (which also began on 27 Nov.); 3). John Felton, who was condemned for Buckingham's murder on 27 and hanged 29 Nov. Birch, i. 437–442.

[2] Samuel Collins, vicar of Braintree in Essex and schoolmaster to Sir Thomas's sons.

the stopp, for it were a needless trouble to [*f. 298*] send a hors from hence to goe that 12 miles and so retourne heather againe. I am sorie to trouble yow with this, but that I see it is so long deferred, which I had hoped would have ben donn long since. I am much bound to you for your loving care of me and mine and desyre it in perticular to this poore child who I hope will be quickly refresht by God's blessing when he is neear your affectionate and tender eye, which obliges me to pray for God's protection on you with the best affection of

Your most dewtyfull sonn   Thomas Barrington

London, November 30, 1628
My wife presents yow with her humble dewtye and my two sisters with all dew respect.

Endorsed (*f. 298b*): To the honourable my very loving mother the lady Johanna Barrington at Hatfeild Pryory give [these]

13 *Sir Thomas Barrington, 6 December 1628*   (*2644, f. 299*)

Madam   Thare is no occasion so urgent as that can make me dispence with silence towards you when any opportunytie gives me leave to tender my service to yow, the best expression whareof (next my dewty and love presented) is to give yow London at Hatfeild in a perspective, which as cleearly as I can I heear doe. Reports hath converted bishop Mountague[1] (but fame outerunns the fact I beleive). The university of Cambridge as it hath ever ben active in complyeing with the present state, so now hath that old grandom of mine shewed more pallable meaneness of spirit and gross flatterye then ever, haveing written a congratulatorye letter to Sir Francis Cottington for his counsellship.[2] Such a busines for the bodye of whole universytie to glorye in the honor of one man no more then singly related to them; I say no more in the discoverye of her shame whose brests I once received a blessing from. The plate fleet is now in Holland, all fought with by the way and all escaped, thankes be to God.[3] The king sends now a shipp with victuall to the Elve, whither Generall Morgaine went lately with men to releive the toune, to whom the toune refused entrye being unprovided of victuall for them selves; a brave busines,

---

[1] Richard Mountague was installed as bishop of Chichester on 22 Sept. 1628. *D.N.B.*
[2] Cottington gained his seat on the Privy Council 12 Nov. 1628. *D.N.B.*
[3] The safe arrival of the captured Spanish treasure fleet in Holland and at Plymouth is reported in Birch, i. 443 (letter of 5 Dec. 1628).

for in all probabillytye those cold seas have frozen them all fast by this time and the way is impassable for Captain Minss (the man that goes now, and is gone indeed with the victuall shipp).[1] And now madam, upon takeing coach and in greate hast, I humblye take leave prayeing for a mutuall blessing from God upon us and so signe me now and ever

Your most dewtyfull and loving sonn

Thomas Barrington

London, Aldersgate West, December 6th, 1628

Endorsed (*f. 300b*): To the honourable my very loveinge mother the ladie Barrington at Hatfeild Broadoke

14 *John Barrington, 13 December 1628*   (*2644, f. 301*)

Deare mother   I have been latelie in Sussex with a frind of mine which hath both caused my neglect of my dutie in wrighting or comming unto yow, and at this present am constrained to stay about my monnie which is dew to mee from the kinge which wee are promised to have the next weeke, so soane as our accompts are all brought in, and so every man is to be cashered.[2] Howbeit it is reported that theare are two reigiments to goe for Venice among whome I do (God willing) intend to goe, and doe to that effect seake for a companie. I am very much bound to my lord generall bye my lord of Warwick's meanes.[3] He hath offred mee large courtesies for to incouradg my going in the very next imploiment which (as wee heare) wilbe about the middle of Februarie at the farthest. With the remembrance of my most humble dutie, I cease, and do beaseach the allmightie to guide yow in all your affaires

Your obedient sonn   John Barrington

London, December 13th, 1628

[*No endorsement*]

[1] Sir Charles Morgan's force had been sent to support the King of Denmark. Before setting off in June 1628 he had feared that money and supplies would be insufficient; now, if the Elbe were frozen over, Captain Mennes would be prevented from reaching him at Glückstadt. *D.N.B.;* Birch, i. 449 (letter of 12 Dec.); *C.S.P.D., 1628-9*, 395.

[2] The writer had taken part in the expedition to La Rochelle. On 28 Nov. the Council of War had ordered Colonels to submit lists of all inferior officers who had served at the Ile de Rhé and La Rochelle so that payment should be made. *C.S.P.D., 1628-9*, 398.

[3] Horace, Lord Vere of Tilbury and Robert Rich, 2nd earl of Warwick.

15 *Sir Francis Harris, 15 December 1628*   *(2644, f. 302)*

Deere ante   I ame humbly to thanck yow for the aparrell I lately received from yow which I will weare owte for his sake that is with God and yours that bestowed it of me. And it came in a needefull tyme, for by reasone of some late sicknes I was brought to a loe ebbe. It was my purpose to have sent yow a new booke of Sir Humphry Loynde his setting forthe which hathe a coherence in some sorte with that booke (caled Via Tuta)[1] which was the meanes of my convertione, beseeching yow to bee perswaded that noe worldely respect moved mee thereunto (for that waye I have disadvantaged my selfe if it weare to bee valewed) but meerely the favor of God towardes mee most especyally, and next the reasones of the aforesaid booke and the perswations of my loveing freindes, whereof your worthy sonne Sir Thomas and his vertuous ladye weare of the nomber, and I canne never forgett the greate love and desire of your selfe and all yours to presentt unto mee the good and badd examples of the tymes, wherein my loveing cosin your vertuous daufter the lady Lamplughe did her parte when I was last at your howse, so that my good aunte bee now (I intreate yow) confident of my resolutione (which would have joyed my most deere and loveing uncle in his life tyme) as I knowe it dothe your selfe owte of your wonted affectione towardes me, as I humbly thanck yow it hathe bine plentifully shewed unto mee, for which I am bound to saye God rewarde yow for it. I have strived, madame, to mache the culler of the clothe and cannott to make me a girdle and hangers against I have another sworde (for that I had broke by an ill accident in my owne defence), so that I would be a sewtor unto yow if the girdle and hangers (which weare of clothe as I take it) made to it maye bee readily founde yow would bee pleased to send them to the place where I received the other things or to my lodgeing, as opportunitye is offered, by Tusdaye or Wedsendaye next if it maye bee. And so commending yow and all yours to the protectione of the allmightie, I remayne

Your ladyship's unfaynedly to bee commanded

Francis Herris

My lodgeing, Mr Ridsleies in Cusseters Alley neere Lincolns Inne in Chancery Lane, Wedsonday, December 15, 1628[2] In some haste being in a lytle payne but hope of ease by phisick of charitie.

[1] Sir Humphrey Lynde, *Via Tuta: the Safe Way*, 1628.
[2] 15 Dec. 1628 was actually a Monday.

Endorsed (f. 303b): To the honored and vertuous ladie the Ladie Jone Barringtonne att Hatfeild Brodeoke, theise

16   *Sir Thomas Barrington, 15 December 1628*   *(2644, f. 304)*

Madame   My distance from the fountaine of newes hath putt me rather into the condition of craveing then gieving accompt of the occurents of time. I have no present now to tender yow, nothing to grace my lines with all but dewtye and love, which I beseich yow thinke as liberally offred to your hands in this barren harvest as in a more plentyfull cropp, sith he that gives all in a little is more free then he that oute of a plentyfull store parts with any thing less then all. My wife and I wish yow hartyly heear, whare the ground conceales the cloudes so continewall liberall streames: we heear of durt but see none. I am glad to heear you are in so good health as to resolve upon a journey, which I shall wish prosperous.[1] And praying for your blessing and comitting us all to God's protection be ever
     Your most dewtyfull sonn and as trewly
                                   Thomas Barrington
Annables, December 15, 1628

[*No endorsement*]

17   *Sir William Masham, 16 December [1628]*   *(2650, f. 310)*

Deare mother   I have sent these lynes to let you know how much we rejoice at your comming to us and how welcome you shalbe when you come. In the meane tyme we desire to heare of your good health and of the daye of your comminge, which we much long for, hoping it wilbe some daye this weeke. So with our humble dutyes and loves I commit you to the God of health and hapinesse and ever rest
     Your obliged   William Masham

December, 16th

Endorsed (f. 311b): To my honourable good mother the Lady Barrington these be given Hatfeilde

---

[1] Lady Joan was to go to the Mashams' house, Otes, at High Laver. Introduction, 17.

18 *Sir Gilbert Gerard, 17 December 1628* *(2644, f. 305)*

Good madam   I am sorry to heare that your lamenes continues and that therby I was deprived of your good company, then which nothing could give mee more content. But madam your comfort is that the lamenes of your feete can bee no hinderance in your jorny to heaven, for although thereby God disable you for worldly imploiment, you are at the more libertie to walke with him and freed from those burthens and cares which God requires at your handes when you are in health, so that such impediments are rather furtherances then hinderances in your spirituell jorny. But heerein I am fitter to bee scholler then a director unto your ladiship and therfore I crave your pardon.

The reyson you have not yet had an answere unto your last letter was not the difficulty of the matter, although for your satisfaction I had the advise of better lawyers then my self, but because I purposed before this time to have bine with you my self, but I was hindered by lamnes of my horses. For answere unto your point of law (notwithstanding the opinion of Mr Necton)[1] I thinke and so doe others that if a surrender bee made and the fine assessed and the tenant admitted there is noe doubt but the fine is due unto the lord and by his death is to bee paied unto the executor, and the entring of the roll and making the copy in the name of the new lord cannott alter the reste, and it is all one as if the fine had bine paied in the lorde's life time upon the admittance, for it being once a debt the death of the lord before the entry of the roll cannott alter the rest. But if the admittance had not bine made as it was in the Ile of Wight that would alter the case, for noe fine is due untill admittance.[2] For your other case of the rent paiable at Whitsontide, there is noe more question then of the wood mony in the Ile of Wight, for that which is due to the father [*f. 305b*] goes to the executor and cannot descend to the heire, for in a stronger case if rent to be paied at Michaelmas and there is forty daies after given to the tenant before you can distraine for the rent, yet if the landlord die after Michaelmas and before he can compell his tenant to pay the rent, which is not untill the fortie daies bee ended, yet this rent goes unto the executor and not unto the heire, and heere upon I have heard of some gentlemen that on Michaelmas and our Lady Day would ever put on there best clothes because they were richer by half a yeare's rent then they were over night, and yet they may die before they can compell there tenantes to paie it, because commonly they

---

[1] James Necton, see letter 185.

[2] Sir William Meux had written to Lady Joan in Aug. about fines on the Isle of Wight estate which had been contracted for before the death of Sir Francis. Letter 5.

have in all leases time after to pay it in. Thus have I at large given you the best satisfaction I could and I hope there will grow noe difference in a thing so plaine, and I dare undertake to satisfy my brother in this.

I thanke you for your great love unto my daughter and I am gladd to heare any good of her, but nothing would so much comfort mee as to heare that shee should doe you any service to expresse her thankfulnes for your love unto her, and I wish now shee is able you would make her continuely attend you.

I have not heard how my neece Mewx proceedes in the busines that was spoken of when I was with you. I saw Mr Goodwin when I was at London and I put my brother Barrington in mind to speake with him, but I heard noe more of it. If all bee at an end I pray send mee word. And now I have troubled you thus long I will conclude with praiers for your health and hapines, and so soone as I have meanes I will God willing waite on you. And so I rest

Your dutifull sonne   G. Gerard

17 December, 1628
Your nephew Thomas Bourchier remembers his dutie unto you.

Endorsed (*f. 306b*): To my honourable good mother the Lady Johan Barrington at Hatfeild these

19   *Lady Mary Gerard, n.d.,* [*December 1628*]   (*2650, f. 253*)

Most deare mother   I am sory your lamenes doth deprive me of your good company this winter which would have beene no small comfort unto Mr Gerard and my seulfe. But God in his wisdome knowes what is best for us. I hope it will be a means to preserve your life because it is so heilthfull a desease.

I pray excuse me for not waiting upon you by reason of the badnes of the ways. As soone as they are fitt to travill I will come and doe my duty unto you in the meane time my prayers shall not be wanting for your heilth and hapines. I must not forgett to give you many thanks for Jugg. I am very gladd to hear shee learns her worke so well. I should be glad to heare shee ware able to do you sum servis. If it please you to make use of any of the oyle of Exeter I will send you sum, it is very good for the goute as I heare. I am mutch bound unto you for my girle at nurse; I pray send me word what shee wants and it shall be sent her. Thus craving your blessing I rest

Your dutyfull daughter till deith   Mary Gerard

I hope Toby remembers my seale you gave me, I thanke you. I pray remember my love to my brother and sisters with Mr Haryson and his wife.

Endorsed [*in the hand of Sir Gilbert Gerard*] (*f. 254b*): To my honourable good mother the Lady Johan Barrington at Hatfield these
Toby I pray give my nurse 44^S for a quarter's wages due at Christmas and give her maid 2^S, and I will repay you when I see you.

20. *Sir Thomas Barrington to* [*Robert Barrington?*], *n.d.*, [*December? 1628*]
(*2650, f. 194*)

Good brother   You shall ever commaund your wellcom whare I can command my owne. I thanke yow for your care of my forrest business, concerning which no more untill I see yow, which I shall be glad of you shall ever find. For Mr Harrison's business I say no more till I see yow neither. Now Sir, haveing this oportunytie, I shall desyre yow to peruse a transcript of that part of a letter from Tobie which concernes Yorkshier busines*, which done, I shall desyre you to read my two letters written to him aboute the same (if he yet have them), for your better understanding whereof give me leave a little to inlarge my selfe. The first was upon this ground: Tobie tooke Nat Sumner's account at Hatfeild, both for the clough[1] (as he tould me) and the fines and the pennygrave,[2] whereof I had the generalls from Tobie and withall notice that my mother was pleased to give me the fines and the Whittson rents**. The steward of Cottingham and Nat being both with me at the receite of the letter, who both tould me that no coppyes were yet graunted the tenants that had surrendred and that theay were not to pay theire fines untill Michaelmas, and for the Wittson rents, though theay went by that name, yet thay could not be demaunded as dew from the bayliff by custom nor destrayned for untill Michaelmas. Heear upon I asked Nat aboute the clough (he haveing tould me it was begun in my father's time), what was layed oute before his death. He tould me aboute 16^{li} within a 20^s as he thought over or under, but Tobie haveing his accompt he could not particularly satisfye me but would perfect his accompt at Hatfeild in

* [*In margin*] for this verte foll.
** [*In margin*] towards the greate charge of the clough

---

[1] Clow: either a sluice-gate, or perhaps in this case, a floating clow, a device for clearing mud from tidal channels, particularly on the Humber; the manor of Cottingham is in question here.

[2] A pennygrave was a collector of manorial dues, chosen in the manor of Cottingham by the tenants from among themselves and paid 10s. yearly, 'but there's none they saie that desire the place for the profitt of itt'. E.R.O., D/DBa E71.

his retourne. All the particulars recited considred, I wrote to Tobie my opinion of somm things, quaeres upon others, [*f. 194b*] and so, super totam materiam, desyred that since I had not the accompts nor seene them, all might be made even between my mother and my selfe, that so I might know what to render dew thankes for. In this what I erred yet I understand not. I confess it might be so related to my mother as there might be a misunderstanding bredd, but could any man thinke me so simple as to intend to fall to expostulations when I know, and knew, that it was in my mother's curtysye and beyond the limitts and commaund of law to give? And had it not ben an easye business to Tobie to have made all even, and if I had ben misinformed by the officers to have written to me againe before he had exposed that to my mother which he thought would displease? I cannot but often remember what St Paule sayth of brotherly love, that (emong other sweet propertyes) it suffreth all things, beleiveth all things. I know yow understand the text and my intention, I am toe large and therefor say no more of that. In my last letter to Tobye I only answered to that displeasuer he tould me my mother tooke at my beleiveing every bodye before theay understand the case, to which I replyed that I desyred not be helde so easye to be ledd (or to that purpose), and for one part which concerned the fines tould him what I was confident verie good lawyers would saye. Need this have ben particularized to my mother? Or had not the fairest and honestest waye ben to have reported me in an ingenuous construction, which could not be, as he writes that I intimated my mother gave nothing. Was this thus rudely implyed, when I only in all my letters desyred an even accompt, a right understanding? I doe [*f. 195*] profess I was farr from such thoughts, but I could not know till I sawe the accompts what was dew on either side, nor till I understood the busynes, and therefore from somm part wrote only by way of admission of what I was informed, as yow may see by my former letters, and that for the maine. But in all this lett me not be mistaken, for I neither seeke to satisfye anye besides my mother that have delte in this business, nor doe seeke her satisfaction but oute of the dewtie of a sonn. For the monie I valew it not a hayre (I thanke God) further then it expresses the love of a mother to me, and that is above valew. For the gift, if I have made my selfe unworthie of it by so honest intentions, wither my judgment hath abused me or else I am toe much mistaken or misapplyed by som meanes to my mother. My desyre is that you would please to imploye your judgment and love to lett my mother know the truth, and then I am confident oute of a clear conscience that the desyres of a just knowledg of dew and an acknowledgment of gift cannot so much offend, I neither slighting of what was so freely offred nor demaunding of any thing as a dew. To conclude, was I such an ass, thinke yow, as to undervalew my mother's intentions, who when the gift was made resolved that all the somm was hers howsoever? I know yow are toe charitable to misconceive me so much in that as well as to beleive that I have not written this tedious tract to any end but that my mother, whose love I tender only for dewtye and loves sake, may know [*f. 195b*] me as I am. For the thing I can say as I ever sayed in all cases between us: if my mother will say 'this is myne', I shall use no peremptorye negatives; only I desyre a trew opinion of my cariage in the matter and then lett her take or give as she pleases.

Good brother pardon me, a full hart must take this large libertye and res ipse postulat. I have learnt patience, else I could easyly remember more from some in this matter then was necessary (but that secret only to yow). When yow have done the good office that I desyre I shall hope to see yow, in the meane while if my mother be now at Oates I pray that yow would stepp to her and right this mistakeing, not, I protest, to any end but for her trew understanding of me and my actions. I could tell yow my thoughts but I leave it till we meet, when yow shall know that I omitt now. Busines of this nature cannot be contracted; I hate my selfe when I am needlessly tedious and therfor hope yow will not now thinke me so to yow. My wive's and my love to yow and yours, whom I love so much, and assure your selfe that I shall ever be

> Your affectionate and faithfull brother
>
> Thomas Barrington[1]

Thare were somm by that can wittness (if I be not to be beleived) that I tould Nat he showld make all even with Tobie, both for the clough and the rest, that so if the other particulars proved my mother's or any of them upon Tobye's and his further conference, yet my mother might rightly understand the mony layed oute in my father's time, which Tobie never mentioned in his letter to me. This will explane me in all if yow rightly consider it.

Tobye's letter:- seeing you asked advice aboute her free gift for the clough and that it was thought to be your right and so her ladyship allowed nothinge, therefor what is dew to her she will expect, and what is dew from her shall be payed.

[*No endorsement*]

---

[1] Beside his signature Sir Thomas has written the initials TBJ.

21. *Thomas Bourchier,*[1] *26 January 1629* (*2645, f. 3*)

Good madame   Though I writte to your ladyship the other daye (wherein I gave yow notice what conference Mr Archer and I had concerninge my coosine Johan Meuxe) yet this bearer havinge busines for my brother with my coosine Hildersham, to whome he must come by your ladyship's dore, I durste not slip so faire an opertunitie of representinge my humbleste dutye to whome I sincerly acknowledge is due a greater debte then my shallowe braine can conceive or barren tongue can expresse. I beseech yow esteem not this as a complemente but beleeve it to be a reall truthe, flowinge from his breste that desires noe longer to live then he is willinge to be faithfull in all your commaundes. I can acquainte your ladyship with noe newes, all I heare is thus much in breife: the kinge upon laste Saterdaye in the banquetinge howse made knowne unto his people that the tundish and pundish is the free guifte of his subjects and the maine reason for his demaundinge it is his necessitye, he also hathe given faire hopes of a succesfull procedinge.[2] I doubte not but yow saye amen to this sunshine. Whatever the evente be in parliment, we have a hidinge place whose strength the malice of the insatiated adversarye cannot weaken; oh madame, how much are we bounde to God that he hathe freely given us Christe by whome we have shelter heer and assurance of glorye heerafter. Madame, if your occasions will permitt I humblye begg a line from your ladyship; yow cannot be ignorant what need I have of such divine councel as yow maye easilye enrich me with, I beseech yow therefore give a drop from your fountaine and tho I am unworthye of such a jemme, yet is he for whose sake I humblye begg it abundantlye able to render into your bosome sevenfolde for what yow doe to me his meane creature. My laste sute is that yow will pardon my rudenes, kindelye entertaininge the expressions of him whoe will firmely and faithfully remaine

Your sincerely observant nephewe to be commaunded

Thomas Bourchier

From my lodginge this 26th of January, 1628

Endorsed (*f. 4b*): To the honourable my noble aunte the ladye Johan Barrington at her howse these be given

[1] Third son of Sir William Bourchier of Benningbrough Hall, Yorkshire, and his wife Katherine Barrington. Table 1.

[2] The king's speech, delivered Sat. 24 Jan., is printed in W. Notestein and F. H. Relf, *Commons Debates for 1629* (Minneapolis, 1921), 10-11.

22. *Sir Gilbert Gerard, 27 January 1629*   (*2644, f. 271*)

Good madam   Meeting with a messenger from Hatfield your
ladiship might take it unkindly if I should neglect presenting my
servise unto you by him, and with all to congratulate your saffe
returne to Hatfield. I hope now you find your abilitie to travaile it
will incourage you to adventure on a jorny to Harrow, which we
should be very gladd of. One occation of my being now in the toune
is to shew unto my brother's counsell such wrightings of yours as are
in my hand and materially to bee used for the drawing my brother's
office,[1] wherein I only lett them see them in my presence and to take
such notes as must serve them, but I will not lett them goe out of my
handes, and if it be necessary that they be at the finding the office I
purpose to bee there at that time also.

I have likewise moved my brother Masham for to give securitie for
my neece's mony and he tels mee it shal be spedely done and that all
thinges are readie, and so I hope they be.[2] For parleament newes I
referre you to the parliament men. My wife and company at Harrow
I lefft well, I thanke God, yesterday morning, and God willing will
returne to them on Thursday. And so wishing you all hapines, with
thankes for all your favours to mee and mine
          I rest your dutifull sone   G. Gerard

27 January, 1628

Endorsed (*f. 272b*): To my honourable good mother the Lady Johan
Barrington these be given

23 *Robert Barrington, n.d.,* [*28 January 1629*]   (*2645, f. 7*)

Madam   I am not a little glad to heare of your welfaire and that
you are soe well as to keepe below. Little newes is heere stirring, only
now (thankes be to God) we have brought the business of religion into
the house and with one consent ordered that it should be the maine
business and first in agitation. I pray God direct us in this soe waighty
business, the success whereof is and wilbe the foundation of our happiness or missery. To morrow the house is to be resolved into a
committe and then to begin this greate worke.[3] I cannot now have
tyme to relate how many excellent speeches were made both yesterday

---

[1] Office of inquest, i.e. the inquest *post mortem* on the estate of Sir Francis Barrington.
[2] See letter 26.
[3] The house went into committee on religion on 29 Jan. 1629, the king gave his answer
to the petition for a fast on 30th. Notestein and Relf, *1629*, 28-9.

and this day in the cause of religion and against both popery and arminianisme. We are to goe to the king to morrow to receave his gratious answer upon the petition of both houses for a generall fast, which we make no doubt of being graunted. Forraigne newes I heare none, only there is a speech that the Hollanders have taken more shippes of late and surprized the convoy that was comeing with money to pay the souldiers in the archduchess' country. I purpose to take the first opertunitie to come downe for a day, then shall you know more. We have greate need of the earnest prayers of all Gode's people for his blessing upon our waighty affaires, especially in this perticular now in hand. It being now very late I am constrayned to be breifer then I would, therfore with many humble thankes for your many favours shewed to me and mine I shall now committ you to the protection of the lord and ever remaine

Your dutifull sonn   Robert Barrington

My brother Gerrad commendes his service to you

Endorsed (f. 8b): To my honourable good mother the lady Johan Barrington at Hatfeild Broadoke give [these]

---

24 *Robert Barrington, n.d., [4 February 1629]*   *(2645, f. 5)*

Madam   Litle newes is stirring since I came to towne: wee are still in the prosecution of the busines of religion, the establishing wherof is the generall resolution of our house before they undertake any other busines. This day there was a petition preferred wherin is expressed the greate encrease of papistes in the farther northerne partes, also in the same petition articles preferred against Doctor Cosins (who I thinke is deane of Durram) for the introduceing popish cerimonies into that place.[1] It was also said that Cosins should say the king had no more to do in matters eclesiasticall then his horsekeeper and yet both this man as also Manning, Sybthorpe and bishopp Mountague have pardons;[2] but I hope it wilbe found out who have ben the procurors of the same. By the next you shall heare more of this busines, it is a very fowle one and I hope will give us ocasion of findeing out further matter against them and others. I had a note from Toby that you forgate to aske me what I had donn about your wooddes and

---

[1] This petition was presented to the Commons on 4 Feb. 1629; John Cosin became bishop of Durham in 1660. Notestein and Relf, *1629*, 124; Birch, ii. 21; *D.N.B.*

[2] The pardons granted to Manwaring, Sibthorp and Montague were also reported to the house on 4 Feb. Notestein and Relf, *1629*, 124.

to whom they were sould and when the money is to be paid. Certainely I tould him I had bought them, but I will not be to confident; however I know he must neede heare of it, I thinke his brother John Bridge had speech with him about it, who desired to have joyned with me in the buying, and soe had he, but that he would not give soe much as I tould him I thought they were worth. I am sure I tould your selfe that I would sell 6 acres and 20 trees. To that end I further tould you I had some of the townesmen with me to view and buy the same, which was John Bridg and John James, who at first made as if they cared not for buying the same, but as we went home I proferred that we three would joyne and buy it. They would give but 44 or 46^{li} for the wood; I said it was worth 50^{li} as I thought, but they refused to joyne with me at that price, wher upon when I came home I tould your ladyshipp what I thought, and that I would give you soe much for the same. Your answer to me was you must trust me with what I did for you, and I thinke I have discharged the part of an honest man. I could have entreated yow that I might have had it at the price others had offered, but I thanke God I have rather valued those thinges I have bought of you at to high then to low a rate; but if I have suffered in it the fault is my owne. It's true they would have had parte with me when I had bought it, but they refuseing before, I refused after. For the money, the usuall tyme of payment for wood sale is Whitsuntide, but I purpose to pay it at Lady Day without faile. I hope this will give you full satisfaction in this busines, which I shall ever endevor to do in all other thinges. Thus craveing pardon for being soe tedious I committ [you] to God and am

Your dutifull sonn   Robert Barrington

My sister Masham hath sent you that which she writt to you she had sent by Pinching.[1] The chiefe cause of my buying your woodd was for hoppoles and to burne my bricke.

Endorsed (*f. 6b*): To my honourable good mother the lady Johan Barrington at Hatfeild Broadoke give [these]

25 *Robert Barrington, 9 [February] 1629*   (*2645, f. 1*)

Madam   I receaved a letter from you by Whyn dated 9th February; the resin why I do express the same is out of a feare that I have

---

[1] Pinching (or Pinchin) is the carrier, for heavier objects as well as letters, whose name occurs most frequently in Lady Joan's account book. E.R.O., D/DBa A15, ff. 2–47 *passim*.

of a miscarriage of some of my letters. I did by Whyn write you all the newes which was then stirringe, as also about the woodd which I bought of you,[1] but I do not perceave by your letter that you have receaved any such from me. I also sent another letter to my wife but have no answer, all which makes me much afraid that these letters came not safe to your hand, which much perplexeth me, for I would be very sorry they should come to other handes. I assure you I am very fearfull to send any letters by him, knoweing his greate carelessnes. I shall not be as quiett till I heare from you againe, I beseech you heerafter let me have speciall knowledg of the receite of my letters as I have now given to you. For the bookes you write of, Toby did send to Mr Man for them, and whither he sent them or not I know not, but if I heare from you againe I shall buy such as you command me. I pray do me the favor to give my wife my thankes for hir care in my busines; I thanke God the confidence I have in hir takes away the care that otherwise might troble me in the greate employment I now am in. There is yet little donn in Parlament. Bishopp Neale is still in question; the last complainte and greatest against him was that upon ocasien meeteing with Doctor Moore, a divine in Hampshire, he said 'I have heard you often preach before the king, and you were wonte to be earnest against poperie and your discourse was pleaseinge to your king, but now you must not, for the tymes are altered.'[2] The doctor is sent for to justifie the wordes, which he will certeynly do. There were many other passages in this busines, but this is the maine and which will touch him neerest. Sherriff Acton was this day committed to to Towre for not giveing sattisfaction in his answers to a committe about the merchante busines.[3] Mr Attorney who was committed to his chamber is againe restored to his place as yesterday. The fast, I make no question but you heare when it is appointed: for the parliament and the cittie the day is Ashweddensday, for the country the Friday before Good Friday, the preachers Mr. Harris lecturer at the church by Westminster, Mr. Harris of Hanwell and one Mr. Fitch Jefferies of the west parte.[4] The lord fitt us for that greate worke. I

---

[1] The reference is to the same writer's letter of 4 Feb. (letter 24): this and the incidents identified in the remaining notes below show Robert's error in dating the letter Jan. rather than Feb.

[2] Richard Neile, bishop of Winchester, archbishop of York from 1631. This and other of More's remarks is reported in Notestein and Relf, *1629*, 50-1.

[3] According to the published accounts, Acton, sheriff of London, was brought before a committee of the house on 9 Feb. but not committed to the Tower until the 10th. Notestein and Relf, *1629*, 52-3, 56-7.

[4] The preachers are listed as Mr Harris of St. Margaret's, Westminster, Mr Harris of Hanwell in Oxfordshire and Mr William Fitz-Jeoffery of Cornwall. Notestein and Relf, *1629*, 42.

beseech you excuse me to my wife for not wrighting at this tyme, haveing almost no tyme. Soe with my praiers to God for you I committ you to him and ever rest

      Your dutifull sonn   Robert Barrington

London, January 9th
I will do my uttmost to helpe my neice Mewx, especially hopeing she will make good what is promised in hir behalfe. Upon prosecucion of the busines of the pardens lately graunted we finde that the bishopp of Winchester hath bin the procurer of them.

Endorsed (f. 2b): To my honourable good mother the Lady Johan Barrington at Hatfeild Broadoke give [these]

26 *Sir Gilbert Gerard, 10 February 1629*   *(2645, f. 9)*

Good Madam   Meeting this bearer thus oportunly I could not but present my duty unto you and lett you know that I left your daughter and all mine well on Monday morning, saving my boy Will at Nurse Bedle's, who hath bine sometime feverish and well by fitts, so that we cannott guesse at his disease, but I hope it's only his teeth.

I have dispatched your busines about your inventory. And for my brother Masham's securitie for Jugg's mony, he tels mee he will doe it, but I cannott tell how, for I persceive by my cozen Hildersham that Toby and he and my brother Masham have never yet perfitted there accounts, so that it's uncertaine what is in either of your handes. I wonder why this hath bine so long neglected, for I did put both you and Toby in mind of it the last summer. And untill that be done my brother cannott give securitie because the somme is uncertine for what he must give it.[1]

For your leese of the tithes, I have thought sithence I was with you that in regard you meane to charge it with paiment of some somes yearly during the continuance, it wilbe best to take it as formerly it was, in names in trust, because it may the more esily be charged with such paiments.[2]

I should be gladd sometime to heare how you doe in a few wordes,

---

[1] See letter 168, n.1 for the complexities surrounding Joan Altham's inheritance from her father.
[2] See Introduction, 3. The lease was in the hands of trustees by 1615. Trinity College MSS. Box 9, II. c.2.

but Mr Steward hath noe leisure to remember such poore folkes as mee. Thus with thankes for all your love to me and mine I rest

      Your dutifull sone   G. Gerard

10 February, 1628

Endorsed (f. 10b): To my honourable good mother the Lady Johan Barington, these

27   *Sir Thomas Barrington, 14 February 1629*   *(2645, f. 11)*

Madame   No forgetfullnes of dewtie or of love hath silencet my pen thus long, but sometimes the want of conveyance, otherwhile the want of time. I know your goodness will valew me according to my generall indevors to express my selfe and not judge me as I may somtimes unwillingly appeear, who shall ever make it my studie (God willing) to approove my selfe to you in all my course and waies. We have no newes but what my brother Robert will more fully deliver then my pen can relate; I will rather choose to write those occurrents that the times minister then, when you are barren of intelligence.

Tobie wrote unto me concerning the monies you expect from me, which trewly I am not yet furnished to discharge; but you shall be assured of my care not to neglect to doe that which may be expected at my hands and I obliged to make good.

My wife presents you her dewtie and love, and my sister both, and I (constrained to conclude by Isaack's importunitie), committ us all to God and will be ever

      Your most obedient sonn   Thomas Barrington

Saint Bartholemew's, London
February 14, 1628

Endorsed (f. 12b): To the honourable my very loving mother the lady Joanne Barrington at Hatfeild Priory give [these]

28   *Lady Elizabeth Masham, n.d., [before 18 February 1629]* *(2650, f. 308)*

Deare mother   I desire pardon for my longe silenc in wrighting to you; indeed I did think to have gon downe this weeke, but haveing gott a very convenient lodging my husband is lothe to lett me goe away, yett Mrs Perkins is grone soe deare that I was very willing to gett my husband from thenc, and I doe much desire to be here att the fast the next Wedensday when the sity joyne with the parliment in keeping that day.[1] I pray God fitt us all ernestly to cry to the lord; we never had such need as now we have, we have no other refuge to fly unto. We may justly fare that we shall cry now and he will not here us, because we have soe longe refused to here him calling to us, and if we doe fall into great misirie we may lay our hand on owr mowthes and confes he hath bin very gratyus in sparing us so long. I pray God give us wisdom to prepare for the worst. I confes I daly se more and more that there is noe hapynes in any thing but in getting asuranc of God['s] love in Christ, and 'tis the only thing, I thank God, which I take comfort in, and I know you will say the like by your self. I pray God increase that comfort which at any time you have felt. I am very glad to here you are soe well. I desire the continuanc of your comfort both in sole and bodye, and shall pray for it as for my one. This with my humble duty, desiring to be rememberd to all my frinds with you, I remaine

        Your ever dutyfull daughter   Elizabeth Masham

When I am like to proseed in any match for Jugg you shall here. We showlde be glad to se you here. My cosin Bowcher hers no more of Mr Archer; Mr Goodwin is fre as yett.

Endorsed (f. 309b): To my honourable good mother the Ladye Barrington these be given

29   *Sir Francis Harris, 19 February 1629*   *(2645, f. 15)*

Good madame   I have just cause to remember dayley youe favors towardes me, and morning and eaveninge I wishe my selfe (weare it God's blessed will) with him whose garment I weare, whoe, amonge other of my deere freinds and alley, would have joyed at my convertione, and bee confident, deere aunte, I humbly intreate yow of my perceiverance and constant resolutione. It was your pleasure, I have harde, any tyme this ij monthes that I should have the gyrdle and hanggers which belonges to the sewte of clothers yow sent mee, and commytted the care thereof to your servant Tobey, whom I never gave any just cawse to be so careles of mee, for as yet I have not received them, thoughe at your worthie sonne his lodgeing (I meane Sir Thomas Barrington's) I have harde often wordes of comforte they showld come within 2 or 3 dayes after. And so intreating yow to excuse this bowldnes, being my costome not to use medyatione of others

---

[1] Ash Wednesday, 18 Feb., see letter 25.

(when I humbly thanck yow, I maye reapayre unto your selfe) I take my leave, with my best wishes to yow and yours, and will contynew
Your ladyship's ever to use and command

Francis Herris

Feeild Lane, Mr Maye's howse in the new brick bildings, Thursday February 19, 1628
Madam, thoughe I muche want them (haveing, to bee playne, none to weare and my purse to weake to buy) yet the former oner of them presseth my desire the more to have them. I beseeche yow to remember my love to Sir Thomas Ellyott and my ladie, whoe I heere are with yow. And in truth in the greate frost I was comming afutt madame, to see yow for 3 or 4 dayes, but a fytt of the stone toke mee.

Endorsed (f. 16b): To the right worshipfull my deare aunte the Ladie Barrington theise

30   *Robert Barrington, 20 February 1629*   *(2645, f. 17)*

Madam   I was very late before I knew of Mr Williams' goeing downe, yet I cannot let him pass without trobling you with a few lynes. The bishop hath appointed me to attend him to morrow morneing about your busines with the colledg[1] and I hope by the next to give you full direccion in that busines. For newes either forraigne or domestick, there is at this tyme litle stirring. Mr Williams, who walkes the citty, wilbe able to say more then I can who have not the least tyme to be from the busines of the house, which, if ever, then now doth require all possible dilligence. He can partly tell you what late rubbs we have mett with, to our greate distraction; I pray God bring us safe of. The next weeke in all probabillitye will discover much; it's praier must helpe us. I heard this day that my brother John had by an accident broken his legg, but how or by what accident, I heare not. My sister Masham tells me she hath written to you about it. I will to morrow enquire more of it. Thus with my humble service to you and praiers for you I rest and am
Your dutifull sonne   Robert Barrington

London, February 20th, 1628

Endorsed (f. 18b): To my honourable good mother the lady Johan Barrington give [these]

[1] Trinity College, Cambridge.

31 *Joan Everard, 24 February 1629*   *(2645, f. 19)*

Most deere mother   Your great love and many favors to mee
maks me ashamed of my self that I can express my thankfullness no
more. Good madam, Mr Everarde would have acquainted you with
this new newes when he was att Hatfeild, but knew not the sertainty
of it nor had no letter that any such thinge was before Tuesday with
senight, and then my Lord of Warwicke wright to his father and the
pattent came dowen.[1] My child has bene very ille againe which maks
me fearfull to stir from hir but, and pleas God, if the weather hold
faire, I purpose to come and se you the next weeke, and then nurse
Mitchell shall see that there is littell hope of me as yet. Thus beseching
your ladyship to remember my love to my sisters and brother, I
humbly take my leave and rest
            Your most obeydient daughter to commande
                                                        Johan Everard

Langleyes, 24 February, 1628
I desire that you would be pleased to send Isac for me, if he may be
spared, about the latter end of next weeke.

Endorsed (f. 20b): To hir Honourable mother the Lady Barrington give
these

32 *Sir Thomas Barrington, n.d., [25 February 1629]*   *(2645, f. 13)*

Madame   If my lines attend not you often enough, it is
not for any want of respect to you or defect in remembrance of that
dewtye which commaunds theise expressions, but the neglect of the
ordinary messinger, with whom it is more then ordinary to see me or
call heear. But I will not spend that little time he now affords me in
apologye. The newes yow heear by my brother were impertinent to
trouble yow in repeateing; what he sees not I only relate, which is a
face of generall sadness for this probabillytie of dissolveing us, all men
that wish well to church or commonwealth mourning for this threaten-
ing evell. Joye only now appears in those aspects that while religion
had so faire a way to advaunce in, were then no way pleased. The
king now pretends (at least) to be immoovable in that resolution
which the house at owr late debate made a dew claime to allter; it is

---

[1] Richard Everard was created baronet on 19 Jan. Warwick's part in obtaining this
and other baronetcies, through the agency (and to the advantage) of Benjamin More,
was noted by Symonds. G.E.C., *Baronetage*, ii. 67; B.L., Harl. 991, f. 31.

farr more easye to avoyde a rock while we are at a distance, then to escape splitting when the shipp is throwen upon it; my judgement cannot propose what is fitt in perticular, but generall wisdom I am suer justyfyes the rather saveing the best goods then by an untimely striveing for all to lett fall that which [is] most precious. This is necessarye and trewly it ought not to be omitted, but (if my opinion deceive me not) might have ben a while deferred. Princes should in pollicye have somm time and way left to evade when point of honour is in competition; if theay acknoledge theire acts past illegall, and theire ministers confess it and pleade ignorance, I know not why it were not better to take reasonable satisfaction for the rest and declare owr right to posterytye by a law, and the errors past, then by laboring to punish more to lett fall the end of our desyres in that and all. Lett us praye, and God will I hope bless our Mondaye's meeteing.[1] Madam I forgett no part of my debt; I shall now shortly be furnished to satisfye yow, God willing, to whom I committ us all and rest

    Your most dewtyfull sonn   Thomas Barrington

Endorsed (f. 14b): To the honourable my verie good mother the lady Barrington give [these], Hatfield Brod [Oak], Essex

33 *Sir Thomas Barrington, 2 March 1629*   *(2645, f. 21)*

Madame   Allthough I love not to be a messinger of evell tideings nor a relator of evells, yet my desyres are so greate to informe you with the occurents of the times as that I will rather make any truth my subject then be silent. This daye in parliament was like the generall of the times, such as hardly ever, no man allmost knowing what to doe; the distraction was so sodaine and so greate, and the case so highly concerning the house. What the perticulars were, you have an eye wittness to report at your leisure. In the generall, I must saye we have a verie greate cause to bless God that we concluded the daye with oute any greater business, the consequence whareof no man can say what it would have ben; yet was so probable to me, that for my part I was in discourse with my selfe what the events would be, of that which was in my judgment so likely. Well, God of his mercye looke on us; 'tis farr more easy to speake bravely then to be magnanimous in suffring, yet

---

[1] The house met on 25 Feb. only to be adjourned over until Mon. 2 March, the last day they were to meet. This letter must be of 25 Feb. and represents Sir Thomas's reflections on the debate and resolution of 23 Feb. Notestein and Relf, *1629*, 93–101, 167–9; for Sir Thomas's even more generalised observations on the events of Mon. 2 March, see letter 33.

he whose hart bleedes not at the threates of theise times is toe stupid. I pray God send us better grounds of comfort, and with all to be armed for the worst that can befall us. I am in somm hast and now I must signe me

　　　　　Your most dewtyfull and loving sonn

　　　　　　　　　　　　　　　　　　　Thomas Barrington

I pray God give us faith and judgment to carye us through this storme.

London, March 2nd, 1628

Endorsed (*f. 22b*): To the honourable my very loving mother the lady Joann Barrington at Hatfeild Pryory give [these]

34　*Thomas Bourchier,*[1] *n.d.*, [*2 March 1629*]　　　　　(*2650, f. 203*)

Honourable madame　　　　　　Findinge it the practice of sainctes in all ages in tymes of peril to excite eache other to looke to theire standinge and to quitte them selves like men, I whoe am a worme and no man, unworthye to be rancked in the number of these worthyes, humblye desire now to awaken my selfe by puttinge your ladyship in minde of these stormes which in the eye of reason this sinfull nation is likely to endure. Good madame, let me humblye beseech yow to weighe seriouslye the miserye which indeed hangs over our heades if thus your ladyship and other cedars take notice of the horrible sinns which crye aloude in the eares of thalmighty for a spedye powringe his vengeance upon this lukewarme nation. If, I saye, such pillars be awakened, how with a holye violence will yow wrastle with our father, not lettinge him reste til he againe looke with an amiable countenance upon this deformed and ingratefull nation.

I am confident that as yow are full of yeares so yow are full of divine experiments, which will not onely shelter your selfe but also those tender plants which by the same spirit crye Abba, father. 'Tis highe tyme for us now to try and examine our selves how the case standes betwixte us and our God. If we finde truthe in our inwarde partes, with what boldnes and sweet welcome shall we encounter our laste enemye which is deathe. Oh madam, this evidence of adoption will make us approache the throne of grace with boldnes, will make us, I saye, confident (notwithstanding these bitter tymes) to finde sweet advantage in the bitterest straite. Oh the excellency of faithe that gives the soule a hidinge place in the deepest deep.

[1] See letter 21.

Tho our sinns crye alowde for vengeance, tho I saye our sinns have a deep die, and in that respecte more justlye challenginge revenge, yet greater is the mercye of our father, of more value is the merits of our ever blessed saviour, then all the sinns of the whole worlde. If therefor we can repente, how readye is God to receive us into the armes of his love, yea, to kisse us with the sweet kisses of his mouthe, promising to scatter our sinns as a cloude, yea, to receive us graciouslye. I beseeche yow therefore madame give not this God reste till he gives yow hope to renewe his sacred covenante, namelye that he will be our God and we shalbe his people. How sweet will this marriage be; the shallowe reason of man cannot sounde the debthe of this excellencye. Now I cease to write ile begin to admire those unsearchable riches which are hid in our lord and master yet open to all those that sincerelye hunger after his appearinge. Madame, my thincks I heare yow saye 'tis strainge that such a striplinge sholde advise your wise gravitye. He before whome I muste appeare knowes that the verye love I owe your soule enforced these lines. I beseech yow give them lodginge and when yow please to sende for me ile bringe all I am to be your faithfull servant in the lord Jesus, to whose protection I commende your ladyship and all yours, in whome I shall continue

    Your obedient nephew   Thomas Bourchier

From my chamber this dismall day of breach of parliment[1]

Endorsed (f. 204b): To the honourable my noble aunte the Ladye Johan Barrington these be given

35   *Arthur Hildersham,*[2] *9 March [1629]*   (*2645, f. 156*)

Good madam   I received upon the 19th of February from my sonn Nathaniel a fair silver bowle, which he tells me your ladyshipp was pleased to send me, and by the scutchion that is upon it and the letters of your ladyshipp's name I well perceiv that it is soe.[3] I heartily thank you for it, and doe not so much rejoice in the worth of the gift

---

[1] See letter 32, n. 1.

[2] The puritan divine, vicar of Ashby de la Zouche, Leicestershire. Through his mother Anne Pole he was related to the Barringtons as well as to the Hastings family. Members of the Hildersham family lived in Hatfield Broad Oak. *D.N.B.; The Letters of Sir Francis Hastings*, ed. C. Cross (Somerset Rec. Soc. 69, 1969), 111; Introduction, 20.

[3] £3 'for a bowle sent Mr A. Hildersham' is entered in Lady Joan's account book under 15 March, 1629, so Hildersham must have written the year according to modern practice in dating this letter. He bequeathed the bowl to his son Nathaniel. E.R.O., D/DBa A15, f. 3b; Leicester Wills, Ashby 77.

it selfe (though it be much more then I have ever been able any way to deserve) as I doe in this, that I see your ladyshipp doth still retain a kinde remembrance of me. The book which I sent you of my lectures on John, as it was of small worth in it self, soe did I stand bound to send you one of them, not only for the many kindnesses which I have of old received, both from your noble husband who is now with the lord and from your self, but because also I knew well that the esteem your ladyshipp hath made of my poor ministry in tymes past would make you apt to take my poor labours in good part, how mean soever they be.[1] The imploiment I have had heer in my ministry for these 5 yeares past hath kept me from visiting you in all this tyme. Now is the tyme come wherein not my selfe only but all of my judgment are cast out as men utterly unprofitable and unfit to God any further service in his church. And through this unwelcom rest from the labours of my calling[2] I shall now have leasure and opportunity to see your ladyship and all your good children once again. In the mean tyme, I rejoice much to hear of your ladyshipp's constancy in the profession and practise of the truth, which soe long agoe with soe great readines and joy you did receiv. And thus (hoping to see you before long) I cease to be further troublesom at this tyme, but shall never cease in my daily prayers to commend you and all yours to the riches of God's mercy in Christ, ever remaining

Your ladyshipp's to be commanded in the lord

Arthur Hildersham

Ashby, March 9, 1629

Endorsed (f. 157b): To the right worshipful my very good lady the Lady Joan Barrington at her house in Hatfeild Broadoke geve these

36 *William Chantrell, 23 April 1629*   (*2645, f. 23*)

Worthy ladie   So many are my obligations to yow and your noble familie that if I should constantly consecrate my selfe to your service it were all to littell to express the largness of your favours, for

---

[1] Payments occur in the account book for single copies of a book by Hildersham on 26 Jan. and 2 Feb. 1629 and for two further copies on 9 Feb. His *Lectures upon the Fourth of John* was entered at Stationers' Hall in June 1628 and published in 1629. E.R.O., D/DBa A15, ff. 3, 3b.

[2] Hildersham's only recorded suspension from preaching at this period was between March 1630 and Aug. 1631 and he seems actually to have visited Lady Joan at Harrow in the early summer of 1630, but the evidence given in n. 1 above for the date of this letter seems conclusive. *D.N.B.;* C. Cross, *The Puritan Earl* (1966), 41; letter 154.

what soever I am in these partes of the world I am by Gode's goodness and your bountie. But my desire is rather to expresse thankfullness then to recapitulate what I owe your ladishipe. Those sounde foundations of true pietie, layd by that hand of that secound Nehemiah who now sleepeth sweetly in the bosome of his Christ, yow will erect, and be carfull to reare up that buildinge in that your worthy familie, that yow may be a mother of godlyness as he was a rich father of graceous imitation.

You know it was not only the comfort but the encomion of the elect ladie that her children were founde walking in the truth.

Rather was the practise of woeman of Samaria that when he[1] had gotten some eye salve to discerne who Christ was then to the cittie to drawe others.

God hath put a large price into your handes, I hope yow will lay it out so prudently that accompt may be easie and your faithfullness procure that mercifull recompenc. Come good servaunt and faithfull receeve your maister joy. My Ladie Bourchier will helpe to excuse my hast, for coming up to [York to] dispatch other busines I found her and her knight to be fitt messengers to convay a letter to your owne handes.[2] The God of grace build yow up to eternall life and fill yow full with all comfortes

 Your obliged servant   William Chantrell

Yorke, 23 Aprill, 1629

Endorsed (f. 24b): To the noble ladie Johana Barrington at Hatfelde Priorie in Essex

37 *Roger Williams,[3] n.d., [April? 1629]*   *(2643, f. 1)*

Madame   Your ladiship may wonder at this unwonted absence! And also aske what meanes this paper deputie? Give me leave (deare madame) to say with David to his brother in the field; is there not a

---

[1] Thus. The handwriting as well as the phrasing throughout the letter shows signs of haste and confusion.

[2] The seal on the letter shows a Bourchier knot between the letters E and G. See Table 1.

[3] Founder of Providence, Rhode Island, and a pioneer of religious liberty, Williams was at this time chaplain to the Masham family. On 15 Dec. 1629 he married Mary Barnard, 'Jug Altham's made', at High Laver; they went to America in 1631. *D.N.B.*, Smith, 27; letter 65. Letters 37 and 38 were printed in full (with a very few inaccuracies of transcription) by G. A. Lowndes in *New England Historical and Genealogical Register*, xliii (1889), 316-20. A large part of letter 38 is also printed in *T.E.A.S.*, n.s., ii. 34-6.

cause? A just, happily a knowne and open cause, I am sure, to your ladiship (who as an angell of God discerneth wisely) a known and open cause. Many and often speeches have long fluttered and flowne abroad concerning your ladiship's neere kinswoman[1] and my unworthy selfe. What little eare I have given that way (further then I have hearkened after your ladiship's mind) all that know me here doe know. Yet like a rowling snowball or some flowing streame, the report extends and gathers stronger and stronger, which causes me this day to stand behind the hangings and not be seene any way countenancing so great a busines which happily may want strength to bring it forth to see the light. It is the command of the God of wisedome, by that wise king Salomon: establish thy thoughts by councell. I presume, therefore, to consult (as most of right I acknowledge I ought) with the soonest with your ladiship, especially considering her loving and strong affection togeather with the report as strong abroad.

Good madame, may it please you then to take notice I acknowledge my selfe altogeather unworthy and unmeete for such a proposition. The neerenes of her blood to your ladiship and godly flowrishing branches hath forc't me to confesse her portion in that regard to be beyond compare, invalueable. Yet many feares have much possest me longe. I have to discover that sinceritie and Godlines which makes the lord himselfe to like his creature, and must make me, if ever. I have receaved some good testimonialls from mine owne experience, more from others, not the least from your good ladiship's selfe. Objections have come in about her spirit, much accused for passionate and hastie, rash and unconstant, other feares about her present condition, it being some indecorum for her to condesecend to my low ebb. There I something stick, but were all this cleared there is one barr not likely to be broken, and that is the present estate of us both: that portion it hath pleased God to allot her (as I heare) is not for present and happily (as things now stand in England) shall never be by us enjoyed.

For mine owne part, it is well knowne (though I would gladly conceale my selfe) how a gracious God and tender conscience (as Balak said to Balaam) have kept me back from honour and preferment. Beside many former offers and that late New England call, I have had since 2 severall livings profferd me, each of them 100ˡⁱ per annum, but as things yet stand among us I see not how any great meanes and I shall meete that way. Nor doe I [f. 1b] seeke, nor shall I be drawne on any tearmes, to part (even to my last parting) from Oates[2] so long as any competencie can be raised and libertie affoorded. I shall impart the utmost to your ladiship (more punctually that ever

---

[1] Lady Joan's niece, Jane Whalley. Introduction, 19.
[2] The Masham's house at High Laver.

yet to any). Beside this meanes I now from hence enjoy, litle is there that I can call mine. After the death of an aged loving mother, amongst some other children, I may expect (though for the present she be close and will not promise) some 20^{li} or 20 marck per annum. At hand (undisposed of) I have some 7 score pieces and a litle (yet costly) studie of bookes. Thus possessing all things have I nothing, yet more then God owes me, or then my blessed saviour had himself.

Poore yet as I am I have some few offers at present, one put into my hand, person and present, portion worthy. Yet stand they still at dore, and shall, untill the fairest end the lord shall please to give to this shall come to light. I have bene bold to open to your ladiship the whole anatomie of the busines. To wrong your precious name and answer her kind love with want would be like gall to all the hony of my life, and marr my marriage joyes. The kind affection of your deare ladiship and worthy niece is of better merit and desert. I shall add for the present I know none in the world I more affect, and (had the lord bene pleased to say amen in those other regards) should doubtles have fully answered (if not exceeded) her affection.

But I have learn'd another lesson, to still my soule as a weaned childe and give offence to none. I have learn'd to keepe my studie and pray to the God of heaven (as oft as I doe pray) for the everlasting peace and well fare of your kind ladiship, whose soule and comfort is in the number of my greatest cares.

The lord, that hath caried you from the wombe to gray heires, crowne those gray heires by making your last dayes (like the close of some sweete harmonie) your best: fruitfull (like Sarah) in old age, out shining all those starrs that shine about you, going downe in peace, rising in glory in the armes of your dearest saviour; to which everlasting armes he often commits your soule and yours who is

The unworthiest (though faythfull) of all that truely serve and honour you   Roger Williams

Endorsed (f. 2b): To his honourable good ladie the Ladie Barrington at Hatfield Priorie these

38 *Roger Williams, 2 May 1629*   *(2643, f. 3)*
Otes, May 2, 1629

Madame   I am forc't (with the sea man) for want of a full gale to make use of a side wind and salute your ladiship by another, being for a time shut out of my selfe. I doubt not but your good wisedome and love have fairely interpreted my cariage in that late treatie, and

I allso trust, quieted and stilld the loving affections of your unworthy niece: we hope to live togeather in the heavens though the lord have denied that union on earth.[1]

Deare madame, let me beg your christian pardon if I shall acquaint your ladiship with a busines of more waight and consequence and much neerer concerning your selfe. I beseech you to reade no further before you resolve to pardon and take with the right hand of love from the lord himselfe a message sent by me his unworthy servant. A better hand might better pen it; a better heart more tender of your peace and everlasting good, none that know you (if I can) shall carie toward you.

What I shall now expresse to your ladiship hath long lyen like fire in my bones, Jeremiah, 20.9.[2] I said I would not make mention of his name in this kind to you, but his word was in my heart as a burning fire, shut up in my bones and I was weary with forbearing and I could not stay.

Good madame, it is not for nothing the God of heaven hath sent such thunderclaps of late and made such great offers at the dore of your ladiship's heart. Distractions about children and their afflictions, deprivall of a deare and tender yoake fellow, weakenesses in the outward and troubles in the inward man, what are they but loud alarums to awaken you?

The father of lights be pleased himselfe to shew you the interpretation of these dreames. Certainely (madame) the lord hath a quarrell against you. Woe unto me if I hold my peace and hide that from you which may seeme bitter at present; it may be sweeter then hony in the latter end.

Incouragements to be naked and plaine your ladiship was pleased to give me at Otes.[3] If ever (deare madam), when there is but the breadth of a few gray haires betweene you and your everlasting home, let me deale uprightly with you.

I know not one professor amongst all I know whose truth and faythfullness to Jesus Christ is more suspected, doubted, feared, by all or most of those that know the lord. Woe to me if I shall conceale what great thoughts of heart the lord suffers yet to be and breake forth in his dearest saincts about you. And yet no hand in this is with me. The God of heaven and your deare selfe only know these secret lines.

It hath almost astonisht me (and I trust will deeply affect your ladiship) that not only inferior christians, but ministers, eagle eyed,

---

[1] See letter 37. The breach between Williams and Lady Joan over his marriage hopes can only have been widened by the plain speaking which follows in this letter. They were reconciled a few months later. Letters 49, 64.

[2] Correctly, Jeremiah 20, v. 19.

[3] Lady Joan had stayed at Otes in early Jan. 1629. E.R.O., D/DBa A 15, f. 2.

faythfull and observant to your ladiship after so many yeares of God's patience toward you, so long profession, such helps and meanes incomparable, should yet be driven to sigh, to say litle, to suspend their judgments, to hope, but feare and doubt.[1]

[*f. 3b*] I know (deare madame) your heart is full at these relations. I beseech you (as David said) on me let your thoughts and the burthen fall, but what have those sheepe done? Where 2 or 3 or few are excepted, the names of so great a number may well be spared.

Three things especially have I often gathered from them: First, feares are that the world hath choakt those blessed seeds that have beene sowne, and keepes the fruite from true perfection. 2dly, a strangenes from the faythfull in spirituall societie: this is the fayrest evidence of adoption, if this pin breake all falls. A 3rd, a stand or stay in the wayes of holynes: young plants of yesterday giving fairer testimonies of greater fruitfullnes.

Deare madame, I beseech you by all those multitudes of tender motherly mercies that are in God and exprest to you, by that inconceaveable patience of the lord toward you, by the bowells and blood of the lord Jesus, by all those sweete cords of love whereby the blessed spirit of God hath striven to draw you, make a stand, and spread my letter (as Hezekiah) before the lord in secret.

If ever (good madame) cry hard, and the lord helpe me to cry for you. Let those 2 peticions, Psalm 51.11 and 71.9, be deare to you.[2] Remember, I beseech you, Revelation 2.2,3; the church of Ephesus was much esteem'd by God for her worcks, her labour, her patience, her not bearing with those that were evill, for that she had borne and for his sake laboured and not fainted, and yet angry was he and he had something against her, and it was because she had left her first love. The lord establish my hope, for I hope it may be but so with your ladiship, only I beseech you lay to heart these few considerations.

1. First: Job, 34.9. He with whome we deale excepteth not the persons of princes nor regardeth the rich more than the poore; for they are all the worck of his hands.
2. Where birth great, maintenance more ample, time longer, and meanes of grace more plentifull, there a great account is of the lord expected. Luc. 12.[3]
3. The lord will doe what he will with his owne. He owes you no

---

[1] The others expressed their doubts about Lady Joan's spirituality more prudently. Introduction, 15.

[2] Psalm 51, v. 11: 'Cast me not away from thy presence, and take not thine holy spirit from me; 71, v. 9: 'Cast me not off in the time of age; forsake me not when my strength faileth'.

[3] Luke 12, v. 48: 'For unto whomsoever much is given, of him shall be much required'.

mercy. Exodus, 33.19. I will be gracious to whome I will be gracious, and will shew mercy to whome I will shew mercy.

4. Call to mind what a cut, what a gnawing worme it will be (the lord, the lord forbid it) if ever you cast up your eye toward heaven and see so many blessed branches in the bosome of Christ, and your stock rejected.

5. Slight not I beseech you all these late loud alarums and sharpe files with which the lord hath striven to burnish you. Ezeckiel, 24.13.

6. Remember I beseech you, your candle is twinckling and glasse neere runn. The lord only knowes how few minutes are left behind, Psalm 95.10. Fortie yeares was I greeved, then I swore in my wrath they should never enter into my rest.

No heart but a trembling heart can get assurance the lord hath not sworne. To that heart he hath sworne to be gracious. In that petition my soule followes hard after him, and still will I wrastle untill you say a blessing is come, a blessing of a heart softened and trembling, of a soule gasping after Jesus Christ, a blessing of joye refreshing to the faythfull and to him who is ever

Your ladiship's most faythfull and truely observant

Roger Williams

Endorsed (f. 4b): To his honorable good lady the Lady Barrington at Hatfield these

39 *Lady Judith Barrington, n.d., [June 1629]* (*2650, f. 164*)

Madam   By Tobie's being in toune I understood your intention the begining of next week to goe to Harrow,[1] sence which time I have been much perplexed in my thoughts that you should the same week goe awaye wherin we resolved to attend you, which hath had the slower publishing by reason of my husband's soe longe unexpected staye I know not whear, for since his goeing into Bedfordsher on Whitsun Monday[2] I have not heard one word whear he is although I have written 2 letters to him, and I have deferd this my writing heatherto hoping of his cominge home. And now I see Saterday come time is so pretious that I must not delaye this sending unto you, which is onely to be an humble suitor to you that you would not now leave

---

[1] Lady Joan left Hatfield on 17 June for Harrow-on-the-Hill, where she stayed with the Gerards for just over a year. Introduction, 17.

[2] 25 May 1629.

us before my actions may assure you of my faithfull respect and love in my attendance of you, wherin you shall not want, God willing, all comfort and contentment that lyeth in my power. And if you should goe now awaye I know it would be such a greife to your sonne that his hart will not easily be quieted againe, he beleeving, it seemes by some encoragedment from your selfe, that you would have [*f. 164b*] patience untell the begining of this terme, and then all our businesses would be put into some good order that we might leave London. You may very well think that though my husband could not come hetherto yett I might, and I had a hart forward enough had I not been prevented by taking care to make my selfe perfectly in health by my perserverance in my coorse of phisick to the last prescription which held untell the Fryday before Whitsuntide, so that in truth before that time I could not stirr without hazarding my health, which hath been but crazy at the best ever sence Christmas. I know you have cause enough to complaine to be left soe longe upon uncertainties; I have been sencible of it, but it must be my part to try to procure your forgetfulnes of all errors or offenses that are past and to entreat you will be pleased to make us happy in your company at Hatfeeld at least this sommer, or ells I shall have litle joye to come thether. And thus hoping to receave a comfortable answear from you, with all affectionate wishes and trew service I rest

    Your most respectively loving daughter to command

                         Judith Barrington

Fryday night

Endorsed (*f. 165b*): To my most honored mother the Lady Joan Barrington at her house at Hatfeeld Pryory this

40 *Sir Thomas Barrington, n.d.,* [*June 1629*]   (*2645, f. 25*)

Madame   You may please to assure your selfe that this season is not so pleasingly consumed in London were not your company a motive above other to call me to Hatfeild as soone as my busyness will possiblye admitt; not many dayes now God willing shall interpose. But I am sorye to heear at this instant (being in my letter) that you are for Harrow; not that it were fitt to confine your desyres, but that I and my wife wish that your convenience of staye at Hatfeild might have mett with owr resolutions to attend yow thare, which will neither be so pleaseing nor so commodious or convenient (especially at owr first entrance) with out you. This sayed, we submitt to your pleasure. The gentlemen prisoners appeared this morning at Westminster: Sir Peter Hayman hath a freedom and Sir Miles Hobart; Mr Coreton hath his libertye (upon petition 'tis voted for Mr Coreton).[1] The Buss[2] is sayed and hoped will be taken. Thus with my wife and selfe presented in all dewtye and affection I committ us all to God

      Your most dewtyfully affectionate sonn

                              Thomas Barrington

Endorsed (*f. 26b*): To the honourable lady the lady Joann Barrington give [these]

41 *James Harrison, 29 June 1629*   (*2645, f. 27*)

Worthy madame   I have much cause to blesse God and to be thankefull to your good ladiship for your great love with the many bountifull expressions of it formerly and of late, both at your goinge from us and my comeinge from you. The lord who hath promised not to forgett the least kindnesse shewed to his will I doubt not recompenc this abundanc of your effectuall love. For my poore self it is little or nothing I can doe, what I am or can shall I hope not be awanting in any service wherin I may be of use to your good ladiship in your furtheranc towards your hoped for happines. My weak prayers I shall desyre and endeavor dayly to present at the throne of grace for you and yours. Being at this distanc I cannot otherwise, eyther in publik or private, performe that meane service to God and your soule which formerly I have (I blesse God not without acceptation and profitt) and hope hereafter in God's good tyme to doe againe. My heart is with you, and as I may I will personally attend you, though in that I am prejudised by the indiscretion of divers of our people when I was at Harrow, whose absenc from the church goeing to High Laver and elsewhere did so offend Mr Parker[3] that good Mr Wilson[4] (who humbly and thankefully remembers his service to your good ladiship) tould me Mr Parker vowed to him that, were it not for the love he did

---

  [1] Hayman and Coryton were released in June, although the exact date is not known, but Hobart appears to have remained in prison until 1631. A letter from Sir George Gresley to Sir Thomas Puckering of 28 June 1629 speaks of the prisoners being moved from one place of custody to another 'to prevent the parliament-men of that liberty which otherwise the law would have allowed them'. H. Hulme, *Life of Sir John Eliot* (1957), 317, 338; Birch, ii. 22.

  [2] 's Hertogenbosch. John Barrington had news of its taking by 21 Aug. but the newsbooks (which have survived only fitfully for this period) report the progress of the siege as early as 4 June. Letter 54; Dahl, 216.

  [3] Francis Parker, vicar of Hatfield Broad Oak. Introduction, 14-15.

  [4] Vicar of Elsenham. See letter 51.

beare me, I should not preach in Hatfeld till they were willing to come to heare him in the afternoones.

Deare madame, goe on with courage and resolution; fixe one ey upon your self, that your soule may ever be sensible of your need of the mercyes of God and merites of the lord Jesus; fasten an other eye upon the unsearchable mercyes of God and the infinit merites of the lord Jesus; in your self be nothing, that Christ may be all in all with you and for you; keepe close unto the lord, let him be the alpha and omega the begining and endeing of every day unto you, behould him ever behoulding you, make his word your rule and his spirit your guide: so shall your course be right and your conclusion sweete: be humble for infermityes and frayltyes, but not too much dejected where the heart is upright: improve all meanes for a spirituall growth, it was a sweete and great commendation of that church of Thyatira[1] that her workes were best at the last. I write not these things as doubting, onely I thinke it not amisse to exhort, which even the best have need of and I know your ladiship will take well. The God of heaven prosper all your holy endevors and fulfill all your Godly desyres upon your selfe and all yours.

My wife (who humbly and thankfully remembers her duty and service to your good ladiship) hath made diligent search for mistris Johanna Jarrotte's[2] samplar but cannot finde it. I hope she will finde it againe. The last tyme that eyther my wife or any of the children saw it, it was in her owne boxe, putt up into it by her self. Thus with the rememberanc of my best service and respect to your good ladiship, desyring that both my selfe and wyfe may be respectyvely and thankefully remembered to Sir Gilbert Jarrett with his worthy lady, my lady Lamplugh and mistris Barrington, desyring by you all to be remembered to the lord I take my leave, ever resting

at your ladiship's command   James Harison

Hatfeild, June 29, 1629

Endorsed (*f. 28b*): To my honorable good lady the Lady Johanna Barrington at Harrow on the hill in Midlesex geve these

---

[1] Thyateria one of the 'seven Churches' of Asia. Revelations 2, v. 18.
[2] Joan Gerard.

42   *Sir William Masham, 1 July 1629*   *(2645, f. 29)*

Deare mother   Though we were sorrye to part with you, yet we
are glad to heare of your good health at Harrow which gives us some
good hope of your speedy returne unto us. We are now at Hatfeild to
welcome our good frends home,[1] but we miss our best frende, the best
ornament of the house, whose presence will quicken much these de-
cayinge partes, and setle well your olive plants in theyre propre soyle,
to their content and the countrye's good. But I shall not neede to
persuade you to make hast to us whose good affection to your proper
place and desire to doe good in that station wherin God hath set you,
will drawe you to us, as the needle to the loadstone. Yet this we desire
conditionally, that it maye stand with your good health and comforte,
which we must preferre before our owne contents. So leaving all to
your wisdome, and you to God's blessing with our humble dutyes, I
rest
            Your obedient sonne   William Masham

Hatfeild, July 1, 1629
I praye present our affectionate love to all our frends with you.

Endorsed (f. 30b): To my much honoured lady and mother the Lady
Barrington at Harrow on the Hill give these

43   *Sir Thomas Barrington, 8 July 1629*   *(2645, f. 31)*

Madame   I am wondrous sorie that my good intentions have no
better success. I can say what my dewtie and love to you is, what my
care to give you no just scandall, but the beleife is yours. If I should
repeate what I have donn and indevored to steear me of this rock, I
should be toe tedious. I had rather trust to the goodnes of your owne
second thoughts, which I am confident will cleear me, especiall when
it is I hope not unknowen to you that my resolution was to have
waited on you with my wife, but was inevitablye diverted from my
intentions, and had not halfe an hower spare after that before my
coming heather. For that which you are pleased to call a wrong, the
not payment of your monyes, I should be sorye that any one should
justly taxe me with such an injurye. You may please remember that I
made you over all my rents in Hatfeild etc, and the 100^{li} to be payed

---

[1] Sir Thomas Barrington and Lady Judith returned to Hatfield in June, after Lady
Joan had left for Harrow.

oute of [f. 31b] the coppye, before I received one penny of either, which you seemed fully satisfyed in. I tould Tobye that I acknowledged it a favor, haveing so many payments to make a Lady Day, and with all that if you needed a speedyer payment I would rather take it up then you should be any way unsatisfyed.* I have heard nothing, but of a desyre to have the tenants quickned, since that. I am now upon my journye, but when I retourne you shall find, God willing, that as those I valew not shall not justly accuse me of any wrong that I will not repaire in this case, so to you I shall ever rather part with any part of my owne then be found any way less then

      Your most dewtyfull and loving sonn   Thomas Barrington

I desyre your blessing along with me, and offer joinct prayers for the continewed blessing of God in your health and in owr journey and retourne againe, by his good favor to us.

Hatfeild Broad Oak, July 8th, 1629

Endorsed (f. 32b): To the honourable lady the Lady Johann Barrington at Harrow on the Hill at Sir Gilbert Garrard's give [these]

44 *Sir William Masham, 8 July [1629]*   (2645, f. 33)

Madame   This daye my brothers and sisters toke theire jornye for Yorkeshire, which maks us now thinke the more of our great losse of your good companye, and maks us longe the more for your returne to us. Hatfeild condoles with us, and Esses longs for that happye daye of setling, which I hope will produce another patriote for them out of that noble family which hath bene honored so long by them. My brother was at this sessions and begines now to affect our countrye business, which gives us good hope that he will parcivare to all our comfortes and his countryes good.[1] I hope we shall not want you to incourage him. I had a good mynd to come and see you now, but that my business is great, espetially now my brother is gon, and besids our sises are approachinge.[2] I will visit you as soone as I can and should be

* [*In margin:*] If I had heard of the tenants' non payment or the coppye monyes to slow, yow should not have been unsatisfyed.

---

[1] See Introduction, 10.

[2] Quarter sessions were held on 2 July and assizes on the 13th. Sir Thomas Barrington is recorded as having attended the assizes. E.R.O., Q/SR and Calendar of Assize files.

glad I might wayte on you home to Hatfeild. In the meane tyme I have sent this bearer to see how you doe and to bring us good tydings of your welfayre, which wilbe welcome newes to us. So with our humble dutye and loves, remembring you in our dayly prayers, I rest
        Your obliged   William Masham

Otes, Juli 8

Endorsed (*f. 34b*): To my honourable ladye and mother the Lady Barrington these be given

45   *James Harrison, 17 July 1629*   (*2645, f. 35*)

My honorable good lady   I humbly blesse the lord to heare of your good health: he in mercy continue it with increase and blessing, filleing your heart with joy and gladnes in the sweete and comfortable behouldeing of his favorable and fatherly countenanc in Jesus Christ. For this purpose I humbly beseech your good ladiship continue still your holy care of maynetayneing fayth and a good conscience, the rootes from which true peace and joy springe; while we ar carefull to nourish the former, we have the latter eyther in sense and feeleing or in assured expectation, by virtue of God's promise to the belevers and Godly, or at least we have them in the true cause and ground of them, and shall in due tyme have the feeleing and experienc of them: psalm 97, last verse. For the mayneteyning of the former the observation of these rules followeing wilbe of good use.
1. Labor to be well acquainted with our owne guiltynes and corruption by a diligent veiw of our hearts and lyves in the glasse of the word.
2. Dayly arraigne, indite and judge our selves before the lord unworthy of his least blessinge, most worthy of his greatest judgements, even of a 1000 hells, by reason of our sinfullnes, originall and actuall.
3. Make we our appeale from the throne of justice to the throne of grace by askeing, seekeing, knockeing with sighes and groanes for mercy and pardon of all our sinnes past and for power and strength against sin for tyme to come, out of a deepe sense of our need and an earnest and high prizeing desyre of findeing favor with God in and through the lord Jesu Christ in these thinges.
4. Keepe a dayly watch over our hearts and wayes, being humbled for fayleings, thankefull for the least measure of true care and indeavor to please God, and power to resist our spirituall enemyes, Satan, the world and our owne sinfull lifes, and dayly endeavoreing by a holy

improveing of all meanes of grace, publike, private, secrett to better owr proceedings in the wayes of God and to be more faythfull and fruitfull unto all pleasing: Colossians, 1.10.

5. Ever behould the lord behouldeing us, endeavoring to walke besemeing his presenc and denyeing our owne wisdome, make we the spirit our guide and the word our rule in all our courses, and by a dayly casting up of our accomptes and making streight with God through Christ, labor to be prepared to gyve up through fayth in his merites and the conscienc of our owne sincerity by his grace a comfortable accompt into the hands of the lord at the last.

6. Wysely and carefully observe God's dealeing with us eyther in mercyes or corrections; let the former, especially in spirituall thinges (as heareing our prayers, strengthening us against temptations, supporting us under afflictions and blessing the lord for spirituall benefitte) be strengthening to our fayth in his promises and providence and incouragementes to wayte upon him in his owne wayes for further mercy; and lett the latter be meanes of humbling us and exciteing of us to endeavor a true reformation of what by diligent search and prayer the lord shall show us to be amisse.

7. If God witnesse with and for us of the sincerity of our heartes and integritye of our lyves, we ought not to be too much discouraged, or to question our being in the state of grace, for imperfections and infirmtiyes in fayth or practise; a heart mourneing for those things and trewly desyreing and endeavouring to honour God more in the obedienc of fayth never wantes acceptation with God.

Good madame, it is my hearte's desyre in absenc and presenc to doe your soule all the service I can; I owe it you many wayes and greyve I can doe noe more. The God of heaven direct your courses with much true comfort towards the heavenly Canaan, he in mercy heale all the diseases of your soule, cleare all your doubtes, remove what ever hinders your sweete peace at any tyme, or in measure and by such degrees as shalbe most honorable to his majesty and best serve to establish your ladiship's heart in the assured hope of glory, draw on that good work of his grace in you unto the end, till grace be perfected in glory, for the sake of him who hath meritted this for you and is at the father's right hand in glory and power to communicate these thinges unto you. Unto him who hath loved and washed you in his blood I doe humbly and heartely commend and comitt you, as to him who careth for you, and in him (my owne and my wyve's duty and service thankefully remembered to your good ladiship) I shall ever endeavor to be

at your ladiship's command   James Harison

Hatfeild Broadoke, July 17, 1629
Pardon my tediousnes, let your love and my intention excuse me. The
lord our good God guide your journey to us in his good tyme with
much blessing.

Endorsed (*f. 36b*): To my honorable good lady the Lady Johanna
Barrington at Harrow in Midlesex geve these

46 *John Barrington, 18 July, 1629*   (*2645, f. 37*)

Deare mother   I am exceeding sorrowfull that I have been
forced by reason of my longe sicknes to be so often importunate to
request your favour in the releafe of my greate necessities, wherby I
know I have beene very chargeable unto yow, without which love of
yours so highlie shewed to mee I could not have imagined what I
should have done for my releafe all this time.[1] I beseach yow not to
esteame your love ill bestowed upon mee hearin; I trust in God I shall
never give yow cause so to doe, but yow shall (God willing) ever finde
mee willing to strive to desearve your love to my uttermost power and
indeavour. I must indeade confess I was more then ordinarie chargeable unto yow latelie (being constrained therunto which I could not
avoide), in which respect I do understand yow are displeased with
mee (which hath much troubled mee) but I do intreate yow if yow
have conceaved any distast against mee hearin that yow would be
pleased to remitt it, assuring yow I will carefully avoyde any thinge
which I can thinke to be displeasing to yow.

I do understand it is your pleasure to know of mee what course I do
purpose to take when God shalbe pleased to inable mee with strength
to goe abroode. I beseach yow not to harbour any other conceite then
that I am resolved to take such a lawfull course as shall be both
pleasing to God and liking to your sealfe; this my desire, for I delight
not in sullenes. But as yet I must with patience waight God his pleasure
for my former strength, for as yet I have not nore dare beare any
waight upon my hurte legg because the bone is not all come of that is
to scale of. I only as yet goe with cruches now and then about my

---

[1] John had broken his leg in Feb. Lady Joan gave him, or laid out on his behalf,
nearly £50 between Dec. 1628 and July 1629. This included £8 to his surgeon in
March. Subsequent payments included a further £8 to the surgeon in Sept. Letter 30;
E.R.O., D/DBa A15, ff. 2–5b, 8; Introduction, 19–20.

chamber. With the remembrance of my humble dutie I commend yow to God his protection remayning

Your obedient sonn John Barrington

London, 18 July, 1629

Endorsed (*f. 38b*): To my honourable mother the lady Johanna Barrington

47 *Sir William Masham, 24 July* [*1629*] (*2645, f. 39*)

Madame This slowe haye weather suts not with our longinge desires to see you and the rest of our frends at Harrowe, which I hope you will accept for the deede, till we can performe with conveniencye. In the meane tyme our harts are with you, our thoughts upon you, and our prayers for you, which is the best service we can doe you, absent or present; ney, these dutyes make us present in the spirit, though absent in the flesh, being a pleadg unto us of our union to the heade and communion with the memberes. It is good to quicken these affections in these dead declining tymes, and whet on one another in love and fayth which are the bonds of perfection uniting us one unto another, and all to Christ, the mirror of perfection, to whose grace and glory I commend you and us all, restinge

Your devoted William Masham

July 24

Endorsed (*f. 40b*): To my much honoured mother the Ladye Barrington these be given

48 *Sir William Masham, n.d.,* [*July? 1629*] (*2650, f. 314*)

Deare mother I ame much bounde to you for your kind letter and desire of our companye. You cannot be so desirous as we are to enjoye yours, and our purpose was to have visited you this weeke, but that a necessary business at Colchester hath with drawen me, being lately put into theyre commision of goale delivery and ernestly desired by the burgesses to be there present this next Mundaye, so that I feare now we shall hardly see you till after haye tyme, by which tyme I hope my brother and sister Barrington wilbe returned, and then we hope to come and fetch you home, where you are much desired and not without just cause, for we are sensible of the want of you. I ame glad the cherryes came so seasonable, but I must returne your thanks, being a pig of your owne sowe, as the proverb is, and crave rather pardon for my boldnes to send you of your owne. But I see acceptation crownes the worke, and doth incourage to future performance, and to present my humble service in these rud lynes to your noble selfe, and my true respects to my good frends with you, whom I long to see and thank them for theyre loves and great desier to see us. And so with my prayers for you I rest

Your obliged   William Masham

I ame right glad to heare of your inclination to Mr Williams who wisheth to you as to his owne soule; a good man is a good frend.

Endorsed (f. 315b): To my much honoured mother the Lady Barrington these be given

49 *Lady Elizabeth Masham, n.d., [July? 1629]*   *(2650, f. 300)*

Deare mother   I humbly thank you for the token you sent me. The ladis at Lees[1] were such abowt their necks with their peticotes and wastcotes. I went with my husband to Chelmsford and Langlyes and so did only supp at Lees. He went in his coatch because Jug has to goe gett hir a payer of bodis. I am glad my husband sent you some of your one cheries and that they cam at soe fitt a time to my sister Robert. My lady of Warwick sends all most evrye day for some, and this day she charged Jug Altham to goe to Hattfeeld and se a baskett-full well putt up for hir; and soe Jug means to preserv some doble cheries for my sister Garard. She preserved 2 pownd of single cheries for my sister before, but I know not whether she will have them or no; if she will not, I will. I am glad you liked my litle pulletts I sent you, I will gett some more fatt to send you. I had hoped to have seen you the next week, but my husband is so importuned by Colchester men to be there on Monday that it hinders my joyrnye because he goeth in his coatch, but when he coms back I hope to have liberty after our haye. I am very glad you have overcom your pashon and will see Mr Willyams. It will be to your grete honer to pass by ofencis, and if we consider how much God forgivs us we canot but forgive such as ofend us, especialy it being the condishon God maks to forgive us if we forgive others. He took noe unkindnes that I colde perceave for your not seing him, he did not speak a word of it tell I asked him. He will

---

[1] Leez Priory, Essex, home of the Rich family.

be very glad to atend you asoone as he can, but it willbe longe first, by reson of much busynes which he hath. Both he and we will not sease to pray daly for hapy being thare and your safe return when the lord shall se it fitt, to whose protectyon I comit you and ever rest

Your obedent daughter   Elizabeth Masham

When I here from my brother Knightly you shall here.

Endorsed [*in hand of Sir William Masham*] (*f. 301b*): To my much honoured mother the Lady Barington these

50 *John Barrington, 13 August 1629*   (*2645, f. 41*)

Deare mother   May it please yow, since my last letter which I desired Sir Francis Harris to deliver unto yow my bone which was to scale is (I thanck God) quite of and the wound allmost dried upp, soe that I hope I shall now be quickly able to goe abroade. I do hope (God willing) to goe for Swede and to have a company for that service, but as yet wee have noe absolute answeare of those condicions are sent to the king, which are carried thither by a Dutchman who is to be our collonell (if wee are agreed upon our condicions).[1] I was demanded by a speciall frind if I would be one of the regiment, to which I have willingly agreed. As yet wee have no certaintie before wee heare from thence, which wee earnestlie expect. The chiefe points wee stand upon are for monie to be paid us heare to rayse our men; and for the time how long they will entertaine us, wee desire to make in our condicions that the king shalbe bound to keepe us in pay three yeares at least. They would pay us (as to some before) halfe our monie heare and the rest a month after our arrivall theare, for raysing our men, but wee hope to have all our monie heare to rayse and transport our men, which is 300[li] to each captain. A captain's meanes is good theare which is twentie five pounds a month, ten to a lieutenant, as much to an ensigne. I shall be wondrous willing to imbrace this imployment if wee can agree to have all our monie heare to rayse and transport our men, else wee cannot rayse them for want of monie. I beseach yow excuse my tediousness, with my humble duty remembred I commend yow to the protection of the allmightie who I beseach to prosper all your affaires, and will ever rest

Your obedient sonn   John Barrington

---

[1] For the high proportion of foreign mercenaries, and the use of Englishmen, in Sweden's armies see Roberts, 205-6.

London, 13 August, 1629

Endorsed (f. 42b): To my honourable mother the ladie Johanna Barrington at Sir Gilbert Gerrard's in Harrow Hill

51   *George Wilson,*[1] *13 August 1629*   (*2645, f. 43*)

Honourable and right worshipfull   My humblest duety and service to your ladiship remembred, my daily prayers to almighty God for you contynued, your many undeserved kindnesses and large favors thankfully acknowledged, for which I confesse ingeniously my selfe to your ladyship strongly obliged, deeply engaged, and therefore am ready by yow to bee commaunded. I have beene resolved since your ladyship's departure from your owne house to have visited yow but hitherto have beene unwillingly hindered; after a while now (I hope in God) to see yow. In the meane tyme, not havinge any thinge more worthy, I made bold with my good freind Mr Harrison and by him have sent your ladyship a brace of phesantes, wishinge they were better then they are yet not doubtinge of your honourable acceptance of so small a token of my far-behind thankfulnes. With my dayly prayers for your ladyship in health and true joyfulnes longe to contynue, with my owne and my wive's due respect to your ladyship and my lady Lamplugh, not forgettinge owr due respects to Sir Gilbert and his worthy lady, as likewise to mistris Mewesie[2] and mistris Joane Gerrard, I humbly take my leave and rest at
          Your ladyship's commaund   George Wilson

13th of August, 1629

[*No endorsement*]

52   *Sir Thomas Barrington, 13 August 1629*   (*2645, f. 44*)

Madam   This oportunytie commaunds my service and the tender of dewtie to yow. I have nothing that is new to yow to wright, but shall refresh my request that we may enjoye you heear as soone as conveniently we may, that being the only incitement to my wife and

---

[1]Vicar of the parish of Elsenham, near Hatfield Broad Oak, from 1622. He was described as an 'able preaching divine' in the parochial inquisition of 1650. Smith, 228 and 'Sequence of Essex Clergy' (typescript in E.R.O.).
[2]Joan Meux.

my selfe to live in this place. The monies dew to yow for last Lady Daye's payment you shall not be long withoute, God willing.[1] Som venison I intend to present yow withall, and if yow will give me leave to be my owne messinger, I desyre and intend it, God willing. My wife presents her dewtifull affection to yow, and I with her my love to my brother Gerrard and sister, expecting him next weeke, God willing. And thus in hast I rest your most dewtyfull sonn

Thomas Barrington

Hatfield Broad Oak, August 13, 1629
My wife, I and all of us salute my sister Lamplugh.

Endorsed (*f. 45b*): To the honourable my very good mother the Lady Johan Barrington at Harrow on the Hill give these

53 *John Barrington to Robert Barrington, 14 August 1629*   (*2645, f. 46*)

Good brother   I made boulde to wright unto yow some few daies since wherin I intreated yow to be pleased to speake once more in my behalfe unto my mother that she would be pleased to extend hir love so far as to cleare me out of my lodging, for my diet which is now neare upon seaven weekes, as allso for my lodging all this time and to my chirurgions, all which I know will be much, especiallie considering how much this my sicknes hath allreadie cost my mother; yet (as I then wroght yow in my last) am I (to my greife) constrayned to intreate my mother's love hearin, which I am loath to wright to hir of, having had so much from hir allready, and therfore do most earnestlie intreat yow this once more to doe your best in my behalfe and as soane as yow may, because I am so much frequented with company heare, which putteth mee to charges which I can no waies avoide but by removing heance, and then would I lodge while I weare something stronger wheare it should cost mee a small matter, that I would trouble my mother no more in this kind, God willing. Indeed (as I formerly wroght yow) I did thinck not to have troubled hir now, but that I am so far short of what I expected to receave that I shall hardly have enough to pay for my cloths and linnen out of this payment, without

[1]Sir Francis Barrington had left the tithes of Hatfield Broad Oak to Lady Joan so that regular payments were due to her from all landowners, but in addition the accounting for the sums due from the estate before Sir Francis died had still to be finally settled at this time.

which I could not be I was in so greate want hearof.[1] If I thought my mother would be angry or offended with this request it would trouble mee very much, and I would rather make any shift then have hir displeasure, yet would I be loath to doe any thing which might turne to my discredit, as I must be forced to doe unles she please to healpe mee. I hope and doubt not yow will doe your best for mee and that my mother will please to heare yow, which earnestlie desiring, as allso intreating yow to pardon my bouldnes, with my trew love to your selfe and my sister, I commyt yow to God his tuition resting

        Your faithfull loving brother   John Barrington

London, 14th August, 1629

Good brother, (if you can) I pray doe mee the favor to procure mee a litle deere marrow, which is to annoint my knee which is so stiffe with long lying out that I cannot bende it, and wee can have none heare; I pray sende it as soane as yow may, and I shalbe thanckfull unto yow. I pray let mee heare from yow of the receipt of my former letter and this as soane as yow may conveniently.

Endorsed (f. 47b): To my very loving brother Mr Robert Barrington, esquire, in Hatfield Broodoke

54 *John Barrington, 21 August 1629*   *(2645, f. 48)*

Deare mother   May it please yow, I wroght unto yow the last weeke of my good hope that I had to be able to goe abroade very shortly in respect I found my legg in so good a case, which (I thanck God) I do finde doth begin to strengthen apace, only my knee and legg are growen so stiffe with lying stretched out so longe time that I am not able to bende my knee. The churgions have used both oynt-ments and baths but what they have done hearin hath done mee but litle good as yet; I must arme my sealfe with patience to wayte the time when God shall please to ease mee of it. It doth not much payne mee but troubles my going, yet I can walke with a staffe in each hand, I thanck God, reasonable strongly. The only newes in thease parts is of the states taking (in the low countries) two of the cheifest townes of consequence the Spanyard had in those parts, the one being Wesell

---

[1] Orders for payment of a small part of the arrears of pay due to those who had taken part in the expedition to La Rochelle were made early in July and a more substantial payment authorised at the end of Aug. £16. 1s. of John's debts were paid by his mother on 3 Sept. *A.P.C., 1629–30*, nos. 235, 236, 419; E.R.O., D/DBa A15, f. 6b.

which is upon the confines of low Germanie; this was done by the advice from those of the towne, who weare weary of the Spanish bondage. The other towne the states of Holland have taken is Bosleduc or the Busse which they had beseiged above six months and is rendred by composicion some few daies since.[1] Thus I have made bould to be tedious in wrighting this newes, which is very good newes to all that do not love the Spanish faction. With my humble duty remembred I commyt yow to God his tuition, whome I beseach to guide yow in all your indeavours, and rest

  Your obedient sonn   John Barrington

London, 21th August, 1629

Endorsed (f. 49b): To my honorable mother the ladie Johanna Barrington at Sir Gilbert Gerard's house in Harrow Hill

55 *Sir Thomas Barrington, 25 August [1629]*   (*2645, f. 50*)

Madame   Your last lines give us yet more confidence of the desyre you have to be with us, which I pray God inable you to accomplish by giveing you health and strength. We are me thinkes like travellers till you comm, unsettled, both in bodye and mind; which we so long have had experience of as owr condition that we should be glad now to find a resting place, yet we are not owr selves till your presence give us a possession. I shall endevor to gett up your monye as soone as may be, and I pray you be confident it shall not be long, neither shall I ever thinke any dew payments made heavye by deferring, I hope, but acknowledg your favor. Madame, as soone as I can with anye convenience, I waite on you, meane while my wife and I joynctly present owr dewtyes and love and I shall ever be

  Your most dewtyfull and lovinge sonn

         Thomas Barrington

August 25, 16[29]
My wife and selfe comend our trew affection to my brother and sister Gerard and sister Lamplugh.

Endorsed (f. 51b): To the honourable my verye good mother the Ladye Johanna Barrington give [these] at Harrow

---

[1] John was ahead of the printed news: the siege of 's Hertogenbosch and the taking of Wesel were reported in the newsbook of 25 Aug. Dahl, 218.

56 *Sir Francis Harris, 4 September 1629* *(2645, f. 52)*

My most worthy aunte   Since I sawe your ladyship at Harrowe
I sent purposely to Sir William Masham and my lady his wife with a
fayre offer of a mache to my cosin Jone Altham,[1] receiving a fryndly
letter of thanckes for my care therein and most willing to entertayne
it, but that there was an other mache in treatye,[2] which if it brake offe
I should forthe with heere of it, but it is nowe 3 weekes past or ther
aboutes and [I] heere nothing from them; but the offer being so fayre,
namely 1,000[li] a yeere in present posessione, and 200[li] a yeere more
within two or 3 yeeres and 1,000[li] a yeere more after a grandmother
(whoe is very aged) and his ladye mother's deathe, as I ame desirous
to presse it with the more earnestnes, yet leave it to God and there
owne judgementes. I wishe the certaynety weare knowen what Sir
William Mewes will give with my cosin his dawfter, whoe is not lesse
in my well wishing then my cosin Altham, and if my cosin Mewes
would bee perswaded to harken to a mache of 7 or 800[li] a yeere, most
in possessione, a goune man (I meane a counselor at lawe), I should
not dowbte but to recommend one of good note and quallitye. I had
byne the messinger my selfe to your ladyship, but that in truthe I have
not byne well since I sawe yow and ame at this tyme very crasey of my
owlde payne, the gravell, and fytts of the stone; which madame,
forceth mee to bee bould to send unto yow for your accostomed
charity, and if yow would bee pleased to send me by this trusty bearer
25[s], it would helpe muche to cheerishe me at this tyme, for some
necessaryes I want, as well aboute my greife as otherwise, protesting
playnely to yow madam I ame in greate want at this tyme, which in
regarde of your former and many favors towardes mee I was most
unwilling to make knowen unto yow, wherein I crave your pardone,
hopinge and purposinge not to bee troblesome agayne or at least this
good whyle to your ladyship.[3] I sawe lately my cosin John Barrington,
whoe mends well. So with my humble service and prayers for your
helthe and happynes, I remayne

Your ladyship's ever to dispose of   Francis Herris

In hast
London, Frydaye September 4, 1629

---

[1] Lady Elizabeth Masham's daughter by her first marriage (see Table 3). The question
of a husband for her was raised as early as 1626 when Sir William Masham, in London
for the session of parliament, had '2 or 3 in pursuite'. At that time, though, he was
prepared to 'rest upon God, who is the great mariage maker'. Eg. 2650, f. 322.

[2] See letters 78–84.

[3] 25s. was paid to him in the week beginning 2 Sept. E.R.O., D/DBa A15, f. 6b.

Endorsed (f. 53b): To the right worshipfull my most honored aunte the Ladye Barrington att Sir Gilberd Garrett's howse, theise

57   *James Harrison, 7 September 1629*   *(2645, f. 54)*

Worthy madame   I humbly and heartely blesse God to heare of your good health, the continuance whereof I desyre as my owne, with the multiplication of all spirituall blessings upon your soule unto a sweete and full supply of all your necessetyes, with gracious increase till you come into the possession of that inheritance of the sainctes in that glorious light where there neyther is nor ever shalbe the least measure of darkenesse; in the assured fayth and hope of which happinesse, goe on, good madame, chearfully in a constant desyre and endeavour of approving your hart and life unto the lord in all sincerity, not casting away the confidence of your hope for infirmityes and frayltyes which will accompany the deare children of God in this pilgrimage, but being well assured that God will never lay these to the chardge of them that mourne truely for them, and in uprightnes of affection unto the obedience of his will and the honour of his name stryve to doe him more and better service, for that purpose attending upon his grace in the use of all good meanes, with hearty prayer for his blessing upon them that they may be inabled thereunto. Good madame I acknowledg my selfe to be yours by just obligation through the many and great favours you have beene pleased to bestow upon me and myne. I heartely wishe I were able to make better requitall by my requests on your behalf unto him who will not forgett your worke and labor of love bestowed upon us and many others, and by better performances of such services and offices as belonge unto my calleinge and are required of me in that relation I stand in to your good ladiship. I longe to se you at Hatfeild; many mourne after and for you, we have great need of you in many respectes. If we might be so happy as injoy you I would not doubt to se the aunceint honour of your family revyved and flourishe againe in constant and setled course of all good and religious exercise with blessing from the lord, both outward and inward, which, if you be wanteing, I have just cause to feare the stay and continuanc of these we now have with us, being, as I conceyve, doubtfull without the comfort of your society. I am perswaded there is noe place where your ladiship can doe God so much service and so much further the publike good as you may doe and will doe if you be here, and I would hope through God's blessing it would be never very prejudiciall to your good, which the lord knoweth both in regard of soule and body I wishe and tender as my owne. I say noe more; many hope, wishe and pray for your good returne. The God of heaven guide and direct you to doe what may best please him and be most for your owne true peace and comfort, as I doubt not but he will, it being the desyre of your soule (as I know it is) to obey him in all thinges. My wyfe is yet on foote, she humbly thanks your good ladiship for former and for your last rememberances, wherby you still binde us more and more in all dutifullnes and thankfullnes unto you. We should thinke ourselves happy, the lord gyving an occasion, to injoy that bould suit I made at my being last with you, which I humbly submitt to your owne good consideration and determination.[1] And so with my owne and my wyve's duty and service to your good ladiship remembered with all thankefullnes, I take my leave, ever resting

at your ladiship's command   James Harrison

Hatfeild, September 7, 1629

[*No endorsement*]

58   *Sir Thomas Barrington, 10 September 1629*   (*2645, f. 55*)

Madame   To express my desyre to give you all dew respect I have sent you a buck by this bearer oute of my poore store, all at your dispose. I hope it will please your eye and not displease your taste; if my judgment faile me not it is full, and I am suer it is young, the best in the forest, tharefor I may wish, but not performe at this time, more. Madame, if I thought Harrow would not be over-troubled with my being thare when so much companye is with my brother I could willingly the next weeke waite on you, and if my judgment will admitt me, will, God willing. However I will not be long absent and meane while rest your most dewtifull and loving sonn

Thomas Barrington

September 10th, 1629
My wife desyres your excuse (with her dewtye) for not now wrighting.

Endorsed (*f. 56b*): To my honourable good mother the Lady Johanna Barrington at Harrow

---

[1] A son was born to the Harrisons later in the month and Lady Joan stood godmother at the baptism. Letter 68.

59 *Sir Thomas Barrington, 17 September 1629* *(2645, f. 57)*

Madame   I am verie sorye that I am necessitated upon my brother Gerard's letter to me, so freely letting me know the unseasonablenes of my intention to have visited yow this weeke, to deferr my waiteing upon yow somm few dayes longer. Besides his desyre to be at home when I showld come, which by his brother Mildmay[1] I understood he would not be all this weeke, theise resons inforced me to send into Hartfordshier and to make my appointment with my brother Litton, who hath both expected and invited me often and long, and tharefor I hope yow will please not to impute my absence to any neglect. I profess my resolutions were alltred by my brother's free and freindly notice, else I had ben with you on Wedensday, which I intend and resolve to be as soone as possiblye I can (God willing). Meane while I beseich you perswade your affections and perfect your desyres for Hatfeild. My wife presents her dewtye and love to you and her wishes that yow will turne our desolation to compleate consolation. Thus I rest

    Your most dewtyfull sonn   Thomas Barrington

Hatfield Broad Oak, September 17th, 1629

Endorsed (f. 58b): To the honourable my very loving mother the Lady Johann Barrington at Harrow on the Hill

60 *Sir William Meux, 21 September 1629* *(2645, f. 59)*

Madame   I must allwaies be thanckfull unto yowr ladyship bothe for my self and daughter, the more seeing yowr care and affection is not lessned towards mee and mine. What I have promised, by God's mercy and goodness I will performe; but good madam, lett there by noe distaste that my childe bee not sent soe farr from mee as either those two places mentioned in yowr last letter, I had rather harcken to my Lady Barrington for her bestowing in Hartfordshire, if there be hope of religion and discretion, which to doubt of I may wrong my lady for her love and respect. When all is don I must submitt my self to God's moste holy will, but once againe I earnestly intreate

---

[1]Carew Harvey Mildmay of Marks in Romford was married to Sir Gilbert Gerard's sister Dorothy. *Visitations of Essex*, 454.

that if itt be possible som neerer match may be had, about her freinds about London or any where betweene this and yowr ladyship. Thus leaving yow to the protection of owr most blessed saviour I rest yowrs in all duty and service

        Your assuredly loving son   William Meux

Kingston the xxjth of September, 1629
I had rather match her to the less estate neere mee then with a greater farr of, and with som hopefull yong lawyer, if itt might please God soe to bring itt to pass. If occasion serve, God willing I will com upp and then acquaint yow with the party that I thinck gave out I neglected my daughter.

Endorsed (f. 60b): To his much honored mother the lady Barrington att Harrow on the Hill give these

61   *Lady Judith Barrington, 23 September [1629]*   *(2645, f. 295)*

Madam   This night I receaved a letter from my husband, whoe is at my brother Lytton's whearby I perceave the favour you intend us of affoording us your company heer on Tuseday next, which I profes seariously I much rejoyce at, for yett the wayes are not very bad and the dayes of a resonable length, soe that I hope the jorny will not be troublesum unto you. And I am the gladder that you please now to make some hast to us that I may attend you the longer time before my jorny to London some fortnight or 3 weeks after Michlemas, whear I hope to finish a good worke that I am interested in aboute my neece Wallop and Mr Heningham, who both, and her father, have much importuned my not failing of meeting of them for some neer consernments to them. I promised them alwayes I would be ready at that call, but knew not the certaine time tell this week that Dickeson came from thence. But I hope a fortnight will dispatche all that is to be done. I am very sorry that my coach cannot attend you as I would, by reason of my man's being now in Suffolk, I kno not whear, who returns not tell the latter end of next week, but if you please to lett Ned Lytton drive, the coach and horses are most willingly at your service, and to this end I have sent this messenger to know. And soe beseeching you to remember my best love and wishes to my brother Gererd and his lady, my sister Lamplugh, with the rest of my good frends, I shall thinge it now longe untell I see you heer and therfore

breifly hasten the tendor of those diew respects which you shall finde
ever from

> Your most faithfull loving daughter to command
>
> Judith Barrington

Thursday night, September 23
Your daughter John remembers her duty to you.

Endorsed (*f. 296b*): To my most honored mother the Lady Barrington
at Harrow Hill this

62   *Sir Francis Harris, 26 September 1629*   (*2645, f. 61*)

Good aunte   First give mee leave to thanck yow for your favour-
able remembrance in your late letters unto mee with gould, which
came aptely to releive mee in a greate strayte; God reward yow for it,
and that I maye live noe longer then when I appeare unthanckfull.
Next, the cause I retourned yow noe soner answere of your letters was
this, that I was styll in hope to heere from Sir William or his ladye as
they partely promysed unto mee; and I have not since there last letter
which was aboute 2 monthe past, merveling, if they have not concluded in a mache they certifyed me of that they doe not imbrace this
fayre offer of myne (which is yet undisposed of) being, in breife, twelve
houndreth pounds a yeere in present posessione and 2,000^{li} more per
annum after his grandmother (whoe is very aged) and mother's
deathe, and him selfe a fyne compleate gentleman every waye and the
parties that deale with mee in it still presse for resolutione, which if I
might knowe thoroughe your favor, I should accounte my selfe
behoulding to your ladyship and Sir William Masham.[1] Touching
my cosin Mewes, she merytts with the best, and where I meane he is
a worthy gentleman, a counsellor at lawe, that hathe formerly seene
her. But the portione beeing uncertayne as yow wryte, that (yow
heere) her father will give her 1500^{li}, is noe certaynety to propound,
unles you will undertake and that it shalbe so. And if I weare worthy
to advise, I wishe Sir William Mewes his comming uppe this next
terme. My cosin John Barrington mends well and this daye I left him
walking in the gardyn. And so with my best wishes to your ladyship,

---

[1] See letter 56. D'Ewes, describing the first (unsuccessful) marriage negociations he
entered on, writes of a family friend who used 'a great deal of faithful care' to make the
match. Sir Simonds D'Ewes, *Autobiography* (1845), i. 322.

Sir Gilberte Garrett and his ladye, and your braunches with yow, I remayne

   Your ladyship's ever to dyspose of   Francis Herris

From Mr Durants in Fullers-rents, my lodgeing
September 26, 1629, in hast

Endorsed (*f. 62b*): To my most honored aunte the Ladye Barrington at Sir Gilbert Garrett his howse att Harrowe of the Hill, theise

63 *Sir William and Lady Elizabeth Masham, n.d.,* [*August/September? 1629*]
                   (*2650, f. 289*)

Dear mother It doth much rejoyce me and many more to here of sum hopes of youre coming to Hatfilde. I hope the lorde will continue the good health he hath in mercy bestowed upon you. You have had a longe experenc of God's mercy to you in that place and I hope that there he will ad many more yeares to those you have and make you a further instrument of glory to him and of good to many of his members who much miss you there. The wett wether hath hindered my coming to you, it making our harvist the longer; as soone as that is done I hope to atend you at Harrow. Mr Williams hath bin very weake of a burning feavor and soe continueth, but I hope there is some amendment. I beseech the lord to prepare us with comfort to brave what he may lay upon us. Thus with my humble duty and harty prayers for your happynes here and for ever, I rest
    Your ever dutyfull daugher Elizabeth Masham

I have not as yet hard from my brother Knightly. I beseech you to remember my love to my brother and sister, and to Mrs More if she be still with you.

I long much to see you. When our harvest is in we shall make hast to you. So with my humble duty and love to all my frends with you, I rest
   Your W.M.

Endorsed (*f. 290b*): To my much honoured lady and mother the Lady Barrington these be given

64 *Sir William Masham, n.d., [August/September? 1629]* *(2650, f. 318)*

Madame   It is a great greife to us to be thus longe absent from
you, yet the occasion (this sad weather, which is like to detayne us
longer in regard of our harvest) adds much more to the same. The
best cure rests in consideration of the cause of this evill, which is our
sinne. And this hand of God upon the cerature (the materialls of
drinke) both pointe out as it were with his finger the spetiall sinne of
our nation, which is drunkenness. We have great cause to be humbled
for this and to be earnest for reconsiliation and reformation, least the
land cast us forth with the drunkards. Justice against this sinne is the
best expiation, according to that of Phynias (Psalm 106. 30); whereof
a president I made this daye in punishing 4 drunkards, 4 drinkers and
2 alehouskeepers in one towne. I could wish the like were practised in
other places, we should then have lesse drunkenness (and lesse judgments).

[*f. 318b*] Mr Williams hath bene very ill of a fever though now (God
be praysed) he is on the mending hand. In the depth of his sicknes
(when he and we all tooke him for a man of another world) he desired
me to remember his humble and affectionate service to you and to let
you know from him, as from a dying man, that what he wrote to your
ladyshipp was out of the depth of conscience and desire of your
spirituall good, which is most pretious to him. These might have bene
his last wordes, which gives you good assurance of the truth of them.
And as I ame now much more confirmed in my former opinion that
what he did proceeded out of love and conscience,[1] so I doubt not but
you are well perswaded of him and will receive him into your former
favor and good opinion. A kinde word from you would much refresh
him in this his weake estate. So desireing your good prayers for him
and us, and for a sanctefyed use of all these warnings, with our humble
dutyes and loves to my good brother and sister and the rest of our
frends with you, I commit you to the safe preserver of Israell and rest
        Your obedient sonne   William Masham

When our harvest is don we purpose (God willing) to come to see you
and to wayte on you home to Hatfeild, where you are much longed
for, and I hope long to be, as your proper place.

Endorsed (f. 319b): To my much honoured lady and mother the Lady
Barrington these be given

[1]For Roger Williams's quarrel with Lady Joan see letters 37 and 38.

65   *Lady Elizabeth Masham, n.d., [Summer/Autumn 1629]*   (*2650, f. 292*)

Deare mother   I am wonderfull gladd that it pleaseth God to
give you your health soe well at Harrow. Mr Dike asked me when I
woulde goe see my nue mother; I perseave Harow hath made you
younge againe. When you dare give us leave to think we are clear we
shall be glad to se you. I thank God we hav had no more ill, the boye
that had them went a brode againe within 2 or 3 dayes. The measels
have bin in most placis abowte us, but thanks be to God I here of none
that dye of them. It is a wonderfull thing to me to think the lord
should lay his hand soe moderatly upon us in these times wherein we
soe much increse in disobedenc to him, and wherin all sorts of sin soe
much abowndeth; but he is a God of longe suffering, yet he will be a
consuming God allsoe to all such as sett lite by his smaller tryalls and
be not broute neerer to him therby. I hope yet you will not forgett
Hatfeeld; the lord is able longe to continue that strenhth and health
ther which you have got at Harow and I hope he will doe soe. I
shall-be gladd to fetch you.[1]
... that all the distempers of our bodys, which must need be many
while we live here, may be a [*f. 292b*] means of the cureing the great
distempers of our soles, and may make us longe for that home whare
all sorows shall have an end and we shall tryumph in joye and glorye
for ever more. I looke evry day to here from my brother Knightly. Jug
Altham longes much for hir cosin Johane Mewexe's company, if you
please to give hir leave to come hither I will send for hir and bringe
hir againe to you. I have inquired abowt Mr Acher and I perseve he
will have none of hir; I pray if you send to my brother Mewix let him
know so much. Yet his sister is come hether who he puts much
confidenc in; it may be if my neece ware here then she mite win hir
love and she will work with hir brother. I like the gentleman exceeding
well by site and discourse. I feare I may be tedius to you therefore
with my humble duty I comend you to God and rest
          Your dutyfull daughter   Elizabeth Masham

I desire to be remembered to all my frends with you. Mr Willyams is to
marye Mary Barnerd, Jug Altham's made.[2] My husband remembers

---

[1] Ten lines are heavily scored through at this point. The passage has been rendered
completely illegible.

[2] Roger Williams and Mary Barnard were married in High Laver church, 15 Dec.
1629. E.R.O., D/P 111/1/1.

his servic to you and his love to the rest. He is in the heate of his harvest.

Endorsed (f. 293b): To my much honoured mother the Lady Barrington at Harrow Hill give these

66 *James Harrison, 5 October 1629* (*2645, f. 63*)

Good madame I know not how to be sufficiently thankefull to God and your good ladiship for vouchsafeing to graunt my bould suit. It shalbe the desyre of my soule and my faythfull endeavour to be alwayes at your command, and ready to performe the best service I may upon every occasion for the furthering of your spirituall good, and to shew my thankefullnes to your worthy sonne Sir Thomas Barrington and sonne in law Sir William Masham, whose heartes the lord moved to graunt my request;[1] blessed be his holy name for this great kindnesse, by his honorable and worthy servantes testifyed to us the most unworthy of all. The lord speed and blesse your good journey to us and gyve your good ladiship abundance of blessing, comfort and content with us, and gyve you such health if it be his blessed will as you may be able safely to adde one further favor to this, to witt that I might injoy your presenc at my house upon Thursday next, which I should account noe small blessing if it may stand with your safety, as if the day be chearfull I would hope it might. Thus with my owne and my wyve's duty and service to your good ladiship, with all thankefullnes remembered, and to all the good company with you, I take my leave and rest always

Your ladiship's servant in the worke of God

James Harison

Hatfeild, October 5, 1629

Endorsed (f. 64b): To my honorable lady the lady Johanna Barrington at Harrow geve these

---

[1] The request may have been that they should stand as godparents to the Harrisons' son in addition to Lady Joan. For an example of two godfathers from gentry families for a clergyman's son, see A. Macfarlane, *The Family Life of Ralph Josselin* (Cambridge, 1970), 145.

67   *Lady Elizabeth Masham, n.d., [early October? 1629]*   *(2650, f. 291)*

Deare mother   I am very sorry you are stayed from coming
amonhst us, yet I am glad you have soe good an ocation to keep you
as to se my sister layed.[1] I hope now my brother Garard will say he is
the cause of your not coming to Hatfeld. My husband had a good
minde to have sent his coatch, tho you sent to the contrary. He was
blamed for not sending it, soe desires are all to have you amonhst us
againe; but the lord knoweth what is best and therfor I desire to refer
all to him, beseeching him to continue you in health both of body and
sole. I am much bownd to you for my husband, I know he will be
fathful in his paying you againe. Thus with my humble duty, desiring
to be remembred to my brother and sisters, I rest
        Your obedient daughter   Elizabeth Masham

I expect to here from my brother Knightly this term. I have not yet.

[*No endorsement*]

68   *James Harrison, n.d., [early October? 1629]*   *(2645, f. 107)*

My honorable good lady   Though it would have beene the
rejoyceinge of many and of my selfe in a speciall measure to have
beene once againe possessed of you, yet the causes of your stay for a
tyme being so important, I cannot but subscribe to the justnes of them,
and upon my could thoughts be persauded that you resolved for the
best, and that God was with you in it. Your presenc wilbe a great
comfort to your worthy daughter in that condition she is in, your
absenc would have added much to her affliction and caused many
distracted thoughtes in your owne good heart. Your assuranc given us
of your affection to Hatfeild and purpose (if the lord continue our
lyves) to be with us in a setled manner when the lord shall be pleased
to gyve you the hoped for blessinge of your stay, doth much refresh us,
and makes us with the more patienc and chearfullnes wayte upon the
good hand of God for that happy tyme; the lord our good God watch
over your good ladiship and the honorable famely where you are for
good every way and be with the good lady to comfort and support her
in all her troubles, and with a sanctifyed use of them so make her and
her worthy husband the joyfull parentes of a blessed seed. Our poore

---

[1] Lady Joan had decided to prolong her stay at Harrow over the winter in order to be
at the birth of her daughter Mary Gerard's child. The child was born in March 1630.
Letter 125.

and weake prayers shall I hope not be awanting dayly for the externall, internall and eternall good of you all, as we earnestly desyre your holy rememberances for us. Good madame I cannot forgett, as your former many bountyes, so this great fruit of your undeserved affection to us, most unworthy of your favors in the least measure; the blessing that Paul wished unto Onesyphorus and his famely doe I with affectionate desyre pray may be the portion of your good ladiship and all yours for your often refreshing of me and myne. Faythfull is he who hath promised who will doe it, blessed be his holy name in Jesus Christ our savior.

Mistris Hildersham is very desyreous, so it may stand with your ladiship's good likeing, to have goodman Litton and his wyfe to be with her for her comfort and helpe.[1] They understand it hath beene made knowne to your good ladishipp and that you are not unwilling with it, for which, with rememberance of their humble dutyes, they rest most thankfull and so hope they may proceed to satysfy mistris Hildersham's desyre, which also wilbe for their good.

For our selves I blesse God we are in good health, my wife well, and your ladyship's litle godsonne a thryving child, the lord be blessed for his great mercy.[2] My self and wyfe with all thankefulnes remember our dutyes to your good ladiship with Sir Gilbert Gerrard and his good lady, my good lady Lamplugh, with our loves to all the rest; the lord our good God be with you all, so prayeth

   Your ladiship's devoted servant   James Harison

[*No endorsement*]

69 *Lady Judith Barrington, [early?] October [1629]*   (*2650, f. 162*)

Madam   The want of your presence amongst us now is so much the worss to be borne because we had soe certainly now propounded to our selves the comfort of you, but you have soe lawfull a cause to detaine you that we ware unreasonable not to be sattissfied, especially sence you are pleased to assure us your company constantly at the springe, which all though we cannot but think longe, yett they are good hopes to make us pass over the dull winter quarter the cheerfuller. And in the mean time I shall not omitt any fitt opertunity to visett

---

[1] Margaret Hildersham was a kinswoman of Lady Joan and of the Littons, a Hatfield Broad Oak family.

[2] For 30 Sept. 1629 the account book has 15s. 'given at Mrs. Harrison's baptizing', and for 18 Nov. 41s. 6d. paid 'for a bowl for Mr. Harrison'. E.R.O., D/DBa A15, ff. 8, 9.

you, which I intend when I come to London if I make any stay thear and that the weather is any thinge seasonable. I begin to finde an inclination to the same infermitie of my lungs that I began withall last winter that will hinder my corage from being to bould with all weathers, but in truth I longe to waite upon you. In the mean while and ever my best wishes and service attend you and so rest

      Your most respectively loving daughter

                                    Judith Barrington

Friday, October [*blank*]

Endorsed (*f. 163b*): To my most honored mother the Lady Barrington at Harrow Hill this

70 *Sir Thomas Barrington, 10 October 1629*   (*2645, f. 65*)

Madame   I am obedient to all your desyres and desire to rest satisfyed with what yow please, yet I must confess this sodaine allteration of your purpose and promise makes me imploye my patience and dewtie; dewtie towards yow injoynes me to be contented with your content, patience houldes me within the limitts of a quiett mind in what soever might otherwayes contradict my desyres. My wife and I had made it our studye to express dewtye and love and to render you all satisfaction, and it so much the more troubles us by how much we ware confident to have wintred together. The house is farr the colder for your absence, because you have made many harts so; but deferred hope though it faint the hart, yet accomplishments of prolonged wishes increase comfort and bring a somer's warmeth of joyes. My prayers attend your health and wellfare, and I, resolveing God willing to see you, rest

      Your most dewtyfull sonn   Thomas Barrington

Hatfield Broad Oak, October 10, 1629

Endorsed (*f. 66b*): To the honourable my verie good mother the Ladye Johan Barrington at Harrow on the Hill

71 *John Barrington, 10 October 1629*   (*2645, f. 67*)

Deare mother   May it please yow, since I last wroghte yow (I thancke God) my legg is much stronger and doth daylie increase in strength, insomuch that I am able to walke with a staff reasonable well, only my knee is not yet recovred, but I hope as strength doth come that will mende. As yet wee have receaved no newes of our bussines in Swede but wee do dayly expect the comming of Collonel Knephusen from theance or else his sending hither;[1] I hope wee shall have such contentment that wee may goe over to searve that kinge next springe, which I doe desire, and shall willingly imbrace any reasonable condicions for my parte. I doe not heare of any newes worth the wrighting at this time. Thus with my humble dutie remembred, I commend yow to the tuition of the allmightie, resting

    Your obedient son   John Barrington

Westminster, 13th October, 1629

Endorsed (*f. 68b*): To my very good freind Mr Issac Ewer, servant to the ladie Barrington, at Sir Gilbert Gerrard's in Harrow Hill

72   *Sir Thomas Barrington, 14 October 1629*   (*2645, f. 69*)

Madame   Allthough your winter's absence from hence hath more then a little afflicted me in single relation to owr selves, yet so much am I obliged to serve your desyres as that I submitt to your pleasuer with as much patience as my judgment can worke in me. And so much doe I desyre to be freindly to my freinds, as that I shall take the more glorye in my suffrings because theay are for the sake of those that love me. Madame, it's now more then time not to abuse you longer with hopes of dew payments, therefor ere long you shall have your mony long dew, and the rest with the first I can receive, God willing. And now my wife tenders her lame legg for an excuse that her hand presents yow not her dewtye, trewly she is not yet well but amending, and so I pray God we may all and cheifly

    Your most dewtyfull sonn   Thomas Barrington

October 14th, 1629

Endorsed (*f. 70b*): To my honourable good mother the ladye Johan Barrington at Harrowe on the Hill give [these]

73   *Sir William Masham, 30 October* [*1629*]   (*2645, f. 71*)

Deare mother   Your last favore added to your former hath so much oblidge[d] me in all love and dutye that I ame bounde upon all

---

[1] See letter 77a.

occasiones to express the same unto you and to let you know how glad I shalbe of any oportunity to doe you service. We have litle or no newes stirring now but what my brother Roberte can tell you, only this which is the act of this daye: Mr Hollice is bayled, having put in suretyes for his good behaviour – himself 1,000[li] bond and his 2 suretyes, Mr Serjeant Ashlye[1] and Mr Noye, 500[li] a peece. I feare now the rest will hardly get out but upon the same tearmes. The consequence of this maye prove ill, yet this is our hope that bad effects will produce good lawes. Lord cheife baron is displaced and yet it is thought he will stand upon his patent, which is during his life and good behavioure.[2] So with my humble duty and prayers for your good health and happiness I commit you to God and rest

      Your obliged   William Masham

London, October 30
I praye present my best respects to my good frends with you and if my brother Gerard cannot helpe me with the mony the next weeke I would intreat you to helpe me with so much in gold if you can. I will see you againe if I can possible.

Endorsed (*f. 72b*): [*torn away*] Barrington these

74 *James Harrison, 31 October 1629*   (*2645, f. 73*)

Good Madame   I account this distanc betweene us as noe small affliction, being therby hindered from performeing that service to your good ladiship which I am by so many bondes tyed unto; I lyve in hope to see the day when I shall have opportunity to gather up these losses, which if it please the lord to graunt, I hope it shalbe my unfayned desyre and endeavour to redeeme the seasons of furthering you towards your journeye's end in that holy way into which you are not onely entered, but in which you have made holy proceedings through the rich grace of our God and father in Jesus Christ. In the meane tyme, as I shall not cease my dayly prayers for you, so as I can I will endeavour to visitt your good ladiship and those worthy frends where you are. The lord our good God powre upon you all the plentifull graces and comfortes of his good spirit and establish your heartes more and more in the assured hope of that life that endureth for ever, in the

---

[1] Ashley's offer to bail his son-in-law Denzil Holles was still news on 17 Oct. Birch, ii. 32.

[2] Sir John Walter, chief baron of the Exchequer. He was still reported as refusing to give up his patent on 15 Nov. 1629. Birch, ii. 36; Gardiner, vii. 112–14.

meane season filleing your heartes with joy and gladnes through beleyveing. Good madame, goe on with chearfullnes, cast your burden upon the lord and commend your cause to him, he will support you under all infermityes, mortify all remaynders of corruption, make up with blessed supply all defectes in grace even to the perfecting of grace in glory, you truely seekeing him, as I doubt not but you doe. My self with my wyfe humbly and heartely thanke your good ladiship for all your love and bounty and for the last great fruits of your love. Be pleased good madame to remember us and your litle godsonne in your prayers. So with our dutyes to your good ladiship and all our worthy frends with you, I rest

    Your ladiship's devoted servant   James Harisonn

Hatfeild, October 31, 1629

[*f. 73b*] Good madame, I have a desyre to plant an orchard in the home pightell if it might please your good ladiship to furnishe me with some trees from the nursery at the Priory. Robert Batesforth telleth me that there may very well be spared a great many more then I shall need and doe noe hurt but good, there are so many. Now he sayth wilbe a good tyme to be doeing such worke. I beseech your good ladiship it may please you hearin to further my desyre, and that I may understand so much by a word or two from Mr Steward as soone as may be. I have a great desyre to come se your ladiship as soone as I can, and I hope over a few weekes to accomplish my desyre. In the meane season and alwayes, the lord our God preserve and keepe you and in his good tyme send you amongst us againe and recompenc unto you abundantly your great love to me and myne, so prayeth he that promiseth always to be

   at your ladiship's command   James Harrison

Endorsed (*f. 74b*): To my honorable good lady the Lady Johanna Barrington at Harrow in Midlesex geve these

75   *Sir Richard Everard, 10 November 1629*   (*2645, f. 75*)

Good madam   Havinge bene deprivd of you alonge tyme in Essex makes it now no small comfort unto us when we can but heare from your ladyshippe, especiallye of your good healthe, which we beseeche God longe to continue, desiringe you to respect it befor all wordlye things. I purpose (God willinge) to come and waite on your ladyship between this and Christmas. I beseech you, good madam, impute not my seldome writinge to be any neglect, but onely want of convenient messingers. Mr Bearde[1] is gone from us to Ipswiche and we heare that Mr Hooker's case will goe very hard with him, the byshoppe is so sett against him.[2] We shall have a great losse of them. My Lady Maynard hath brought my lord another sonne, at which there is much joye.[3] This is all the news our countrye affords. I beseeche your ladyship if you have any good news to make us partakers of it. Thus with my humble service presented unto your ladyship, I desire ever to continue

Your most observaunt sonne   Richard Everarde

Langleyes this 10th of November, 1629

Endorsed (f. 76b): To his honourable mother the Ladye Barrington give these

76   *Lady Joan Everard, 10 November 1629*   *(2645, f. 77)*

Most deere mother   I thinke Essex to be a very solitarye place now, beinge bard not only your companye but alsoe of hearinge from you so oft as I mighte doe when you were at Hattfilde. I should be very glad to wright offener, but that I know not which way to send a letter saife. It would much rejoyce me to here of your good health this winter, which I much disire and praye for. I thank God I and my children are well. We have no good newes hear, but ill; Mr Beard is gone from us and we are left in a petifull condition and may well say with Johoshaphat, we know not what to doe but our eyes are upon the lord, for the means that we have is very pore and we have litel hope of any other.[4] Thus desiringe your praers for us I ever remaine

Your most obeydient dauther   Johan Everarde

November 10, 1629
My father and mother remember ther service unto you and all your good companye.

[1] See letter 76.

[2] The petition from Essex clergy to William Laud, as bishop of London, in favour of Thomas Hooker, town lecturer at Chelmsford, is of the same date as this letter. Hooker left Essex for Holland and then New England in 1630. *C.S.P.D., 1629–31*, 92; Smith, 30–5; *D.N.B.*

[3] William, 1st Lord Maynard, of Easton Lodge, Essex, married Anne, daughter and heiress of Sir Anthony Everard. Their eldest son was born in 1623. G.E.C., *Peerage*.

[4] If the reference is to a lecturer at Great Waltham, paid by the parishioners, Beard was eventually replaced in 1632 by John Fuller. Smith, 26.

Endorsed (f. 78b): To my honourable mother the Ladye Barrington
give these

77 *John Barrington, 12 November 1629*   *(2645, f. 79)*

Deare mother   I understood by Mr Bridge your desire of my
going downe into the country, which commandment I shall most
willinglie obsearve as soane as ever I can cleare my selfe out of towne
of some small debts, which I hope I shall shortlie doe by meanes of my
brother's letter to my lord treasurer.[1] I have herinclosed sente yow a
coppie of a letter wee receaved from the sergeant major generall of the
kinge of Sweden's army,[2] and allthough wee are for the present prevented of our expectacions, yet wee hope before the springe to have
our desire that way. I beseach yow however to be assured that my
desire is greate to be in inployment, yet I ought to loake for such an
one as I may be able to live by, which I will not fayle to doe to my best
if our hopes of Swethland do fayle. Moste parte of the English which
went over last sommer into Swethland being placed in the front of the
king's army weare cut of by the Polanders, however that cannot daunt
us;[3] allthough the kinge is very much blamed for placing such younge
souldiers in the front, yet wee thinck the best. Thus with my humble
dutie remembred I betake yow to the tuition of the allmighty who I
beseach to propser yow in all your godly indeavours and rest
          Your obedient sonn   John Barrington

London, 12th November, 1629
Since my wrighting of this I heare there is a frind of mine come from
Sweden who was a captain there. He reports the peace is ended twixt
Sweden and Poland and allmost all the English officers are dead, some
slayne others by famine and pestilence, that he was constrayned to
come home by reason of that extremitie; the like he hath related to the
kinge.[4]

Endorsed (80b): To my honorable mother the lady John Barrington at
Sir Gilbert Gerrard's in Harrow Hill

[1] Richard, Lord Weston. Weston lived at Skreens, Roxwell, in central Essex and also
held property in Hatfield Broad Oak. *D.N.B.*; Colvin, 68–70.

[2] Letter 77a.

[3] Gustav Adolf had been heavily defeated by combined Polish and imperial forces at
Honigfelde in June 1629. Roberts, ii. 394.

[4] The six year truce of Altmark between Sweden and Poland had been signed on 16
Sept. after negotiations lasting all summer. Roberts, ii. 398.

77a   (*2645, f. 81*)

A coppie of Collonell Kniphasen's[1] letter to Lieutenant Collonell
Hone

Sir   The day that I parted out of Prusen from the kinge of
Sweden (which was the 13th of the last moneth) yours of the 10th of
August came to my hands. I had sooner given yow newes of my
dispatches if it had not beene that his majestie had with-helde his
resolucion by reason of the treaties of peace which weare then in hande
by the interposicion of the embassadors of theare majesties of Greate
Brittaine and France. His majestie of Sweden having receaved the
regiments my lord Marquay[2] and Collonel Konyngham have promised to rayse, seing likewise that the regiments of Allmans are greatlie
diminished, he hath for this present remitted the leavie of the English
and Scottish nacion and hath given mee orders to make a certaine
leavie of the Allman troupes out of those that the States of the Low
Countries did entertayne the last sommer into theare service in case
they shalbe willing to licence them; and to this purpose am I arrived
in thease quarters, and have not fayled for[th]with to advertise yow
therof, assuring yow that I am very sorrie that I canot for this present
tyme have the honor of your companie which yow thought mee
worthie of. I do purpose in November to returne towards his majestie
into the kingdome of Sweden, he having obliged mee with the chardge
of Sergeant Major Generall of his army, and if soe be towards the
spring-time theare shalbe any leavie of your nacion, I shall not leave
to follow it to the kinge of Sweden and likewise to make knowen by all
meanes the obligacion I owe to yow and the rest of those gentlemen
which had a desire to follow mee. I shalbe very joyfull to entertayne
your newes. When yow please to wright unto mee send your letters to
Emden to my house called the Clouderbourgh. For the present I will
conclude with my commendacions to yee all, and remayne

Your very loving frind   Knyphusijn

Harlengham in Frizeland, October 5th, 1629

78   *Lady Elizabeth Masham, n.d.,* [*November 1629*]   (*2645, f. 90*)

Deare mother   I have sent this bearer desireing to here of the
continuanc of your health. I showlde be glad to here some hopes of
your coming amonkst us againe. I wolde wilingly waite upon you with

---

[1] Dodo von Inn und Knyphausen, Swedish general.

[2] James, Marquis of Hamilton offered his services to Gustav Adolf late in 1629.
D.N.B.

my coatch to fetch you home. I shall pray hartyly to God for your safe
returne hither. I had lately a letter from my brother Knightly and he
gives me better hopes of the young man, withall expresing the younge
and olde man's great desire of the proseeding with this match and hir
well aproving of our family, wharupon we will proseed in further
treaty if you think good. His father desiers to meet my husband to
make conclusion of matters of estate, but we desire to do nothing
withowt your advise. These shallbe our demandes, which we will
stand upon if you think fitt, 300^{li} maintinanc besides hir one lands and
soe much in joynter. I think it is as little as can be demanded, thay
being alowed no borde with his father. The olde man offers to settle
1200^{li} a year upon his sonn and his ayers mayles, but I think it fit to be
settled upon the isue whether maile or female, specially considering
he hath more lande which he may settle upon his younger sonne if his
eldest dye withowt isue maile. I pray consider well of these things and
send me your opinion by this bearer. I shall desire your harty prayers
to God to direct us to doe that which may be most for his glorye and
all our comforts. 'Tis a waity busynes and God canot be to much
sought in it. I am now going to wright to my brother Knightly and
therfore I must here conclude, with my humble duty and ernest
prayers to God for your happynes here and hereafter, and so I rest
                Your dutyfull daughter   Elizabeth Masham

I beseech you to remember my love to my brother and sisters. I have
sent you a cople of little pulletts, the best I have at this time.

Endorsed [in Sir William Masham's hand] (f. 91b): To my much honoured
mother the Lady Barrington, these be given

79 *Lady Elizabeth Masham, n.d., [November 1629]*   (*2645, f. 84*)

Deare mother   I have received a letter from my brother
Knightly and it seemes Sir Robert Bevell thinks our demaunds very
unreasonable.[1] I did write to you what thay ware, 300 a yere joynter
added to hir owne and hir land to hir owne ayer, but he would have
it presently asured upon his sonn and his ayers and then he would ad
so much joynter to hir owne, or elce if he may not hav hir lande he
would make hir noe joynter at al, but she showld have hir owne againe
if hir husband showld dye befor hir. I perceive by every one that he is
a very worldly olde man, he is not willing by any means that his sonn

---

[1] Sir Robert Bevell of Chesterton, Huntingdonshire, K.B. 1626. V.C.H., *Hunts.*, iii.
139; H. Ellis *Visitation of Huntingdonshire.* (1849), 9; W.A. Shaw, *Knights of England*
(1906), i. 163.

sholde live with him after he is maryed, I know not what the reson is. I woulde be glad to doe as well as I can for Jug, for I perseive ther is nothing will come from him but what is agreed, for we must have nothing to his curtysye. I desire you seriusly to consult with my brother Garard and to help me with your best advise; I will send no answer of my letter till I here from you. Ther is no perticulars in the letter, but in genrall that we come nothing neer what he expects in our demandes. I desire your hartiest prayers for the busynes. 'Tis a wayty matter and I desire of the lord that if it may be for his glory it may come to pas, elce not. Thus with my humble duty and my love to my brother and sisters I comit you to the lord and ever rest

      Your obedient daughter   Elizabeth Masham

Mr Willyams desirs to have his best service remembred to you. My husband is at Colchester.

Endorsed (*f. 85b*): To my much honoured mother the lady Barrington at Harrow thisse

80   *Lady Elizabeth Masham, n.d.,* [*November 1629*]   (*2645, f. 92*)

Deare mother   I have better considered of my brother Knightli's letter, which is very hard to reade, he writing so bad a hand, but I perseve ther is not soe great a differanc between Sir Robert and us as I thought ther had bin. Jug is desirus to keep hir owne land, tho she have the less joynter, and I think hir owne inheritanc willbe better for hir preferment in a second match, if God should take away hir husband withowt iswe, than her joynter. Sir Robert ofers 300 maintinans and so much joynter aded to hir owne if she oute live hir husband and have isswe by him, other wayes not, which I se no reson for, because he shall injoye hir land for his life. I dout not but my brother Knightly will prevaile with Sir Robert to yeald to our resonable demaunds. I have writ to him and when I here his answer you shall know more. I hope God will dispose all for the best. Thus with my humble duty praying for the continuanc of your health, especialy for the thriving of your sole, hoping ere long to se you, I remaine

      Your obedient daughter   Elizabeth Masham

I desir to have my kind love remembred to my brother and sisters and the rest of my frinds.

Endorsed [in Sir William Masham's hand] (f. 93b): To my much honoured
mother the Lady Barrington these be given

81 *Sir William Masham, 19 November [1629]* (*2645, f. 86*)

Deare mother   I hope you have receaved my last letter since
Tusdaye last, wherin I did express our intended meeting on Tusdaye
next with Sir Robert Bevell, when I should be glad of my brother
Gerard's good asistance in the business. I wrote to him to that purpose
and doubt not of his ready performance therein. My wife is somewhat
better, and therefore I intend (God willing) to hold my former resolution to be at [*blank*] on Mundaye next. So with our humble dutyes
I commit you to God and rest
    Your obedient sonne   William Masham

Otes, November 19

Endorsed (f. 87b): To my honourable ladye and mother the lady
Barrington these be given.

82 *Lady Elizabeth Masham, 24 November [1629]* (*2645, f. 88*)

Deare mother   I thanke God my throate is somewhat better,
though not so well that I can write you an answer my selfe.[1] I ame
glad to heare of your good health, for which our prayers are still
presented at the throane of grace as we desire the continuance of yours
for us, and for a blessing upon this great business in hand, hoping we
shall injoye your good direction and my brother Gerard's good asistance. My brother Knightly and I have treated long and proceed to
agreement in part of joynture 300ˡⁱ and so much present maytaynance.
The mayne difference rested upon provision for daughters, which I
hope now wilbe accorded as you approved when I was last with you,
so that now I hope ther wilbe no more speach of my daughter's parting
with her land, which she would by no meanes yeald to. Nether do I
hold it fitting for many reasons: some I will mention, as her owne
advantage upon a second marriage, and her children's, who maye

[1] The letter is in the hand of Sir William Masham, signed by Lady Elizabeth.

challendg a right in it. So with our humble services and best loves to all our frends with you, craving your blessing upon me and myne, I commit you to God and rest

Your obedient daughter   Elizabeth Masham

November 24
I pray tell my sister the maide hath broke her arme and is now in service. My throat is somwhat worse since the writing of this. My husband presents his service to you and love to all his friends with you and hath wrote to Mr Tarlinge.

Endorsed (*f. 89a*): To my honourable ladye and mother the Lady Barrington these be given.

83   *Sir William Masham, 28 November* [*1629*]   (*2645, f. 94*)

Deare mother   I ame sorry it falls out so that we have bene thus long delaye by Sir Roberte. It is tyme now to thinke of some other. There is 2 in proposition, Sir Fredrike and Mr Pykerine; I have bene lately moved touchinge Sir Fredrick, as for Mr Pykerine I know not his intention. I should be glad to receive your direction on Mundaye next, for I ame to goe downe on Tusdaye. Ther shalbe no indeivore wanting on my parte, as ther hath not bene hetherto, being ready to doe for her as for my owne. I doubt not but God in his tyme will provide one for her sutable to her desires, in the meane tyme we must submit to God's will, who disposeth all things for the best of his children. We have litle newes, only 2 censures: Sir John [Stowell] is censured 500^{li} in the star chamber for some wronges to Sir Robert Phillips, and Jefs is fined 1,000^{li} in the King's Bench and to acknowledg his fault at all the barres, for some wronges to Sir Edward Cooke.[1] Ther is nothing don against the gentlemen: they pleeded against the jurisdiction of the King's Bench and Mr. Allwaye hath demurred upon theyre plea. Theye are to argue the 2^{d} dye of the next tearme. The judges have delivered theyre opinions in generall and that it is the opinion of the juges of England that some parliament men have bene punished out of parliament for crymes don in parliament.[2] This maye be granted, and yet nothing to the point in question:

---

[1] 'One Jeffes' was convicted of libelling Sir Edward Coke in 1630. *D.N.B.*
[2] Mead reported to Stuteville in a letter of 12 Dec. 'On Saturday (this day fortnight) Sir John Eliot, Mr Holles, and Mr Valentine joined with Mr Attorney in the demurrer concerning the jurisdiction of the King's Bench; and the day appointed for arguing the same is the second day of the next term'. Birch, ii. 44; see also Hulme, 329.

those presidents that are in that kind will fall out to be don by direction or authoritye of parliament. So with my humble duty and love to all my frends with you, with many thanks to my brother Gerard for his paynes, I commit you to God and rest

Your observant William Masham

London, November 28
I praye send Sir Robert's letter on Mundye inclosed in yours. I praye burne this.

Endorsed (*f.95b*): To my honourable ladye and mother the Ladye Barrington at Harrow these be given

84 *Sir William Masham, 30 November* [*1629*]   (*2645, f. 96*)

Madame   I ame as sorry as you can be, for I have lost all my labore which I was willing to undergoe to doe her good. And for that point of sellinge her land, nether my wife nor her selfe would give consent to it, and I had no reason to persuad her to it, which every man thinks unreasonable, that she should so far prejudice her selfe or her heyres. But for myne parte I never did diswade her, for in all those proceedings I desire to avoyd that, not to persuade or disuade, only to doe your commands and what my wife and daughter shall desire me to doe. And therfore I praye expect no more from me, for I would be left to beare a greater burden, that if things succeede not according to expectation I should beare the blame. And wheras you laye the b[r]each upon that of not selling the land, I conceive other wise, that if hir affectiones had stood right at first this could not have directed them, considering that this point was yealded to by Mr Knightly. But ther is more in it then you know: my brother [*f. 96b*] Knightly told us now at last that he hath bene to see another gentlewoman, who it maye be liks better, not approving our waye, which he maye hold to strict. God is the great marriage maker, and therfore we must submit to his will in all these proceedings who over rules all for the best good of his children. For Mr Pykerine (which I like best in respect of the man) it seemes now by the letter we can rest no longer upon him, and for Sir Fredrike, I desired my brother Gerard to informe him selfe well before his going out of towne, which it seemes he could not; and therfore I should be glad his occasiones would give him leave to come some tyme to morrow to be more fully informed of Mr [Grymnell], and that there we might make some conclusion of this business. In the meane tyme I will speake with one that hath lately moved the business to me. So in great hast, being full of business, with my humble dutye and love to all my frends with you, I commit you all to God and rest

      Your obedient sonne   William Masham

November 30

We have litle newes, only that you write of I feare is to true. The manner as I heare was this, that my lady giving her yonger sonne good counsell, and advising him to leave his ill companye, he fell into a rage, and so thrust her through with his rapier and honge naked by hir bead sid.[1] This is all I heare, you shall know more by the next. I praye commend my best love to my brother Gerard and my sister and desire him to come up to morrow, his presence will do much in this business.

Endorsed (*f. 97b*): To my honourable ladye and mother the Lady Barrington these

85 *James Harrison, 30 November 1629*   (*2645, f. 98*)

Good madame   Since I came home there was brought unto my handes a letter written from a reverend and worthy minister in Suffolke, one unto whome I have been much bounden ever since my first comeinge to Cambridge, by whome I understand that there are in the towne and parish where he preacheth, many poore Christians who are in want, and though there be divers rich there, yet they have not any willingness to helpe these poore. The burden lyeth sore upon this worthy minister, who hath ever had an open heart to doe good to such; he intreateth me to imparte my interest in some that are able and willing to help in this case. I confesse, considdering your ladiship's bountyfull hand to me and myne, for which we shall ever rest thankfull, I have the lesse heart to importune you for others, but I considder it is a labor of love to the members of Christ, which he takes as shewed to himself, and that it is a fruit that will further your reckoning, and I have good experienc of your ladiship's readynesse to every good worke, I am bould therfore to intreate your good ladiship to further this good worke of relyving the sainctes as the lord shall move your

---

[1] Mead's letter of 12 Dec.: 'The gentleman whose son slew his mother is Sir William Donnington of Hampshire ... This unhappy young man was his second son, and had been a scholar at Oxford a very debaunched gentleman, and some say drunk at this time, others in a frantic melancholy. His mother came up into his chamber to reprove him for some misbehaviour in this unfit mood, and so occasioned this heavy accident.' Birch, ii. 46.

good heart and you in your wisdom shall see fitt.[1] I shall make bould to intreate the help of some of your worthy braunches and with safety to convey to him what God shall bring to hand. Thus craving pardon for my bouldnes, with my owne and my wyve's duty thankefully and respectively remembered to your good ladiship, praying the lord to blesse your good ladiship and to graunt us in his good tyme to injoy you with us, I rest at your ladiship's command

    James Harison

Hatfeild, November 30, 1629

Endorsed (f. 99b): To my honorable good lady the Lady Johanna Barrington at Harrow in Midlesex geve these

86   *Sir Thomas Nightingale,*[2] *5 December 1629*   (*2645, f. 100*)

Honored lady   Certen of the inhabitantes of Langley, your ten-antes, who have endevored to suppresse a disordered alehouse there kept by one John Malyn, and to that end did first obteyne a warrant from the Lord Howard and the Lord Maynard,[3] but by the advice of Mr Barley[4] he neither did nor would obey their said warrant, whereup-pon both my self and they did appeall to the quarter sessions holden at Chelmesford at Michaelmas last. And by the generall quarter sessions there he was againe suppressed,[5] but contrary to the order there, by the incouragement of the said Mr Barley, he doth still vittell, and for the further vexacion of the said townsmen, Mr Barley hath caused the three weeks cort for your ladiship's half hundred of Clavering to be kept there. And he and the said Malyn, with two of Malyn his brothers, do so vex and molest the said townsmen with accions of trespas upon every pettie and smale occasion; the said Malyns had three trialls in trepas in one day. Now there importunities doe move me (as one sensible of there greavances) to write unto you, to intreat

---

[1] *Cf.* postscript to letter 89. No payments in response to this request appear in the account book.

[2] Sir Thomas Nightingale of Newport, Essex (in the Barrington's half-hundred of Clavering), sheriff of Essex 1627–8, created baronet Sept. 1628. *Visitations of Essex*, 258, 462; E.R.O., Q/SR 263/2–7; Colvin, 183; G.E.C., *Baronetage*, ii. 53.

[3] Edward, Lord Howard of Escrick (youngest son of the 1st Earl of Suffolk of Audley End) and William, Lord Maynard of Little Easton, both J.P.s from north-west Essex.

[4] Thomas Barlee of Elsenham. See letter 117, n.1.

[5] There are presentments against Malyn for keeping a disorderly house and for giving short measure in the Essex session records for Midsummer and Michaelmas 1629. E.R.O., Q/SR 267/25 and 268/30.

you to manifest your authoritie (for the good and quiet of the said townsmen) to cause Mr Barley to desist from advising and giveing way to such malitious suites, and to remove the keping of the said cort to some place more convenient for the said half hundred, or otherwise (if reformacion be not had) upon your comaund, then to displace the said steward so bent to oppresse your ladyship's tenantes. And my self shall accept it be a great curtesie, and the said tenantes shalbe ever bound to your ladiship for the same. Thus referring these thinges to your worthy consideracion, I rest

      Yours ever to commaund   Thomas Nightingale

Newport the 5th of December, 1629

Endorsed (*f. 101b*): To the right worshipfull my verrie good lady the Ladye Barrington at Harow on the Hill or elsewhere

87 *John Barrington, 18 December 1629*   (*2645, f. 102*)

Deare mother   I doe most humblie thanck yow that yow have beene pleased to healpe mee in this extremitie in furnishing mee with monie to cleare mee out of towne, which I will not faile to restore in Februarie when I receave my monie dew to mee from the kinge.[1] Sir Francis Herris hath certified mee of a command in the Ile of Man of a castle which is in the gift of my lord Strange, I shalbe very joyfull if yow will please in any way to instruct mee to compass so much happines to my sealfe, but Sir Francis will more largelie relate this to yow upon Monday, for he assures mee tomorrow he will fully informe himselfe herof.[2] I shall ever be willing to conforme my selfe to your will and pleasure in the taking of any course of life. I had thought to have gone before now into Essex to my brother Masham's [*f. 102b*] but my chirurgion, by reason of the weaknes of my legg and being but latelie cured of the last sorenes, did counsell mee not to depart untill he had made mee a strengthing plaster and a remedie to hinder the breaking out of the skin, which I am to have tomorrow; then I will not fayle to goe downe. In meane tyme I beseach yow not to blame my stay two daies or three daies more then your command is I should, for I doe assure yow I have written the trew cause and I will with all

---

[1] £15,000 to pay arrears to troops was issued (under a Privy Seal Dormant dated 2 July 1629) to the Treasurer for the army on 10 Feb. 1630. *A.P.C.*, *1629–30*, no. 272.

[2] See letter 91.

expedicion hasten downe. Meane time I doe (with my humble dutie remembred) commyt yow to God his protection and rest

   Your obedient sonn   John Barrington

London, 18 December, 1629

Endorsed (*f. 103b*): To my honourable mother the ladie Johan Barrington

88 *Richard Smith,*[1] *20 December 1629*   (*2645, f. 104*)

Good madam My dewtye remembred. I besech yow to pardon my bouldness, for I confesse I have presumed to much of your pacyence, but that neede that constrayned me. For the truth is I have scarse yet recovered that losse that my greate rents brought uppon me these hard tymes that was about five or six years agoe, and if that worthy knight (whose reward is now with the lord) and your ladiship had not delt so favorablely with me as yow did, it had indangered my undoinge, where as now, by Gode's blessinge, I hope I shalbe able to live in some comfortable manner, for which I shalbe bound to pray for your ladyship. And to shew my thanckfullnes wherin I may, I have sent up by Nathanyell Sumptner sixtene pounds, which is as I remember the last payment. I had sent it soner if I could have gotten a convenyent messanger to have payed it. Thus ceasinge further to trouble your ladyship, daylye prayinge for your longe and happye dayes, I humbly take my leave, this xx^th of December, 1629

   Your ladyship's to Commaund to his power

             Richard Smyth

Endorsed (*f. 105b*): To the honorable and vertuous good Ladye Joan Barrington at Hatefeld in Essex be these given

89 *James Harrison, 22 December 1629*   (*2645, f. 106*)

Good madame I know not how to be sufficiently thankefull to your good ladiship for your great bounty to me and myne, at all tymes and upon all occasions, it is my desyre to be truely thankefull, as for all, so for your last great favor bestowed upon your litle godsonne. It is my earnest suit unto the lord to be the more provoked by all your

---

[1] Lessee of Cottingham park, E.R.O., D/DBa E71: 'Notes taken by George Smyth of his going to Cottingham, 1632'.

love, to be more frequently and fervently before the throne of grace on your behalfe and the behalfe of all yours, that the lord may be pleased to powre downe his blessings upon you all, and in speciall upon your good ladiship, dayly addeinge unto that blessed worke of his grace in your heart, and abundantly supplyeinge all needfull comfort unto you. Accept, I beseech your good ladiship, from my self and my wyfe a small rememberance of our bounden duty and thankefull respect which we send you by this messenger, a brace of phesantes (the third is from good Mr Wilson whose letter[1] is hereinclosed), a couple of capons and a cake. We heartely wishe they were better, or that we had any better thinge to send, but we are assured you wilbe pleased to accept the affection of the senders. The lord our good God gyve us to injoy you many good and happy dayes and in his good tyme bringe your good ladiship amongst us. Thus with my owne and my wyve's duty and service with all thankefullnes remembered to your good ladiship, humbly craving your prayers for us and for your litle god-sonne, who blessed be God is a thryving child, I humbly take my leave, promising ever to be till death

> Your ladiship's devoted servant in the work of the lord
>
> James Harison

December 22, 1629
Your bountifull contribution to the releyve of the necessityes of the servantes of God (for which I humbly and heartely thanke your good ladiship) will I doubt not be receyved with much thankefullnes and many prayers to God for you.[2]

[*No endorsement*]

90   [*George Wilson, 22 December 1629*][3]   (*2650, f. 366*)

[Hono]rable and right worthy   My humble service to your ladyship with my wive's remembred, our hearty thankes for your many undeserved great favours acknowledged. Not havinge any thinge more worthy your [worship] we present our due respect and dutifull esteeme of your ladyship's bounty towardes us in this younge phesant cock, humbly intreatinge your honourable acceptance as comeinge from heartes desirous daily of your health, life, praier,

---

[1] Letter 90.
[2] See letter 85.
[3] Identified from Wilson's hand in letter 51 and dated by comparison with letter 89.

comfort and all that's good for yow here and hereafter. And thus with our due respect to Sir Gilbert, his worthy lady, the lady Lamplugh, mistris Mewis and the rest worthy, we humbly take leave and leave your ladiship and all them in the mercifull handes of God

[*Signature cut off, no endorsement*]

91   *Sir Francis Harris, n.d., [23 December 1629]*   (*2644, f. 309*)

From Mr Oynions at the Hande and Penne in Saint Gyles, towards Holborne, Wedsonday before Chrismas

Deere aunte   Late sicknes (which is caled the Irishe diseise) hathe hindred me, els I had seene yow for a night at Sir Gilberd Garretts, but I hope by my letter to expresse my selfe to your content and to knowe your pleasure by this bearer, els I will make bould to stepe over for a dyner tyme this Chrismas. First, touching my cosin Mewes,[1] I could have tendred unto yow good maches 6 or 7 score myles offe, but I perceived your mynde and desire (and please God) was otherwise, so that I have byne vygolent to steere an other waye within the distance of 3 or 4 score myles from Lo[n]don, and in truthe I hope before the ende of the aprocheing terme to accommodate it if please God to send likeing of boothe sides. But the first thing, the persone and his famely and condistione and his estate, which haveing one or two in hande I ame well informinge my selfe to present them to your and her father's considerations; and by the message which Tobey delivered unto mee that her grandfather was deade lately it is now conceived her portione wilbe £2000, which if I maye knowe your pleasure to incist uppon that poynte, it will in theise tymes expedite a good mache.

Madame I lately propounded to your sonne Sir Thomas Barrington a place of creadit and command with sufficyent profytt to live plentifully for my cosin John Barrington, which is to bee captayne governer under my lord of Darbey in the Ile of Manne, some 4 owers sayle from the northe of Ingland, a place I well knowe.[2] And trewly madame, considering there is like to bee none forryne imployment (for within theise few dayes certayne newes is come that the states have caceired

---

[1] Joan Meux.
[2] The lordship or admiralty of Man had been in the family of the Stanleys, Earls of Derby, since 1406. James Lord Strange (7th Earl of Derby from 1642) took over the government of the island in 1628. G.E.C., *Peerage*, iv. 205; *Private devotions . . . of James Seventh Earle of Derby*, ed. F. R. Raines (Chetham Soc., lxvi. Manchester, 1867), xxxiii.

15 thousand men with commanders)[1] I knowe noe cource better then to obtayne suche a thing, and I knowe for the love all men boore my deere uncle, as I perceive likewise they did in the Ileland, my cosin wilbe well liked, therefore I wishe Sir Gilberte Garrett (whoe Sir Thomas Barrington conceiveth to be inward with my lord Strang or that noble famely) to informe him selfe howe things stand and to laye for it for my cosin John; and I will doe my best indevors, which is not so powerfull as I wishe, yet something it is, with the officers there, and not forgott, I thinck, by my lord Strange first begane in his travells.[2]

Lastly good ladye, I ame ashamed to tell yow that my late danger-ous sicknes hathe made me paune some things given mee, because it is a kynde of beging of yow which I must not doe as yet because of your late favors towardes mee, but in trothe I ame like to weare noe other clothes then that your ladyship last gave me of my honored uncles unles some freind reedemes me a doblett and hose of black, which lyeth for 21s. My cosin John hathe sent your ladyship a scarfe[3] which hee would not cutt till yow sawe it; hee is gone to Otes, and shortely wilbe at Sir Richard Evered's. This bearer is hee I sent unto you formerly. In hast I rest your ladyship's ever to command
      Francis Harris

Endorsed (f. 310b): To my honored deere aunte the ladye Barringtone at Sir Gilberte Garrett's, theise

92   *Tobias Bridge,*[4] *23 December 1629*   *(2645, f. 108)*

Madam   I have accordinge to your ladyship's appointment sent the capons with some other thinges, wherof yow shall receive a per-ticuler note, as also from whom they come. I beseech the lord to continue your ladyship's health and stomach, that they may bee eaten with as much joy and mirth as ever capons weare at Hatfeild among your neighbours, who long for and pray for the enjoyment of your companie againe. Mrs Barrington hath sent yow a small token, hop-

---

[1] The Dutch attempted to negotiate a truce with Spain after the siege of 's Hertogen-bosch (1629) until they formed an alliance with France in June 1630. Roberts, ii, 428.

[2] Lord Strange was sent abroad, visiting France and Italy, after a private education. Raines, vii, viii.

[3] A scarf was an item of military as well as civilian dress at this time.

[4] Bridge, Lady Joan's steward and principal servant, had a substantial house in Hatfield. The Francis and Joan Bridge who received gifts from Lady Joan (the latter an expensive silver tankard in 1637) can be presumed to be his children. Bridge died in 1645; his widow remarried in 1647. Introduction, 17, 18; E.R.O., D/DQ 14/191, T/A 160/10 and D/DBa A 15, ff. 30, 39b, 68b; P.R.O., P.C.C. wills, 98 Rivers.

inge she shall be excused for not wrightinge, her belly beinge soe bigg that she can scarse reach the paper. I pray God vouch safe her a happie howre of deliverance, she desires all your prayers for her. Mr Barrington is gone to Bumpsted to his farme.[1] I have made bould from my selfe and my wife with our humble service to present unto your ladyship a poore token of remembrance of my dutie, which I owe unto you for your many noble favours, which are as soe many tyes and obligations, that I shall ever acknowledge my selfe bound and shalbe ready to performe any service that may lye within my power, soe long as it shall please God to vouchsafe me life, duringe which tyme I will never cease to bee

Your ladyship's devoted servante ever at commaund

Tobias Bridge

Hatfeild Broadoke this 23th December, 1629

Endorsed (*f. 109b*): To my honorable good lady the Lady Johanna Barrington at Harrow upon the Hill give [these]

93 *Lady Joan Everard, 25 December 1629*   (*2645, f. 110*)

Most deere mother   I am very glade to heere so good newes, that you have your health so well this winter; I praye God to continue it longe. I thanke God I and my children are very well now againe, ther was not any in the house that had the measels but they. Good mother I give you many thanks for your good counsel, I beseech the lord to give me a hart so to seeke him that I may be harde and that I may make a holy and sanctified use of all his fatherly chastisments, knowinge that all things shall worke together for good to his children. I should be glad to hear when my sister Garard looks hir, because of nursh Michiel. I doe not looke me tell the begining of May. Thus desiringe you to pardon my rude lynes, I ever remaine

Your obedient daughter   Johan Everard

Langleys, December 25, 1629
I desire to be remembred to my brother and sisters.

Endorsed (*f. 111b*): To my much honored mother the Ladye Barrington senior give these

[1] Robert Barrington owned the manor of Lacheleys in Steeple Bumpstead. Morant, ii, 354.

94 *Sir Thomas Barrington, 29 December 1629*   *(2645, f. 114)*

Madame   My first knowledg of this bearer's journye towards
you made me differ my intentions of sending purposely to you, and by
him to present you with so much balsom as I could gett in London,
which allthough it be not answarable in quantitye to my desyres and
indevors, yet the qualytie may render som answarable satisfaction,
haveing with som labor obtained it of a freind who hath made greate
tryall of it; that which wants tharefore makes the worthe of the
remaineder the greater. I wish and praye for a merrye new yeear unto
you, and your safe and comfortable being emong us in it, and so many
as God shall see best for us to enjoy such and so greate a blessing. The
children of theire owne ernest desyre have presented you with theire
owne, and that meearly so [*f. 114b*] in matter and forme too, even to
my sonn Oliver who would not so much as have it lookt on till he had
finished. You will please to thinke I would not perswade them so much
to trouble you, but I was unwilling to discorage them in that loveing
indevor which was so meearly spunn oute of theire owne good natures.
My wife offers her dewtie and love to you, humblye desyreing your
excuse for her not wrighting, for that in good truth her present toyle
is verye greate.

My brother Riche remembers you lovingly, who hath ben heear
theise two dayes oute of his love and upon a busines relateing to my
neice Alltham which you shall know shortly, one Mr St. Johns[1] (but
it must yet not be imparted to anye because the success is [*f. 115*]
doubtfull). He is religious, honest, of sweetness in nature, discreet, his
estate in land som 300^{li} by the yeear, his practise I beleive neear
double, handsom for person, probable to rise, my Lord Bedford's only
favorite[2], who promises that nothing shall hinder it for joyncture if his
estate will make it good. I thinke it's not to be slighted considering his
present meanes are [so] competent by his prefession and [his] likely-
hood to rise so greate, considring how he is befreinded. I desyre to be
remembred, and so doe my wife and sisters, to owr brother Gerard
and our sisters, and my neice and uncle, and cosen Brewster, who I
assure me is now with you. And thus I kiss your hands and pray to
God to bless you and us all and am allwayes
          Your most dewtyfull and loving sonn
                                        Thomas Barrington

Hatfield Broad Oak, December 29, 1629

---

[1] Oliver St. John, the future chief-justice, and the final, successful, candidate for the
hand of Joan Altham.

[2] Francis, 4th Earl of Bedford, St. John's patron, acted for him throughout the
negotiations.

Endorsed (f. 115b): To the honourable and my verie good mother the Lady Johan Barrington

95 *John Barrington, 30 December 1629*   *(2645, f. 116)*

Deare mother   May it please yow, as soone as I possibly could I have according to your command repayred into the country and am very much bound unto my brother Masham and sister for my courteous entertaynment. I have understood your pleasure concerning my sealfe and that yow would have mee enter into some setled course of life; I do intreate yow will be pleased to beleave what I have formerly declared by my letters unto yow, which is that I shall be ever desirous to be instructed hearin by your sealfe and will not be wanting in the following of the course yow shall be pleased to advise mee, howbeit I shall nevertheles be diligent my sealfe in learning some good way to proffit my sealfe, and shall carefully follow it with my best indeavours. I will be no farther tedious unto yow, but with my humble duty remembred I betake yow to God his tuition and rest
         Your obedient sonn   John Barrington

Oates, 30th December, 1629

Endorsed (f. 117b): To my honourable mother the ladie Johan Barrington at Harrow Hill

96 *Sir William Masham, 30 December [1629]*   *(2644, f. 307)*

Deare mother   I could not omit this fayre oportunity to express my duty to you and let you knowe how we longe for the springe of our hopes in the approach of our sonne which will make all things greene and flourishinge at Hatfielde and Otes, which have longe faded in the winter of your absence from us. Yet this is some comforte to us, that the heate of your presence is so refreshinge to that worthye branch of your stocke which now is branchinge out farther, and requires all helpe from her frends. Among the rest we are willing to cast in the mite of our poore prayers for her happy deliverance, that so your returne to us maye be with an addition of comforte in the increase of the olive plants which God hath set rounde about your table. My brother Rich is now at Hatfeild[1], and for that proposition which he hath made, I

---

[1] The Earl of Warwick and Sir Nathaniel Rich acted as intermediaries. Letter 109.

referr it to my wive's relation.[1] Only I will tell you what newes I heare, that it is hoped my Lord of Holland wilbe Lord Admirall; I could wish rather his brother, whom I hold fitter, yet I hope he wilbe advised by him and other his good frends whome you knowe well. My Lord Carlile and his lady hath labored much for it to be bestowed upon my Lord Chamberleyne, that so he might succeede him, but could not prevayle, whereupon, and other discontents, my lady Carlile hath left the courte.[2] There are other occurrents of the French great prepara-tions by sea and by land against Italye, and some propositions of the Hollander for the recovery of the Palatinat, which I presume you heare of, being nearer the well heade of newes, and therefore to tell you of these and such like things were to cast water into the sea. So to end with my paper, with our humble dutyes and prayers for receiving of all comforts with the new yeare, I rest

　　　　　Your obedient sonne　　　William Masham

December 30
I praye commend my love to all my cosins with you. All there frends her salut them.
I praye present my affectionate love to my good brother and sister and let my wive's letter excuse myne, being late at night.

Endorsed (*f. 308b*): To my much honoured lady and mother the Lady Barrington, these be given at Harrow.
I praye let the napkines be sent back by this bearer.

97　*Lady Elizabeth Masham, n.d.*, [*30 December 1629*]　　　(*2645, f. 120*)

Deare mother　　　I rejoyce to think the time drawes neer that we shall injoye you at Hatfelde, where you are much desired. I shallbe very glad to here that my sister is safly delivered and then I hope you

---

[1] See letter 97.
[2] John Beaulieu wrote to Sir Thomas Puckering on 30 Dec.: 'The admiral's place is not yet disposed of, but likliest by the common rumour and appearance to fall upon my Lord of Holland than upon any other. The Countess of Carlisle keepeth yet at Essex House; but it will not be long, it is thought, before she come back to court'. The post of Lord Admiral was one of the offices that had become vacant with the murder of Buckingham. On 11 Jan. 1630 the Venetian ambassador reported that the contenders were the Earl of Pembroke (the Lord Chamberlain), whom Carlisle favoured since he hoped to become Chamberlain himself, and the Earls of Dorset and Holland. Neither Holland (a 'court' man) nor his elder brother Warwick (the leader of the 'county' opposition in Essex) was appointed, though Holland had been made both Captain of the King's Guard and High Steward of the king's revenue in 1629. Birch, ii, 49; *C.S.P. Venetian, 1629–32*, 263; G. E. Aylmer, *The King's Servants* (1961), 126.

will come cherfully. I thoute good to lett you know of a proposition of a match for Jug propownded by Sir Nathanell Rich. The gentleman's name is Mr Sant Johns that was lately in prison in the tower.[1] I here very worthyly of the man, but it semes his estate is very small, not above 200[li] a yere, and besids his father was a base sonne (as I have hard) of the Lord Sant Johns. Sir Nathanell and he are both at Hatfeld and meane to take our howse in the way to Pergoe,[2] and when he informes me more fully then you shall here, for I will doe nothing withowt your advise. He is a lawyer, but young, and therfor I think his practis is little, yet I beseech you to consider well of it and keep it very secrett. And let me crave your prayers to God that he will be pleased to direct all as maybe most for his glory and all our comforts. Thus with my humble dutye praying for your increse of comfort in sole and body, I remaine

> Your dutyfull daughter   Elizabeth Masham

I have sent you a small remembranc of my duty, sum plaine gloves.

Endorsed (f. 121b): To my much honoured mother the Lady Barrington these be given

98 *Sir Francis Harris, 1 January 1630*   (*2645, f. 130*)

Deere aunte   I hope I have found a sewtable mache for my cosin Mewes in the county of Kent, aboute 25 myles from London. His estate estymated (at resonable rate) 1,000[li] per annum and better, hee is of good worthy famely and his father wil setle uppon the marryage the aforesaid estate and allowe his sonne to live 300[li] per annum, and so muche to make his wife a joynter. I ame injoyned as yet not to name the partye, but very shortely I will, and informe my selfe of all things. But the questione is whether your ladyship will undertake that her portione shalbe 2000[li], for that is the portione studd uppon, being sed hee maye have 1000[li] more newly profered him, but that those from whence my cosin is discended are honored and loved. In conclutione I humbly thanck yow for your token in Sir Gilberte Garret's letter,

---

[1] St. John had been imprisoned in Nov. for his part in the discovery in Sir Robert Cotton's library of a paper setting out a scheme for the extension of royal power through the military, including 'propositions ... to bridle the impertinancy of Parliament'. This was explosive material for 1629 and St. John had shown a copy to Bedford and others in the opposition group. The paper was eventually found to have been written in 1614 and not, in any case, to have emanated from the crown. Gardiner, vii. 138–141; *C.S.P.D., 1629–31*, 95–6.

[2] Pyrgo Park in Havering, Essex, home of Sir Thomas Cheeke.

which I protest was farre from my thoughtes to expect, onely I discovered to your ladyship my hindrance by sicknes and yow with your compastionate eye and phisick did helpe to cure me, for which God blesse and reward yow for it.

Touching my cosin John Barrington, your sonne, I will doe him all the fryndly offices of a kinsman, which is but lytle in respect of my desire. I did also propound it by letter to Sir Thomas Barrington and hee aproves of the place.[1] And so desiring to heere from your ladyship by this bearer, Poynter, I humbly rest to doe yow all service so longe as I ame

      Francis Herris

In muche hast from my chamber, Mr Oynions howse in St Giles, in the new brick bilding next dore to the Hande and Penne, January first, 1629

Endorsed (*f. 131b*): To my honorable and honored aunte the Ladye Jone Barrington theise

99   *Lady Elizabeth Masham, n.d.,* [*18? January 1630*]   (*2645, f. 126*)

Deare mother   I acknowledg my self very much bownd to you for your care of Jug Altham in this watye busines, wherin I woulde be loth to doe anything withowt your advice and aprobation. I conffes the man moveth me much to aprove of it, but I know God comandes me to have a care in the second place of the outward conveniencis; tho I desier to acsept of much less with such a man, yet I shallbe much taxed of hir friends if I look not for a compedency of owtward estate. I think thar may be prity well, for thare 2 lives, his and hirs, will make between 4 and 5 100li yearly besides what he may get in law, but some say hi cannot get much yet. But Sir Nathanell Rich tolde me he thought Mr Saint Jhons colde not spend less then 500li yearly him self now he is a single man, if that be soe then hir estate willbe but little to pay howsrent and maintaine howskeeping if thay keep any, or elc to sogiorn in another bodie's howse. Thay cannot gather much to purchas for posteryty. I beseech you to way all things well and give me your considerat advice. She hath good frinds to advise for hir with you, my brother Garard and my brother Mewix, who I know desire to seek God's honor in the chefe place, and then God gives leav to seek other things as may be fitt to make our pasadg the more comfortable to that place whare we shall have no need of these vanitis. The lord fitt us for soe gloryus a place. I am very glad to here you have your

---

[1] See letter 91.

health soe well. I much longe to se you, I hope the time will not be longe. The lord send my sister a safe deliveranc that you may come with more joy. Thus in hast with my humble duty and harty prayers for your increse of happynes here and especially in the life to come, I rest

Your ever obedient daughter   Elizabeth Masham

I desire to be remembred to all my brothers and sisters. I beseech you if you think it not fitt to proceed in the busines that you will write your minde to Jug, for she desirs to be directed by you.

Endorsed (f. 127b): For my much honoured and most deare mother the Lady Barrington at Harrow these

100   *Sir William Masham, 18 January [1630]*   *(2645, f. 134)*

Madame   I could not let passe this bearer without some mention of our dutye to you, who maye challeng so much at our hands, and expression of thanks for your last kinde tokens which, together with your former favors, being cast up amounts to so great a summe that deserves to be written in the table bookes of our hartes, never to be forgotten. We dayly expect my brother Gerard and your advise by him in this great business, which reqiers the best helpe of our frends. So in great hast with our humble dutye and love to all our frends with you, not foregetting you and my deare sister in our dayly prayers, I commit you all to the good blessing of God and rest

Your obliged sonne   William Masham

Otes, January 18

Endorsed (f. 135b): To my much honoured lady and mother the lady Barrington at Harrow

101   *John Barrington, 18 January [1630]*   *(2645, f. 132)*

Deare mother   May it please yow, I having notice of so fitt an opportunitie as by this bearer would not let it passe without the presenting of my most humble dutie unto yow in a few lines, having no other subject at this present to wright of, onlie I do desire againe to let yow know (as often I have made knowen by my letters unto yow) that as your desire and will is I should undertake some setled course so yow will please to beleave mee that I do most earnestlie wish I could finde out a way to free my selfe from idlenes, and to live in such a course wherby I might give yow satisfaction and content to my sealfe. My labour and care herin shall not be wanting in the seaking out this way, but as yet I heare of none worth the undertaking, unles it fall out our bussines for Swethland goe forward which is revived againe since I wroght yow of the last newes thence. If yow shall please to desire my undertaking any other course I shall most willinglie submit my sealfe to your command whatever course it be. I do hope wee shall have imployment this springe for Swede, if not else where, but as yet I heare of none, only New England which I do utterly dislike, yet I will conforme my sealf to your will if yow will please to command it

        Your obedient sonn   John Barrington

Oates, 18th January

Endorsed (f. 133b): To my honorable mother the ladie Johan Barrington at Harrow Hill

102   *James Harrison, 18 January 1630*   *(2645, f. 136)*

My honorable good lady   I humbly and heartely blesse God for the continuance of your good health, the same our good God longe continue it, if it be his blessed will, with increase of all spirituall blessings and comfortes upon your good heart, that you may still be an instrument of much good amongst us, who longe greatly after you and shalbe most glad to injoy you, in a speciall manner and measure my self, unto whom the lord hath made your good ladiship a cheif comfort and stay, for which his goodnes by you I stand bound and I hope shall ever be most willing, to my poore power, to performe all that service and duty that it shall please him to inable me unto upon every occasion, though without me I doubt not but the lord, as he is able, so he will ever be most ready to supply all your wantes and to keepe you safe even unto his heavenly kingdom, through him who hath purchased it for you and is your advocate at his right hand. In his mediation comfort and strengthen your heart, seeking pardon of an power against all sin and a sweete increase of all that heavenly wisdom, fayth, love and zeale with all other graces that may adorne your latter dayes, and carry you on with true peace and comfort to the end of them, ever to the injoying of the end of your fayth and hope, the salvation of your soule; faythfull is he who hath called you, he will doe it. Good madame, pray for me in these straytes, I desyre to doe the will of God, I blesse his name, his law is in my heart; it is not the world I regard, but my liberty and the good of his people is deare and precious to me. Thus with my owne and my wyve's duty thankfully remembered, I rest

Your ladiship's unworthy yet faythfull servant   James Harison

Hatfeild Broadoke, January 18, 1629

Endorsed (f. 137b): To my honorable good lady the Lady Johanna Barrington at Harrow in Midlesex give these

103 *Lady Elizabeth Masham, n.d.,* [*January 1630*]   (*2645, f. 124*)

Deare mother   I doe acknowledg my selfe much bownde unto you that you woulde be pleased to joyne with me in this waitye busines for Jug. I receaved a letter senc from my lorde, but it was only to desire forbearanc of his answer of our letter till sumtime this week. Mr St Johns writ to me that my lord was lothe to diny to grant sum inheritanc, nether woulde he as yet promise it, but he woulde consider of it. I asure my selfe that the lord will dispose all for the best in his d[e]we time. Hir unkle Altham sent to us that if we ware willing he woulde bring a lorde to hir, but I feare few lords have the maine, I mean the trew feare of God, which I prefer before all the honer in the world. When I here my lord's answer I will with all convenient speed waite upon you. Thus with my humble duty, desiring to be remem-berd to my brothers and sisters, I comit you to the lord and rest

Your ever dutyfull daughter   Elizabeth Masham

Endorsed (f. 125b): To hir honourable mother the lady Barrington at Harow Hill these

104 *Lady Elizabeth Masham, n.d.,* [*January 1630*]   (*2645, f. 170*)

Dear Mother   I had purposed to have writ more largly at this time, but I have bin soe imployed senc my brother's coming (being sent for to Mrs King's labor etc.). Allso now, when I was wrighting a letter to you, I am prevented by a letter from my Lady Cheeke to send sudenly for nurs Michell to goe to hir bicause hir one midwif is far from hir. But I have fully related my minde to my brother in Jugg's busynes and I desier your ernist prayers and continuance of your best advise. I acknowleg myself much beholding to my brother for his love and I hope he will continue the same in his best help. Thus with my humble duty, in great hast, hoping you will excuse me at this time to your self and my sister, I rest

Your dutyfull daughter   Elizabeth Masham

[*In the hand of Sir William Masham*:] I present my humble dutye to you, havinge sent my letter by Mr Bridge before. I hope to see [you] the next tearme. I trust my brother Gerard canne [excuse] sufficiently in this business.

Endorsed (f. 171b): To my much honoured mother the lady Barrington these

105   *Sir Thomas Barrington, n.d.,* [*24 January 1630*]   (*2650, f. 184*)

Madame   This short time of distance since I was with you hath produced nothing either new or worthy of your eye, only the greate affaire of the King's Bench is to morrow to be tryed between the king and our parliament men.[1] The time is fixt, God send such an issue as may most gloryfye him and benefitt king and subjects. This day my cozen Dunch maryes his brave mistress, a gentle-woman of portion, education and proportion paralel to his estate and credit sufficient for his long delayed matrimonye.[2] My wife and my selfe are solemnely invited to morrow to be thare when is the festivall, this day not allowing it, and the joyneing of hands being alltogether private. Madame my intention and desyre is to see you againe before my jornye to Hatfeild (if I can find any time from my busynes) haveing had so little libertye by reson of my lord to discourse with you of diverse particulars which I resolved to impart to you, som of mirth, som for meear notice, som of (though small) busines. My wife tenders her dewtye and service to you, desyring your excuse for her not waiteing on you haveing no horses of her owne and being so lately perplext with those hyred, as Tobie knowes. Owr love to all our freinds, and so I rest

Your most obedient and loving sonn

Thomas Barrington

Endorsed (f. 185b): To my most honored mother the Lady Barrington at Harrow Hill

[1] Eliot, Valentine and Holles appeared before King's Bench on 25 Jan. 1630. Hulme, 329; Birch, ii. 56–7.

[2] Edmund Dunch, son of Sir William Dunch and of Mary, daughter of Sir Henry Cromwell, married Bridget Hungerford, an heiress with a reputed fortune of £60,000. Noble, ii. 162.

106   *Lady Elizabeth and Sir William Masham, 26 January* [*1630*]

(2645, f. 122)

Deare mother   Senc my brother Garard was here I reseved
another letter from my lorde of Bedforde, wherin he preseth much for
a meeting; and rather then faile he woulde come downe to me, which
I think altogether unfit; therfore I returned him this answer acording
to that which we resolved of with my brother, which is to this efect
that there is litle hope of proceeding, for that which may be resonable
for us to disier might not be thought resonable for my lord to grant,
nor convenient for us to accept, besides the uncertain isue of his busines
in the star chamber,[1] and another proposition made in this kinde,
against which lyes noe exception; tharfore I desire to be free to treate
with another. I doe intreat my brother to ingage me further to him by
shewing me this favor, to meet my husband at London on Thursday.
I beseech you let me still crave your ernest prayers to God that he
wolde bring that to passe which may evry way be most for his glory
and hir and our comfort. I thank God I finde hir very wiling to be
directed by hir frindes. I confess the [f. 122b] gentle man is worthy of
much honer in regarde of the mayne, but how inconvenient it may be
for hir posterity to injoye that which by right belongs to my lord's one
children (if he showlde give any thing for inheritanc) I woulde have
well to be wayed, for tho in my lord's dayes she may injoy it with
comfort, yet I know not what discomfort she may reseave from his
children after him. I am in hast, being layte and Mr Saint Jons being
here,* tharfore with my humble duty I rest
                Your obedient daughter   Elizabeth Masham

January 26
I beseech you to remember my love to all. I woulde have writ to my
brother but that I wanted time.
I present my humble duty to you and love to all. I hope to see my
brother Gerard at London on Thursdaye.
                Yours   William Masham

* [*Added in margin, in the hand of Sir William Masham:*] He goes up to London this
Wensdaye with my husband.

---

[1] See letter 97, n. 1 for the circumstances of St. John's imprisonment in the Tower.
On 15 Nov. the king decided to release the prisoners and prosecute the matter in the
court of Star Chamber. Late in Nov. Cotton's library was searched, the original of the
offending paper found, and the truth of its origins revealed. But the prosecution process
had already begun and nothing was done to halt it. In the event, the coincidence of the
date fixed for the hearing (29 May 1630) with the birth of the future Charles II offered
an opportunity for a royal display of mercy. *C.S.P.D., 1629–31*, 96; Gardiner, vii. 138–
141.

Endorsed (f. 123b): To my much honoured mother the Lady Barrington these be given at Harrowe

107   *Henry Cromwell,*[1] *28 January, 1630*   *(2645, f. 138)*

Dearest sister   I received your letter at Ramsey church dore as I was comming from performing my last dutie to my brother Phillip, who was buried this present day at Ramsey: he departed this life on Sunday last about one of the clocke in the afternoone. He led a religious life, died most religiously, so as we may assure our selves that he is now in the place of joy. God graunt us that live hearts truly to imitate the good examples of good people gone before us, that living in the feare of God we may die in his favoure. He hath left behind him many children with small meanes; a hundreth pound a peice will be the uttermost can be wrought for them out of his estate.[2] One daughter he hath left heer which I cold wish you wold be pleased to take to you, at least wise till she may be provided for, for otherwise she wilbe in great danger to be lost for education. She is your brother's daughter, it will be a deed of extraordinary charitie, and I doubt nott but God will repay you doble. I will nott presse you any farther, but leave it to the worke of God in you. As for the writings you send for concerning my neice Jane Whalley[3], I only saw them once long since, at the keeping of a court at Screaveton, but never saw them since, neither can I imagine in whose hands they are if they be nott in my brother Cromwell's. [f. 139] I praise God I am now in the way of recovery after a long and most dangerous sicknes. I am able to ride abroad a little, to eate my meat with a reasonable stomacke and to digest it, and my sleep is convenient, so as by the help of God I am in some hope of a perfect recovery. I was most glad to see your letter, and to understand of your health and wellfare, which I beseech the lord to continew. If God graunt me health and reasonable strength, I purpose this next summer to visitt you. My prayers and best wishes shall daily attend you. I desire to be most kindly remembred to my nephew and neice where you now are. And so with the remembrance of my best love to your self, I rest

Your ever loving brother   H. Cromwell

28th January, 1629
[*No endorsement*]

[1] Henry Cromwell of Upwood, Huntingdonshire, Lady Joan's brother. Table 2.
[2] Sir Philip Cromwell, who lived at Biggin House, Ramsey, died 24 and was buried 28 Jan. He had six sons and four daughters, though only two daughters survived him. Noble, ii. 30-2; V.C.H., *Hunts.*, ii. 68, 72, 189.
[3] Jane Whalley was to marry in May 1630. Introduction, 19.

108 *Lady Judith Barrington to Mrs Necton[1], 28 January 1630*

(2644, f. 268)

Sweet Mrs Necton   I hope you have receaved my former letter of my intention now to be at Mr Martin's if all things may fall out conveniently and I have now directed thease unto you to begg I may now receave an answear, because we intend to be in London on Tuseday or Wensday next, and I beseech you lett Mr Pahanesin know my husband will bringe up with him a fine gelding for his frend, such as a frend may put into another's hands; and withall lett him know, as the best entertainment I can give him, his mistres is well and joynes with me in all harty good wishes to him. And so beging pardon for thease abrupt lines, which I am constrained to hasten, with my affectionate love [to] you and your husband and my pretty godaughter I rest

Yours faithfully to serve you   Judith Barrington

Hatfield, 28 January, 1629

Endorsed (f. 268b): To my much esteemed frend Mrs Necton in Aldersgate Street neer the Halfe Moone tavern

109 *Sir William Masham, n.d., [February? 1630]*   *(2645, f. 118)*

Madame   My Lord of Warwicke, Sir Nathaniel Rich and my selfe are comming to you this morning and I thought good to send this messenger before to give you notice. Some of us thought to have bene with you yesterdaye, but that my Lord of Bedford altered his resolution of sending his letter by us and meanes to come to you him selfe. You neede be well armed. I feare thinges will not answer your expectation. The best answer for the present wilbe that when you have my lord's propositions you will advise with frends and then returne your resolution. So in great hast, speeding to you whom I long to see, with my humble dutye I rest

Yours obliged   William Masham

I must intreat you maddam and my wife to take this great busines upon you (whom it most consernes) for it is to great a burthen for me to beare.

I pray burne this.

---

[1] Wife of James Necton, who acted as an agent in London for the Barringtons on many matters. Letter 185.

Endorsed (*f. 119b*): To my much honoured lady the Lady Barrington these

110   *Sir Oliver Cromwell,*[1] *2 February 1630*   (*2645, f. 140*)

Good sister   I am glad to hear of your health. Now our nomber is very [s]maule, for my brother Phillipe departed this life the 24th of Januarie. I geve God thankes my brother Henry is well recovered of his longe sickness. As for the writinges which conserne the portions of my neces by my sister Waley, I have non, neyther was acquaynted what they were.[2] I will send your letter unto my brother Henry, who it may bee can geve yow better light. Thuse with my ever true affectionat love I rest

    Your most lovinge Brother   O. Cromwell

Februari 2ᵈ, 1629

Endorsed (*f. 141b*): To my beloved sister the Lady Barrington theise

111   *Ezekiel Rogers, 2 February 1630*   (*2645, f. 142*)

Madam   My late seeing you in the south had written such a newe impression of you in my minde that for a good while I thought myselfe still speaking to and with you, but now methinkes 'tis high time to visite you againe and this way rather then not at all, the which I holde my selfe the more bounde unto, not only in regarde of your love and kindnesse both of olde and still, but because the lorde hath bereaved you of your heade and helper whom you so long injoyed, beside that I thinke I am as well acquainted with your state and temper as most are, both in regarde of that good the lorde hath done for you, as also your wants and weaknesses, so that if the lorde will voutsafe me a gratious and holy hart and fittly inlarged toward your cases[1] (which I hartily begg for your sake), I might hope to doe you some good. I have bene long a wittnesse how much the lord hath shewed his well-wishing to your soule, besides those actuall workings

    [1] Sir Oliver Cromwell of Ramsey, Huntingdonshire, the eldest of Lady Joan's brothers.
    [2] See letter 107.

of his spirit which hath bene a comfort to many, though it seemes that for the matter of assurance he hath not dealt so largely with you as with many of his saints, wherby as you are hindred of much comfort which others doe injoy more constantly, so you cannot have so large a measure of love to your God againe when you doe not so certainly and confidently beleeve that many sins are forgiven you. Hence also it is that you are oft in doubtings and feares, which your naturall temper doth much increase, but weaknes of faith is the maine cause: as Christ tells us, O thou of little faith, why didst you feare? Againe hence it is that the opinion that others have of you doth sometime sway you more then your owne knowledge as I observed when I was last with you by occasion of that letter which you shewed me, and with it also I confesse some weaknes of your owne.

Well, thus I have mentioned somwhat concerning your disease[2]. Now what is the remedy (you will say)? Surely no one like to this, that you labour still more to gett a sure grounde of comfort to builde upon. And there is but one grounde of our faith, which is the promise made in Christ to poore sinners. Many evidences there are, but no ground but that. This therfore must be your scope, unweariedly to followe the lorde and beseech him to let you see more cleerely your interest in this promise to discover to you what is the cause why he withdraweth that from you which he imparteth to others, which you may well see is somwhat in your selfe, and therfore matter of humiliation. [f. 142b] And be not discouraged if you gett not satisfaction so soone as you desire, or weary of taking paines. Let me tell you from some little experience, that the lorde so sought will sooner or later be founde. I thanke my God even since I sawe you I have founde some fruite of prayers made seven yeeres agoe or more. Oh this constant and uncessant plying of him, looking to his promise, in humility content to waite his leisure, doth bring to passe that in time that we woulde not part with for a kingdome. I might give you many rules, as I have also done heretofore, but this I pray you thinke of seriously. And as you finde that the lorde hath or doth further cleare this to you, so marke well in the next place that your foundation or groundworke you ought not to question. I say though your walking and faylinge therin you may and ought to question and to challenge your selfe about them, yet your

---

[1] i.e. cases, or questions, of conscience, as in William Perkins's *A case of Conscience, the greatest that ever was; How a man may knowe whether he be the Child of God or no* ... (1592). Rogers uses the word in the same sense in letter 192.

[2] See introduction, 15-16.

standing and foundation you ought not. When the lorde hath once given you a promise, it shalbe allwayes as true as ever it was, though not in your owne feeling. To this grounde adde as many evidences as you can: the through change that you finde in your selfe, the power you have gotten over corruptions, the wittnes of your conscience concerning your uprightnes and desire to please God in all things, what soever it cost you in displeasing others or your selfe, your joy in God's presence and ordinances, your willingnes to leave the world to goe to him, with your delight in his saints because of his stampe upon them, though their disposition naturall be not so sutable to yours, and the like. But I see though I desired brevity my letter groweth ere I be aware. If you (to contract) can gett this furniture, you neede not care what man or devill shall thinke or censure of you, for your hart being fixed, you shall not feare, but retire your self into the sanctuary of a good conscience which will ple[ad] for you against all.

I doe not knowe where you now abide, but I beseech your ladyshipp to have speciall care that you have full satisfaction in the ministery you live under, and make much account of the society of God's saints, putting your selfe forwarde in conference with freedome. I mus[t] needes take liberty to say that in my time at H[at]fielde I thought you much wanting to your selfe in the choise of your neighbours for converse, many being such as coulde helpe you by telling what God had done for their soules. The servants that are about you [f. 143] would also be of the choisest for Godlines, and then much countenance rewarde and bearing with their infirmityes. I hope I shall not neede to call upon you for bounty to God's poore saints; the truth is this poore country doth farre more in that kinde then Hatfielde did in my time. Madam, my hart wittnesseth for me how glad I shoulde be if I might any way further you in the worke of your faith. Your time and mine cannot be long;[3] the lord teach us to husbande it so that when death cometh it may be welcome. I shoulde be glad to see you once againe and to spende a day in private for our mutuall refreshing, as I have written to some others. But ever God will supply all your wants. To him I committ you, and with my service rest

Your ladyshipp's to command in him   Ezekiel Rogers

Rowly, February 2, 1629

Endorsed (*f. 143*): To the honourable the lady Johan Barrington

[3] Rogers died in 1661.

112 *John Barrington, 10 February 1630* (*2645, f. 144*)

Deare mother   May it please yow, since my comming to London I have understood by a letter receaved from my brother Robert Barrington how exceadinglie I am bounde unto yow, that yow are pleased to be intreated in my behalfe by my friends and to be so willing (notwithstanding so many former favours yow have pleased to heape upon mee) to continew your favours towards mee, for which I do present yow my humble thanckfulnes in thease poore lines;[1] and yow shall (God willing) finde mee ever carefull to strive to expresse this thanckfulnes in my submitting my selfe to whatever yow shall command mee. Wee cannot as yet have our pay, neither are certaine when wee shall. Wee heare no other newes but that of certaine the French fleete and army in them are at sea and have beene thease six daies and are bound for Mantua; they are 120 sayle of great and small shipps, but 25 or 30 great shipps, the rest but small boates.[2]

I beseach yow excuse my tediousnes. And so with my humble dutie remembred unto yow and my prayers for the continuance of your good health, I remayne

    Your obedient sonne   John Barrington

London, 10th February, 1629

Endorsed (*f. 145b*): To my honorable ladie and mother the ladie Barrington at Sir Gilbert Gerrard's house in Harrow Hill

113   *Sir William Masham, 12 February 1630* (*2645, f. 146*)

Deare Mothere   Your lettere was delivered my lord on Tusdaye night with my wive's hand to it and approbation acknowledging our selves much bound to you and the rest of our frendes with you for your great love and care expressed in this businesse, and I doubt not but your grandchild will see the fruit of it one daye, to all our comfortes. On Thursdaye night my lord sent for me and told me that he would confere with Mr St. John and the rest of his frends and see what maye be don further to give satisfaction, so that he did intimate theye would rise somewhat higher, though I feare not much. I told his lordship of this messengere goinge to you and if his lordship pleased he would conveye his answere to you, but he desired 3 or 4 dayes respect.

---

[1] The account book records bills of £10 and 16s. 6d. paid for him by Lady Joan in January and £6 given him in mid-Feb. E.R.O., D/DBa A15, ff. 9b, 10, 10b.

[2] News that there was possible danger to England from a French fleet was reported by John Pory in a letter of 12 Feb. Birch, ii. 58.

When you heare from my lord I praye let us know his resolution with all speede, for delayes in this business are prejuditiall to both sides. And if we heare first you shall know the same, that so there may be still a concurrence of frends as there hath bene hitherto in this great business and all litle enough to give it a quicke and good dispatch. My horses come up this daye and I have many occasions of my owne, besides the country business, that call me downe to morrow and I see litle hope to put this business to an issue as yet, which makes me the more willing to goe, havinge attended it thus longe to the neglect of myne owne, and shall still be ready upon all occasions to doe you and youres any services, espetially for her whom I accounte as my owne.

Oure newes is little, only they call up gentle[men] of severall coun-tyes to fine for knighthoode[1]. This morning the gentle[men] are to put in theyre plea, which I heare wilbe spetiall expressing the maner of the facts.[2] Young Dr Burges was questioned yesterdaye in the High Commission for [not reading service *struck through*] deniing to reade service, by reason of his indisposition of bodye, before the lecture at St Mary Overyes wherupon the congregation was dismissed with a great murmure and called againe to heare the king's instruction reade.[3] What was done against him as yet I knowe not. I pray God give a good issue to these things, generall and particular. So with my humble dutye to you and love to all my frends with you, I comit you all to God and rest

                    Yours   William Masham

February 12

Endorsed (*f. 148b*): To my honourable ladye and mother the ladye Barrington these at Harrow

114 *John Barrington, 12 February 1630*   (*2645, f. 148*)

Deare mother   May it please yow, I receaved your letter by Mr Masters and (according to your command) have sente yow as speadie

---

[1] The commission for fining those not taking up knighthood had been set up on 28 Jan. Rymer, xix. 119.

[2] Pory reported to Mead that Sir John Eliot, Holles and Valentine were to be given a last opportunity to plead on this day, but that although a plea was prepared none was made. Eliot was returned to the Tower on 27 Feb. Birch, ii. 57; Hulme, 337.

[3] Cornelius Burges was rector of St. Magnus, London Bridge, from 1626. The instruc-tions regulating lectures issued in December 1629 stipulated that no sermon could be given before divine service had been read according to the authorised liturgy. St. Mary Overy (St. Saviour, Southwark, now Southwark Cathedral) paid a regular lecturer at this time. *D.N.B.*, Gardiner, vii. 151; P. Seaver, *The Puritan Lectureships* (Stanford, 1970), 154.

an answere as I could. Yow may please to know then that to this effect I did intreate my brother Masham to confer with Mr Johnson[1] (who is one of the cheifest in that imployment) and by him my brother understood that they had no purpose to entertayne any companie, only he said they had three or foure souldiers out of the Low Countries which as I conceave are ingeniers, which are skilfull in the making of fortifications, to whome they allow twentie pounds a yeare. I am sure they are no men that leave the least command theare, to goe for so meane a reward so far, but some ordinary men that have beene servants to ingeniers theare. Soe Mr Johnson resolved him they did entertayne none other but in the way of a plantacion, which is a meere uncertaintie, which by some is approved, but by the greater parte and the best intelligence I can have utterly disliked. As I have formerly written yow shall dispose of my sealfe according to your pleasure, to which I wholly refer my sealfe, and if yow so please I shall resolve upon my journey into the Low Countries, which is I am sure a certaintie. In the meane tyme I shall dispose of my sealfe according to your appointment. And so with my humble dutie unto yow re-membred, with my thanckfull acknowledgment of your love in heaping so many favours upon mee, I commyt yow to the lord his tuition, who I beseach to continew your health and to bless all your Godly indeavours, and so I rest your obedient sonn

    John Barrington

London, 12th February, 1629

Endorsed (f. 149b): To my honourable mother the ladie Barrington at Harrow Hill

115 *Sir Thomas Barrington, n.d., [February 1630]*   (*2650, f. 189*)

Madame   This toune is so barren of newes, as if the frost [had] foreclosed the streame. The only intelligence I can derive to yow is the French king hath advaunced his foote forces to Piamont and the cardinall demaunds high conditions in his behalfe thare. His naval power is in dayly preparation, he haveing dessigned 30,000 crounes by the yeear to fortyfye him selfe at sea,[2] and towards the effecting heearof hath procured 20 or 30 familyes of the best shipp wrights that

[1] Isaac Johnson, of the Massachusetts Bay Company, was concerned that members of the party to sail in March 1630 should have a knowledge of fortifications. A. P. Newton, *The Colonizing Activities of the English Puritans* (Yale, 1912), 80–81.

[2] This news was reported by Mead to Stuteville in a letter dated 13 Feb. 1630. Birch, ii. 59.

he can obtaine into his countrye. Besydes this, he finding that the only way to improove his strength for the seas is to take of that contempt which the nobless of Fraunce held formerly all marchandizeing in (that so the publique of the better condition applying them selves to trafique might necessaryly add increase to his kingdom in shipping), he hath him selfe immediately professed that he will trade at sea as a marchant and hath innobled thareby that qualytye and will no question in probabilytye be much more powerfull at sea, of which the French embassador knowes for he allready professes against owr king's sole regalytye on the narrow seas, or his master his rayseinge sayle to our king's shipps. But his indevors have not yet raysed his ambition high enough (as all men thinke) to attempt us with a bodye of a navye, yet God open the eyes of state to foresee the perill of this groeing evell. And so with my humble dewtye and my wive's I rest

     Your most obedient and loving sonn

                                        Thomas Barrington

(*f. 109b*): Madame, my wife is so unwilling and carefull not to intermedle with or dispose of what is yours that she will not be perswaded to make your old peuter new with oute your consent, which being graunted it shall be the same in nomber and waight; the charge will be myne as well as the comodiousnes, now especially when we expect som freinds of worth before Easter. I desyre your answar to this resonable request for my wive's satisfaction.

Theise be delivered to the honourable my verye good mother the Lady Johan Barrington at Harrow

116 *John Barrington, 19 February 1630*   (*2645, f. 150*)

Deare mother   In regarde my occasions have detayned mee thus longe in this towne I have made boulde to let yow know the cheife cause hearof, which is to know the lords' order concerning our payment and the certayne tyme, that so I may accordingly repaire hither, and God willing at the beginning of the next weeke I will make bould to see yow. For wee are heare in feare of greate deductions out of our money, which I would gladlie know before I go heance, that I may frame an answere against the tyme to avoyde any deduction.[1]

I heare of no newes in this towne worthy of your knowledge. I do desire yow will please to accept of my humble acknowledgment as of divers former so of your late readines to extend your bountie unto

----

[1] See letter 87, n. 1.

mee. So with my most humble dutie remembred I betake yow to the lord his protection who I beseach to guide yow in all waies, and so I rest

Your obedient sonne   John Barrington

London, 19th February, 1629

Endorsed (*f. 151b*): To my honorable ladie and mother the ladie Barrington at Sir Gilbert Gerrard's in Harrow Hill

117   *Henry Wiseman*[1] *to Sir Thomas Barrington, 22 February 1630*
(*2645, f.152*)

Right worshipful   My dutie remembred. My brother Barlee hath appoynted a courte to be kepte heere at Elsenham in his owne name, the 2° of March nexte, and one Mr Newcumin of Starforde is his stewarde, and he hath made a warrante to warne the courte aganste that tyme, and this laste saboth daye it was warned. I did acquaynte Mr Scote[2] here with, and his occasion will fitt to keepe the courte that daye, for the prevention of Mr Newcomin's kepinge the courte. I muste intreate you to wrighte a letter to him on Thursdaye nexte to spare his labor, for that it is my Lord of Warwicke's plesure, and the rest of the committes,[3] to continue the oulde stewarde, for that he knoweth beste the title of the courte and the custome for ratinge the fynes, and withall I muste desire your company heere at the courte the 2° of March, and if it may be I woulde gladly intreate Sir William Masham's company likewyse, for with out your presenc my brother Barlee will not suffer the courte to be kepte, and therefore I hope you wilbe both intreated to be heere on that daye, consideringe how nedfull a thinge it is for the good of the tennantes, ther estates lyeinge in daunger, and likewyse for raysenge of mony to satisfye the agremente made by the committes. Mr Scote sente me the graunte under the greate seale, which I have sente by this bearer, desiringe your man may shewe it to Mr Newcumin. And in your letter to him I muste desire that I may not be named, for it may be he will shewe it to my brother Barlee. I oughte to have wayted on you my selfe, but my

<hr>

[1] Henry Wiseman of Barworth, Northamptonshire, was the brother-in-law and guardian of Thomas Barlee, who had inherited the manor of Elsenham, but who had subsequently, in 1608, been declared a lunatic. Morant ii. 571; *Visitations of Essex*, 2; J. E. Cussans, *History of Hertfordshire* (1870–81), Hitchin Half-Hundred, 156.

[2] Lady Joan Barrington's manorial steward. Introduction, 21.

[3] Commissioners in the lunacy of Thomas Barlee. The Earl of Warwick was distant kin to the Barlees.

brother is so jeleous of my goinge abrode, that if he should knowe I have any hande in the busines it wilbe a continuall bretch betwene us, which maketh me the more boulder to wrighte and sende my sunn to wayghte on you. And thus beinge desirous to be remembred in my best servis and wishes to your good selfe and my honoured ladye, I reste

Yours to be cummanded   Henry Wyseman

Elsenham, 22 February, 1629

Endorsed (f. 153b): To the right worshipful Sir Thomas Barrington, knit and barronet at Hatfelde give these

118 *Lady Elizabeth Masham, 1 March 1630*   (*2645, f. 154*)

Deare Mother   I have resceaved an answer to owr last letter to my lord of Bedford by the hand of Mr St. Johns which I have sent you hereinclosed with owr joynt replye to the same, which I hope will drawr my lord somewhat higher. As yet his offer is to lowe in respect of provision for posteryty, to whom our care must extend as well as for the present. I must acknowledge your former love expressed in this bisines acording to your constant care of me and mine and still I intreat the continuanc thireof, especially in your great ocation which may suffer much by your not joyning with me, who now have most need of your good helpp, and the rest of my frindes. When I have received my lord's answer I purpose (God willing), if my brother have any spare rome for me, to come to you and consult abowte this busines. Jugg hath a good afection to the gentleman, yet is very disirous of sum good inherytanc for her posterity and hath hir selfe expressed as much to him. Thus intreating your harty prayers for a good isue of this waity busynes and desiring your hand to this inclosed, I rest

Your ever dutyfull daughter   Elizabeth Masham

March 1, 1629
We present our humble dutis to you and our love to our frindes.
My lord intimated to my husband that he must add to his former offer, therfore I wonder he doth not express so much in his last letter. My brother Altham sent to us to stand for more estate then was offered. I pray send me my lord's letter which he sent me last sealed up in yours.

Endorsed (f. 155b): To my much honoured mother the lady Barrington these be given

119 *Lady Elizabeth and Sir William Masham, n.d., [March 1630]*

(*2645, f. 128*)

Deare mother   I was fully resolved to have waited upon you this Friday at Harow, at farthest, but it hath pleased the lord to hinder me by a very sore colde which I have got, soe that I dare not as yet venture out of dores into the ayre, nether can I goe now tell after the sesions. I hope you will except this as a just excuse. I have writ my excuse to my lord in a letter to Mr St Johns and have desired his answer by letter to us, and I will send it to you when I have it. Thus being not well able to inlarge my self further, with my humble duty and love I rest

Your dutyfull daughter   Elizabeth Masham

I must also fill up my wive's spare paper with the like excuse of a great cold, which I tooke at the assises,[1] so that I can not write so lardgly to you as I desired, only to present my humble service and duty to you to whom I owe more then my selfe

Yours obliged   William Masham

I meane to wayte on you after the sessiones.

I pray remember our best respects to my good brother Gerard and my deare sister, whom we forget not in our dayly prayers, together with your selfe and other our good frends. We salute my sister Lamplugh and the rest of our frends at Harrowe.

Endorsed (f. 129b): To my honourable mother the Lady Barrington these be given

120 *Sir Thomas Barrington, 18 March 1630*   (*2645, f. 160*)

Madame   Haveing this verye daye received letters from diverse parts, everye one relateing somwhat new, I am the more willingly invited to wright because I am supplyed with som subject.

From court the newes is that the king by his councell hath made a strict order that the forraigne ambassadors houses be attended by

---

[1] Assizes were held at Chelmsford on 10 March 1630. E.R.O., Calendar of Assize Files.

pursuivants to attach all that goe theither to mass, and that the queen's chappell is not priveleged now for any but her househould.[1] From Ireland the newes is of like nature: the 2 justices have so suppressed the preists, jesuites and fryars that neither public mass is sayd nor any of this rabble presumes to walke abroad with theire former confidence, so that thare is greate hope of much better times in that kingdom, thankes to be God. The lord prymate[2] hath bledd lately with such violence in his tongue, as that he was compelled to have it seared twice, for the first brake oute in new veines, but God be praysed he is perfectly well and hath begott a wondrous reformation in his northerne parts of Ireland, whare the light of trewth is broken forth in greate luster. From Hampshire we heear Mr Dorrington is condemned, and (suerly 'tis thought) by this time executed. He shewed little remorse at the assises, for though he at last desyred time to repent, yet he was verye violent in his goeing back to the prison after judgment.[3] Two others thare being condemned tould the judg theay hoped within a few howers to be devills in hell to torment him. An other swareing a greate oath or two that the judg had delt ill with him, called to Sir Henry Wallop saying Mr Sheriff pray send for som drinke for me, sorrow is drye. Thus theise vild wretches dyed ('tis to be feared) as theay lived. The Spanish treatye goes on slowely, the Dunkerk[er]s have lately taken 3 of the best shipps of Newcastle and have blockt in theire whole fleet and made them repair to the counsell boord for a convoye. The new French ambassador, intertayned with greate respect, had his audience upon Fryday last. Thus I committ us all to God and am ever your most obedient and loving sonn

  Thomas Barrington

Hatfield, March 18, 1629

Endorsed (f. 161b): To the honourable my verye good mother the Lady Johan Barrington give [these]

121 *Lady Elizabeth Masham, n.d., [March?, 1630]*   (*2650, f. 306*)

Deare mother In respect that the sicknes is abated at London and soe my lord of Bedford is not like to goe into the country till after the term and alsoe my self being still much trobled with my colde, my

---

[1] This news was similarly reported in a letter sent by Beaulieu to Puckering on 18 March 1630. Birch, ii. 67–8.

[2] James Ussher, archbishop of Armagh.

[3] He had been accused of murdering his mother. Birch, ii. 70.

desire is to staye my coming to you till I have got a litle more hart, which I hope will be the next week when my husband coms back from his great joyrnye owt of Hamsheer. I have bin wonderfull ill of a very sore cough but I thank God it begins to break away. I am very sory to here of the great loss we all sustaine by Mr Michill's death. I beseech the lord that the sudin chaingis may meake us carfull to be well prepared, that so our comfort may not be to seek when we shold have most use of it. Thus with my humble duty, much desiring to be with you if the lord will give me leav, I comit you to the lord and rest
  Your dutyfull daughter Elizabeth Masham

[*In the hand of Sir William Masham:*] My purpose was to have seene you now with my wife, but seeing she cannot come I must intreat you to excuse me till my returne from Warnford and then I purpose, God willing, to wayte on [you]. In the meane our prayers shall not be wanting for you and our frends with you and for a happye meeting and conclusion of this business. In hast, with my humble duty, I rest
  Yours William Masham

I pray commend our best loves to my deare brother and sister and to the rest of our friends with you.

Endorsed (*f. 307b*): To my much honoured mother the Lady Barrington these be given at Harrow

122 *Lady Elizabeth Masham, n.d.,* [*March? 1630*] (*2650, f. 287*)

Deare mother It is a great comfort to me to hear of your good health and I rejoyce to think that the time draws on apace of your coming to Hatfild, which I here you are resolved of. I hope in God you shall finde such good content that you will not be willing to depart againe. I desir that you may. I wold not you should have any thing now to greve you and make this litle time of your uncomfortable, 'tis fit you shold have all the comfort from your one children, and I make no question but you shall; and for the spetiall helpe in the best things which is first and most to be sought I think you canot hav it better in any place. I pray God send my sister a comfortable deliveranc, then I am sure you will com with the more cherfullnes away.[1] Thus in great hast, with my humble duty, praying for the continuanc of your hapynes, I rest
  Your ever obedient daughter Elizabeth Masham

[1] See letter 125, n. 1.

I beseech you to remember my love to my brother and sister. My husband and sister remember their servicis.

Endorsed (*f. 288b*): To my honored mother the Lady Barrington at Harrow Hill give these

123   *James Harrison, 18 March 1630*   (*2645, f. 158*)

Good madame   Haveinge so fitt a messenger I should much have forgotten my selfe not to have written, though I have notheinge to write but my humble and hearty thankes for your good ladiship, for your still continued and continually wittnessed abundant kindnes to me and myne, as many other tymes so at my last beinge at Harrow, for which my self and myne have great cause to be thankefull to God and you, and as we are able to be suitors to his majesty that it would please him according to his promise to recompence your great love with blessings of all sortes, especially in spirituall things, and to continue you in the land of the lyving for his owne glory, your owne further comfort, and the great good of many. It much rejoyceth me to consider the shortenes of the tyme that now remaynes till we shall injoy you; the lord bringe that great worke to a good issue that hath caused your stay, that wee may have our mouthes filled with prayses unto our good God, and he in mercy prosper your journey to us and your abode with us. Thus with my owne and my wyve's duty and service to your good ladiship thankefully remembered, as also to Sir Gilbert Gerrard and his lady with hearty thankes for their great love in my kinde entertaynement and many favors, with the like to my lady Lamplugh, I take my leave, ever resting
          At your ladiship's service and command   James Harison

Hatfield, March 18, 1629
Your litle godsonne thryves well, I blesse God. Let him injoy your prayers for him I humbly desyre your good ladyship.

Endorsed (*f. 159b*): To my honorable good lady the Lady Johanna Barrington at Harrow in Midlesex geve these

124   *Lady Elizabeth Masham, n.d.,* [*March 1630*]   (*2645, f. 168*)

Deare Mother   I am hartyly glad to here of God's mercy to my sister. I shoulde have bin very hapy to have held hir back, but I am glad it is so well over. I thank God my coulde is pretty well gon, yet I have not stured into the ayre. I purpose, God willing, to be with you the week after Ester that together we may make sum conclution of this busynis.[1] If I sholde here that my lord of Bedford is like to goe shortly into the country before the terme, then I meane if God give me leave to be with you the later end of Ester week. Thus, not dareing to hold down my head longe to wright, desiring the continuanc of your prayers for the good sucses of this busynes, I humbly rest

Your obedient daughter   Elizabeth Masham

My husband remembers his servic to you.
I beseech you to remember us to all our good brothers and sisters. My lord stands upon his former ofer without any inheritanc and I feare he will do no more. We shall se when we meet.

Endorsed (f. 169b): To my honourable mother the ladye Barrington at Harrow these

125   *Sir Richard Everard, 24 March 1630*   *(2645, f. 166)*

Good madam   I am very glad to heare of your ladyship's good healthe, as of my sister Gerard's good deliverye.[2] I am sure my wiffe wilbe very glad to heare it. I praye God send her as quicke speede; she growes very bigge and somtimes is somthinge ill. I would desire mistris Michaell to send me worde as soone as she returns to Hatfeilde. We have buried Sir John Rousse.[3] I praye good madam tell my cosin Mewx I wilbe very carfull of her businesse. Thus with my humble service presented to your ladyship, my brother Gerarde and sister, I desire ever to continue

Your most observant sonne   Richard Everarde

Hattfeild, 24 March 1629/30

Endorsed (f. 167b): To his honourable mother the Ladye Barrington give these

[1] Easter Day was 28 March 1630.
[2] The Gerards' son Henry was baptised 1 April 1630. *The Registers of St. Mary's Church, Harrow-on-the-Hill,* ed. W. O. Hewlett (1900), i. 225.
[3] Sir John Rouse, who had acted as receiver general to the Rich family, appears to have lived in Great Waltham at least in the early 1620s. His burial is not recorded in the Great Waltham parish register. Alnwick MSS. XII, 7. Box 1 (a source kindly indicated to me by Mr Christopher Thompson); Thomas Barnes, *The Gales of Grace* (1622), epistle dedicatory.

126 *John Barrington, 24 March 1630*   *(2645, f. 162)*

Deare mother   I understand by Mr Brewster he sente Sir Phillip
Pagnam's letter unto my brother Gerrard, which doth mencion a
meeting of the states at the Hague about a treatie of peace, but I
understand by some that came latelie from theance that it is not likelie
a peace wilbe concluded, but is quite rejected by the greater parte of
them.[1] I do assure my sealfe if Sir Phillip and my Lord Veare come
not over this weeke or the next they cannot come this sommer, it being
generallie beleaved the army wilbe on foote at the beginning of May.
Thearfore I shall (God willing) resolve the beginning of the weeke
after Easter to wayte upon yow at Harrow, with my brother and sister
Masham, and from theance as yow shall please to appoint mee soe to
dispose of my sealfe, for it is my earnest desire to be abroade in action
and not to live in this maner at home, which desire of mine I doe
assure my selfe doth correspond with your will. With my humble dutie
remembred and praiers for your health I commyt yow to the lord his
mercifull tuition, remayning
             Your obedient sonn   John Barrington

Hatfild, 24th March, 1629

Endorsed (*f. 163b*): To my honourable ladie and mother the lady Barrington at Harrow Hill

127 *Sir William Meux, 2 April, 1630*   *(2645, f. 179)*

Madam   I suppose itt needless to profess my willingness, nay
rather my earnest desires, that my daughter should be well bestowed,
but in these partes good and fitt matches are soe rare as that itt makes
me hopeless to bestow her neere me. If any may be herd of about yow,
the first that comes (having yowr approbation) I should be unwilling
to refuse, fearing the longer she staies, the harder itt will be to preferr
her. Yet I know that itt is the lord that disposeth all things, and when
he sees itt fitt will doe that which is best. I intend God willing to be
with yow ere long, att which time I shall further impart my self. Good
madam, give Jack som good councell, and God of his infinite mercy
mak him to receive itt effectually. Itt's late and therefore I must bid
yow good night. The lord of heaven preferre yow and send us an
happy meeting,
             Yowr assuredly loving son   William Mewx
Kingston the 2^{ond} of Aprill, 1630

[1] See letter 91, n. 3.

Endorsed (*f. 180b*): To his much honored mother the Lady Barrington att Harrow on the Hill give these

128   *John Barrington, 5 April 1630*   (*2645, f. 172*)

Deare mother   May it please yow, I did determine to have beene with yow at the beginninge of this weeke, but my sister Masham's indisposicion causing hir longer stay of hir journey doth likewise cause my deferring comming unto yow, partly in regard my sister desires my company (my brother being gone toward Hampshire) to accompany hir to Harrow and partly because I doe not conceave that there is any very urgent occasion that I may not defer my voyadg into the Low Countries a few daies longer. If in the meane while I shall have any notice that yow are pleased to have mee this weeke to returne to London and so dispose of my selfe more spedily for my journey, I shall intreate my sister to dispense with mee, and I will at first notice attend yow. In the meane tyme, with my humble dutie remembred, I remayne

> Your obedient sonn   John Barrington

Oates, 5th April, 1630

Endorsed (*f. 173b*): To my honourable lady and mother the Ladie Barrington at Harrow Hill

129   *Sir Thomas Barrington, n.d.*, [*early April? 1630*]   (*2650, f. 187*)

Madame   Lett me beseich you to interpret my not attending you (before my long intended journye) to the urgence of my occasions at London which, upon my word, detained me in howerly imployments untill my coming downe, and now the sessions till late this verye night have kept me in imployment,[1] and tharefor I have sent this bearer purposely to understand your health, as theise to excuse my absence, who if God bless me with life and health will visit you imediately after my retourne. My wife presents her dewtye and love to you and I my hartye prayers for owr comfortable meeteing. And so with my love to my brother and sister Gerard and sister Lamplugh, I committ us all to God and rest

> Your most dewtyfull sonn   Thomas Barrington

[1] The Easter quarter sessions at Chelmsford met on 6 April. E.R.O., Q/SR 270.

Endorsed (*f. 188b*): To the honorable my verie good mother the Lady Johanna Barrington give [these] at Harrow on the Hill

130 *Sir Francis Harris to* [*Lady Judith Barrington*],[1] *9 April 1630*

(*2645, f. 174*)

Worthy ladie, my most honored cosin   It hapned I could not give yow suche satisfaction in your busines as nowe I canne, by reasone of the gentleman's occasions (I meane that skillfull gentleman in phisick) and a resolutione aboute a lodgeing for yow, but I have nowe brought him to a certaynety with much willingnes and hee wisheth your comming uppe with all convenyent speede, hoping yow will defer it noe longer then the next weeke, the soner the better, for it is likely to growe hott. Hee dothe so muche regarde your convenyencie and contentment that, seeing my Lady Coope cannot accommodate yow as she desired, hee will come unto yow once a daye for a weeke into Aldersgate Streete, within which tyme hee dowbtes not but to doe yow muche good and give yow suche derections as he hopeth yow shall have lytle neede of his muche helpe (especyially of his presence), observinge the rewles hee will tell yow, for hee saythe, and please God, to expedite his pacyents is his costume and ayme.

Your carryer's uncertayne comming uppe disapoynted me of sending to yow. And for your other busines I have byne myndefull, namely Mr Somes (whoe seemes muche to respect yow) hathe sett by an excellent peece of muskerdyne of his owne chosing. And for your coche horsse, the Earle of Lynsey or a knight in Westminster would gladly buy them, so that if yow purpose madame to use them in your coche at your comming uppe, spare them what yow cane, for they wilbe the better to the eye and so for sale, for they have present uses for them. Therefore madame if I weare worthy to advise yow, they should not bee used in the coche comming uppe if yow cane possible spare them, especyally one of them, the darker culler that stood next the walle when I was there, for I tould your grome hee stood with one of his fore fytt like a fenser, which hee sayde was a defect in the farryer in shoing, but sewer I ame suche a thing maye hinder the sale of them 4 or 5^{li}. I lodge uppon occasione of busines neerer your lodgeing and shalbe ready to doe yow any service within my poore reache. And eaven so I hartely salute Sir Thomas my honourable cosin, your deerest, your

---

[1] At the head of the page Sir Thomas Barrington has written 'My most dear frend my service' and Lady Judith has used the back of the paper to keep accounts.

ladyship, lovely mistris Jane your sister, and my other alley, with
wishes of all your prosperityes, remayninge
Yours unfaynedly to command   Francis Herris

From Mr Okelie's, a pynemakers, one Claftonwell, neere the maye-
pole, Aprill 9, 1630, Fryday, in hast

[*No endorsement*]

131 *Lady Anne Bourchier,*[1] *17 April 1630*   (*2645, f. 175*)

Madame   Your favoures from time to time heapt apon me
makes me stodey which waye to shew my thankfulnes to you, if by a
poore token. Your bounty furder ingage me and by writing I am
alltogether unabel to exprease it, onely acknowleg it and wait for an
opertiunity to shew it in any kind that I am abel. I much desier to
hear of your health, which I will allwayes praye for. I bles God I am
now well recoverd, but I was very weake of this last child a longe
while, and the child two, but nowe he grows very stronge.[2] Thus not
trobeling you any longer to read my cribling lins and bad English,
with my best respects to your selfe I rest your truly loving nece to
command tel death
Anne Bourchier

April 17, 1630

Endorsed (*f. 176b*): To my much honored ant the Lady Barrington att
Hatfild give this

132 *Lady Judith Barrington, n.d.,* [*April? 1630*]   (*2650, f. 158*)

Madam   You must pardon my troubling of you soe soone
againe, for Toby will not think himselfe well used sence he brought
me a letter if he maye not returne one againe, and I am easily
perswaded upon all occasions to be glad to tendor my service to you.
This place affoords nothing now, nothing worth the relation to you,
this colde weather I think freezing actions as well as spoyling all our

---

[1] Wife of Sir John Bourchier of Benningbrough: see Table 1.
[2] The eldest son of Anne and Sir John Bourchier was born in 1627. They had two
more sons. William Dugdale, *Visitation of the County of Yorke* (Surtees Soc., xxxvi. 1854),
140.

hopes of stoare of plums, soe that I will onely renew to your memory the trew affections that every body heer owes you. And so hartely praying for your welfare I rest ever

Your most respectively lovinge daughter

Judith Barrington

Munday

Endorsed (*f. 159b*): To my most honored mother the Lady Barrington at Harrow this

133 *John Barrington, 28 April 1630*   (*2645, f. 177*)

Deare mother   May it please yow, I have this day according to your command beene with my brother Barrington and did confer with Sir Edward Horwood[1] who promiseth to doe mee that courtesie he may. If yow finde it fitting, I shalbe readie to passe over with him, but I am very much unfurnished of all necessaries, which I am very loath to importune yow for in regard I have allreadie beene very chargeable unto yow; but I am now constrayned to intreate yow will be pleased to assist mee, which I shall strive to desearve as much as I am able, for indeed I was so exceadingly disapointed in the expectacion I had of much mony from the king that I could not either furnish my sealfe with any necessaries neither performe my promise in repaying yow as I promised, which I humbly beseach yow to pardon and not to have an ill opinion of mee for not performance, for (if yow please to give credit to my protestacion) I assure yow I had not twentie shillings left by reason of abatments for diet in the countrie for my sealfe, [*f. 177b*] some other deabts which was layd upon mee as receaved by mee which I never did receave, and cannot however get redress from the commissioners. I can shew you (if yow so please) the particular of what was deducted from me and paid (in unavoidable deabts) by my consent, which I could not honestly avoyd, wherfore my right earnest request is that yow will please not to conceave ill of mee in the not being better furnished with meanes to helpe my sealfe nor performe my promise unto yow, for nothing could happen more unexpectedly unto mee then being disapointed of my expectacion from the king of what I made account to receave.[2]

Sir Edward Horwood departeth the next weake; for my part I

---

[1] One of the four standing colonels in the army in the Low Countries. *D.N.B.*

[2] £25 was paid out for him and entered in the account book under the date of this letter. E.R.O., D/DBa A15, f. 12.

shalbe willing (if yow please) to goe with him but I must confess I had
rather to searve in my Lord Veare's company, however I will submit
to your plesure. With my humble duty remembred I will rest
   Your obedient son John Barrington

London, 28th Aprill, 1630

Endorsed (f. 178b): To my honourable and very good mother the ladie
Barrington in Harrow Hill

134 [*Sir Thomas Barrington, May 1630*]   (*2645, f. 181*)

Madame Allthough I wrote this morning to you concerneing
my brother John, yet (on the sodaine) it was so confusedly as that I
feare you hardly could hardly [*sic*] apprehend my meaneing. The
reson why I did not formerly applye my selfe to my Lord Veare was
because he was not in toune, nor did I heear of his coming over; since
then I heard it reported that he was resolved to make his abode in
England, which heearing contradicted since I did speake with Sir
Edward Horwood, I am resolved by your favor to claime my Lord
Veare his makeing good of his tender to my father at his being at
Hatfeild, but I hope you may trust my judgment so farr as that and it
shall not be donn so as may admitt any prejudice or exception, nor so
far as can give any impediment to owr first indevors towards Sir
Edward Horwood. But I am still in hast; my wife and I tender you
owr dewtye and love
   Your most dewtyfull sonn

My point points at my nephew St John's his appointment and I pray
for his happyness. My Lord Bedford is well.

[*No endorsement*]

135 *John Barrington, 7 May 1630*   (*2645, f. 182*)

Madam May it please yow, I was to have spoken with my Lord
Veere, but was disapointed by reason of his early departure out of his
lodgings, and therfore must have patience untill this night or to
morrow morning, at one of which tymes I doubt not but I shall have
opportunity to deliver your letter, and then I will not fayle to give
yow account of his answear unto it. I heare since my comming hither
that Sir Edward Horwood departed from hence upon Wednesday

night to Gravesend and I do beleave the fayre wind yeasterday carried them away. With the next shipps (God willing) I purpose to goe, which I hope wilbe ready at the beginning of the weeke at Gravesend, else I will seeke in some other place for shipping to transport mee over. In meane tyme and ever I shall desire to remayne

Your obedient sonne   John Barrington

London, 7th May, 1630

Endorsed (*f. 183b*): To my honourable and very good mother the ladie Barrington at Harrow Hill

136   *Sir Thomas Barrington, n.d.,* [*May, 1630*]   (*2645, f. 184*)

Madame   In obedience to your desyres I have this morning perfected my suite to my Lord Veare and have tendred to my lord my brother in person, whom he verye curteously intreated, and promised me that he would not only looke upon his merrits in future with a just eye, but allso that he would have a perticular respect unto him for his freinds' sakes, and he hath promised my brother to wright over by him to recommend him into his companye (meane while) till he goe over him selfe, which will not be sodainely I beleive. My brother being the convoye of theise I shall need wright the less, but referr it to his relation. Thare remaines only now a faire disingagement towards Sir Edward Horwood, which I will no wayes neglect, God willing. Madame, I shall be most readye to serve you in any thing, trust me as you find me. I have a motion made unto me for Mr Pimm[1] to have Barrington Hall till winter. Now my wife, oute of her provident care of your selfe and us, thinks that the feare of the sickness disperseing is cause enough to desyre to keepe that house free for a refuge[2], and I confess I have intimated as much; if you are of the same opinion I shall persist. Newes heear is barren, only the French yet prosper in Italye and the Hollanders in the West Indyes, so the Spaniard is cufft on both cheekes and is not patient in suffring, but groes poore by it. This after noone my deear sister Higham calls your selfe and me to give a more sufficient answar before a master of the Chauncerye, and trewly I will be thare in person and hope to speake suff[ic]ient to cause to their shame. Higham is upon sure grounds, for

---

[1] Sir Thomas Barrington's association with John Pym became closer in Jan. 1631 when Sir Thomas became a member of the Providence Island company, of which Pym was treasurer. *C.S.P.Col, 1574-1660*, iii. 7-10.

[2] London experienced only a minor outbreak of plague in 1630 but its beginnings caused considerable concern in late April. J. F. D. Shrewsbury, *A History of Bubonic Plague* (1970), 355-6.

he (as I heeard) hath a bond of Dousett to save him harmeless in all suites for his wife, tharefor he takes all the wayes he can for to increase the charges of the suite; and trewly if you please we will make him draine the tann fatts to feed his counsell and the old tanner glad to displaye his greate pawes for the favor of an end, and since theay goe vexatious wayes I will trye to counterworke them[1]. Thus in hast I committ us all to God

Your most dewtifull and loving sonn

Thomas Barrington

Endorsed (f. 185b): To the honourable my verye good mother the lady Barrington give [these] at Harrow on the Hill

137   *Francis, Earl of Bedford[2], 7 May 1630*   *(2645, f. 186)*

Madam   My cosen St. John telleth me that hee hath reseved favors from you by heapes, which I shall desier yor Ladyship toe beleve that I vallew them at noe less then if you had bestowed soe many kindnesses and so much plate[3] uppon me, which I am confident his love and service toe you and yors shall in sume mesuer aunsewer his debt toe you and the obligation of

Yor Ladyship's affeccionat servant and frend

Francis Bedford

Bedford House this 7 of May, 1630

Endorsed (f. 187b): To my honoured frend the lady Barrington at Harrow give this

138   *James Harrison, 12 May 1630*   *(2645, f. 188)*

Good madame   Besides the unseasonablenes of the weather and the unfittnes of the wayes for travayle, my owne bodily diseases and

---

[1] Francis, the third son of Lady Joan and Sir Francis, married a daughter of Richard Dowsett. Little is known of him. Noble states that he settled in London and then pursued a distinguished military career in the civil war, ending up as a field-officer in Jamaica. This letter, however, is evidence for his death and his widow's remarriage. Table 3; Noble, ii. 41. See also letter 203.

[2] Francis Russell, 4th Earl of Bedford.

[3] Lady Joan's gift was a basin, ewer and two livery pots, costing £66.14s; E.R.O., D/DBa A15, f. 12, entered under the week of 5 May. The precise date of the couple's marriage is not known.

want of health hath for a while hindered me from visitting your good ladiship and the worthy famely where you are and from whenc we hope you intend shortly to come to your owne habitation, in which journey I shall take much content to attend you and to come to Harrow to fetch you, if I may, as I hope I shall, know the tyme which, as I hope it is nigh, so I know it will be the cheareing of many. The lord our good God guide and prosper your way to us and direct and inable us so to performe what belongs to our partes as may gyve your good ladiship such content as may with thankfullnes confirme your resolution of continueing with us, which, as I hope it will be indeavored on all handes, so for my owne part, as I am much bounden, it shall be my true care not to be awanteing in any duty and service that the lord shalbe pleased to inable me to performe for the furthering of your best good both in publike and private. I am very sorry to se my good lady Lamplugh so ill in regard of bodily weakenesse, I hope the lord will in his good tyme gyve her the comfortes her soul desyres and bringe her with rejoyceing in his rich grac in Christ out of this sadnes; my poore prayers and best indeavors dayly shall not be awanting for her good, but the care will requyre as well bodily as spirituall phisick, nyther alone wilbe so avayleable as both together, the lord being pleased (as my trust is he is) to gyve a blessing. Mrs Lucy[1] hath had a feavor, but is fynely recovored blessed be God; it doth much cheare her when we speak of your ladiship's comeing. She remembereth her duty and craves your blessing. Thus humbly and heartely beseecheing the lord dayly to adde unto your spirituall stock of grace and comfort and to recompenc your great and undeserved bounty to me and myne,[2] with the rememberanc of my owne and my wyve's duty and service to your good ladiship, with Sir Gilbert and my lady, desyring all your prayers, and your ladiship's in speciall for your litle godsonne, I take my leave and rest alwayes

at your ladiship's command   James Harison

Hatfeild, May 12, 1630
If Sir William Masham and my lady be not come away, we desyre with mistris Joane Masham, who is merry and well, to be remembered to them as we doe to both the new secretaryes for whose happinesse every way our poore desyres neyther are nor shall God willing be awantinge.

Endorsed (*f. 189b*): To my honorable good lady the Lady Johanna Barrington at Harrow in Midlesex geve these

---

[1] Sir Thomas Barrington's daughter. Table 3.
[2] Besides the gifts at the baptising of the Harrisons' son Lady Joan had also lent them money: £10 was paid back on Lady Day 1631. E.R.O., D/DBa A15, f. 3b (end reversed).

139   *John Barrington, 15 May 1630*   *(2645, f. 190)*

Madam   I have seene your letter to my brother Barrington
wherin I perceave your desire to have me suddenly to transport my
sealfe over into the Low Countries, which command I shall not faile
to obey so soane as possible I may, for I am readie for the first
opportunitie of a shipp to transport mee, which I thought would have
beene this day, but I was informed yeasterday by the master that he
cannot be ready thease foure daies. I beseach yow to be pleased not to
conceave ill of mee in regard that I have not meanes to transport my
sealfe, for I must wayt upon the shipping. If then I neglect the
opportunity let mee bee blamed, for my desire is not to stay long
heear. In meane tyme I beseach yow to have a charitable opynion of
me. I perceave yow are displeased that I went not over with Sir
Edward Horwood, which I could by no meanes, for he went away
sooner then was expected, and if I had beene heare then I could not
have gone with him, for I was unprovided then of all necessaries. I
therfore desire yow would not entertayne an ill conceipt of mee without cause, and for my part I desire no longer to be regarded of yow
then I shall strive in all things to my utmost power to give yow content.
And so with my humble duty remembred I commyt yow to God his
tuition and remayne
         Your obedient sonn   John Barrington

If yow shall please to afford mee your letter at the stacioner's in
Lincolnes Inne gate, I shall receave them if yow please thither to send
them.
London, May 15th, 1630

Endorsed (f. 191b): To my honourable and very good mother the lady
Johan Barrington at Sir Gilbert Gerrard's house at Harrow Hill

140   *John Barrington, 21 May 1630*   *(2645, f. 192)*

Madam   May it please yow, I was so suddenly and unexpectedly
posted from London, by reason of the sudden departure of a shipp
bound for the low countries, that I could not wright yow from London;
as allso I am by my Lord of Dorchester ingaged to deliver the king's
packet at the Hage which I could not refuse (alethough it be far out
of my way and will be chargeable to mee), for I did by my brother's
meanes obtayn my passe from him. And so he hath layd the chardg
upon mee to travell to the embassadors at the Hague, which (God
willing) I shall faithfully performe. And withall I pray yow to be

assured that in this course I now goe I will strive to give yow a good accompt. I beseach yow excuse my great hast in thus rudely wrighting yow, and that yow would please to use a farther meanes to my collonel the Lord Veere. I pray God send us a good passage, cleare from our enymies, which wee much doubt. And yow shall heare from me, God sending mee well to our garrison at Dort. My humble duty I desire to remember, with my prayers for your good health and happines. So will ever pray

Your obedient sonn   John Barrington

From aboard shipp at Gravsend now ready to set sayle, May 21th, 1630.
Wee are constrayned to depart without convay by reason of hast.

Endorsed (*f. 193b*): To my honorable mother the Lady Barrington, at Sir Gilbert Garrard's at Harrow Hill. Leave this with Mr Brewster at the Dutchy office in Grayes Inne

141   *Lady Judith Barrington, n.d.,* [*May? 1630*]   (*2645, f. 194*)

Madam   I have noe hart to lett a frend soe neer us pass to you without some few lines of my respects to you. Whear I owe soe much, this is the least I can doe, and your lovinge care of my safety in our returne from London, with your kinde letter, challenged my thankfulnes before now, as well as the account to lett you kno I think we fared the better for your good wishes, for I see you wear mindfull of us. And soe shall I be now to gett your gardin and all things to your contentment against you please to do us the favour you have promised, which now draws on soe fast that our hopes grow stronge. My daily prayers attend you that we may enjoye with health, which I am confident this ayre will be no enemye to, and I am sure you have many harts that doe attend for that good daye. Mine must be in the first ranke and shall ever dispose of me and my actions to render me

Your most respectively lovinge daughter to command
Judith Barrington

Thursday
My sisters remember thear best services to you.

Endorsed (*f. 195b*): To my most honored mother the Lady Barrington at Harrow this

142   *William Hook,*[1] *25 May 1630*   *(2645, f. 196)*

Madame   Being sensible of that blessing which the lord hath given me through your ladiship's hands, I desire first to looke upward to his majestie, then backward to your much honoured selfe with a vow of thankefulnes. How unwillingly were you departed from both my wife and my selfe, desirous as we were (if it could have bin) of an everlasting fruition of your presence, endeavouring our selves in this necessity of our absence to preserve your ladyship in our continuall remembrance. For my selfe I cannot but acknowledg, with much praise to God and respect to your selfe, that I have admirably found the finger of God's mercy and providence, both in the entrance, proceeding and close of my now finished suite, and desire to be instructed which way I may be expressed yours. Madam give me leave to specifie the special ties of your bounty and kindnes towards me since my last being at Harrow in more then one respect, your purse, your servants, your prayers, advise (to say noe more), have ministredd to my selfe and your niece.[2] Part of my poore requitall shall be presented unto you in my tender regard of the welfare both of her body and soule. I doubt not of your ladiship's continuing prayers and intercession for our good. What I canot write I have striven by word to commend by the bearer to your ladyship, resting in the profession of my selfe

Your ladyship's unworthy servant   William Hooke

Upper Clatford this 25th of May, 1630

Endorsed (f. 197b): To the much honoured lady the Lady Johan Barrington at Harrow these be given

143   *Oliver St. John, 26 May 1630*   *(2645, f. 198)*

Madame   Suffer me I beseech you to become a sutor for my letter, that togeather with the rest of the packet you would be pleased to give it the reading. It desyreth to informe your ladyship that I was lately att London and had an intente to have seene you but having promised a sett time of returne to my wife the busienesse that drew me up would not afforde me one howers freedome till my promised time

---

[1] William Hook, rector of Upper Clatford in Hampshire, married Lady Joan's niece Jane Whalley earlier in May. Hook later went to New England but returned to become Cromwell's chaplain in 1656. Foster; E.R.O., D/DBa A15, f. 12b; *D.N.B.*

[2] Lady Joan gave Hook's wife £100 in the week of 19 May. E.R.O., D/DBa A15, f. 12b.

was come. I intende, God willing, ere long to wayte uppon your ladyship and hope that in the meane time you will be pleased to receive my humble and sincere acknowledgment of those many free, greate and undeserved expressions of your love and affection unto me. Requitall from me I know you expecte none, what I am able is only as one of your beadsmen and dayly orators to intreate him whoe is able that he would restore them agyne with tenfould increase uppon your head. Deare madam give me further leave I humbly beseech you to promise my selfe and to remayne

Your ladyships faythfull and thankfull servant

Oliver St. Johns

Oates, 26 May, 1630

Endorsed (f. 199b): To the honourable lady the Lady Johan Barrington att Harrow these

144   *Sir Richard Everard, 28 May 1630*   *(2645, f. 200)*

Good madam   Assuringe my selfe that your ladyship hath longe expected to heare of our welfares, especially my wife's, and we, beinge as desirous to heare of the continuance of your healthe, doe present these, advertisinge you that it hath pleased the lord to give her some strenghte againe and to make her prettie heartye, beinge able to walke about her chamber. She was the first fortnight very weake and ill, beinge troubled with an every daye ague. She hopes the lord will make her perfettly well against your ladyship comes to Hattfeilde, that she may meet you there. She hath brought me a very fine fatt girle; she never was so good a nurse to any as to this. Thus with mine owne and wive's humble service and dutye presented to your ladyship, with our best respects and wishes to all the rest of our good frends, I desire ever to remaine

Your most observaunt sonne   Richard Everarde

Langleyes, May 28, 1630

Endorsed (f. 201b): To his honourable mother the Ladye Barrington senior give these

145   *Josias Knight to John Kendal[1], 30 May 1630*   (*2645, f. 202*)

Mr Kindal   I reseved your later consaring Flamsted rent[2] an I
have sant up four scor pond by Mr Nell, whar of ten pond wos Mr
Rollnd, twant too pond god man Casle and sixtin pond Mr Sanders,
and nine pond Braden an twat thre pond godman Bridin, an too pond
Mr Cotan. As for wod mone, thar is littel or none radi besid that I
hafe paid out. As for my one honderd pond, it is not ridy, but I due in
tind to pa it in fift pond at Michaelmasse nixt an fift pond at our lady
da, or to gife sattisfi for. An thus I rist
        Your lofing frend   Josias Knight

Maye the 30, 1630
Deliver this to Mr Kidal I pray

[*No endorsement*]

146   *William Chantrell, 7 June 1630*   (*2645, f. 203*)

Noble ladie   Should I forgett your auncient favours I might
justly be cast out of the societie of men, for what I am in these
northeren partes I am by your means under our great and loving God.
Littell can these partes afford to yow, your higher and hotter hilles
glide downe all newes to us, only madame my hope is yow daily looke
for your changes. Well knowe yow all flesh is grass and the benignitie
of it as the flowre of the feilde. How soone are wee cut of? But here is
our hope and anchorhold: I know my redeemer liveth and I shall see
him with these eyes of mine, as Job sayth.
        Littell reson hath the weakest faith to feare death, it being that
usher that leades to our father presence wher there is joy for ever more.
        I had purposed to have visited your southeren partes and presented
my service to your ladishipe hathe not God intercepted my jorny with
those venimous arrowes shott into our universitie to the scatteringe of
these young impes[3]. The good lord shalbe pleased to reverse them. I
shall addres my selfe therunto by his rich mercie in Christ to which I

---

[1] Steward to Sir Thomas and Lady Judith Barrington. See Introduction 18

[2] All those named were landowners in Flamstead in Hertfordshire where Lady Judith
Barrington leased the tithes. They include Edmund Neele of Ing's Place, Harpenden
and Thomas Saunders of Beechwood in Flamstead. Introduction 5; V.C.H., *Herts.*, ii.
307.

[3] Cambridge suffered its worst outbreak of plague in 1630; it was publicly known on
10 April, sermons and exercises were stopped on 19 May and the university officially
dispersed six days later. A Samuel Chantrell matriculated pensioner from Trinity
College in Easter 1631. Birch, ii. 78; Shrewsbury, 357–8; Venn.

commend your ladishipe as to the strongest towre for your sweetest and surest comfort and rest

　　　　　Your old and true servaunt　　　William Chantrell

Junii 7°, 1630

Endorsed (*f. 204b*): To my noble patroness the Ladie Johana Barrington give [these]

147　*Mary Whalley*,[1] *9 June 1630*　　　　　　　(*2645, f. 205*)

Madame　　　It was your noble freenes to send master Ewers[2] to London in my sister Hooke's behalfe. Hee promised to have beene in London on Munday last. His not coming is the cause of theise lines, to beseech your ladyshipp to send some to asist mee. Your honoure cannot be ignorant that it is to heavie for mee to beare a lone. I have gone so farre in it that I am unwilling to proseide any farther by my selfe, therefore I beseech yow send one with all speede to your humble servant and

　　　　　obedient neece　　　Mary Whalley

Holborne Bars, Mr Frenche's, June 9, 1630

Endorsed (*f. 206b*): To the honourable the Lady Joane Barrington my dearly honoured aunt at Harrow on the Hill most humbly present theise

148　*Sir Oliver Cromwell*[3] *to Sir Thomas Barrington, 12 June 1630*
　　　　　　　　　　　　　　　　　　　　(*2645, f. 207*)

Sir　　　I am very glad to hear of my sister's health with yours and your noble lady. My brother Henry is upon recoverie out of a later trouble which he had with a payne in his eare, but of late hath not gone abroad. I had an ague this springe, but God be praysed I am well recovered, and have not gone to visitt any freind as yett, but

---

[1] Daughter of Richard Whalley. Her sister Jane had recently married William Hook; even before the marriage the girls' Cromwell uncles had been unhelpful on the question of portions. Their father's financial affairs had been in disarray for many years. Letter 1, n.l. and letters 107, 110.

[2] Lady Joan's servant Isaac Ewers. Introduction, 18.

[3] See letter 110.

content my selfe at home now I am growen old. I thinke my lady and
your selfe feared the unsaverie ayre of Ramsey, which then hindred
your comminge out of your way, and can yeald yow noe thinge
befittinge yow, and therfore I will not invite but tell yow they bee very
good freinds which will come to see me, a poore man without a wife,
and know not how to besturre me if ladyes come, yett what yow are
pleased to doe, yow must take your fortune. And when yow are hear
with your lady yow doe commande freely

   Your most lovinge uncle and servante O. Cromwell

Ramsey, 12 June, 1630

Endorsed (*f. 208b*): To my honored nephew Sir Thomas Barrington,
knight and barronett, theise

149 *Henry Cromwell,*[1] *13 June 1630*   (*2645, f. 209*)

Dearest sister   I am more then much beholding unto you for
your great kindnes in sending to visit your poore brother that hath
bine visited with long sicknes and much weaknes. Yett (I praise God)
I am now somwhat recovered, both in health and strength, and I
assuredly hope in some sort I am by God's gentle hand of visitation
fitted and prepared for a better life, nothing doubting but God will
perfect his worke begun in me by the operation of his holy spiritt. I
desire your prayers for me. If God graunt me some small abilitie of
bodie I purpose to see you, though it be with much weaknes. It is
somewhat painful to me to write, pardon therfore my briefnes. Thus
with all kind remembrance of my true love to my nephew and neice
Jarrett[2], with all the rest of yours with you, I rest

   Your ever loving brother H. Cromwell

13th June, 1630
My 2 daughters desire to have their duties remembred unto you.

Endorsed (*f. 210b*): To my most respected kind sister the Lady Johan
Barrington at Harrow theis be given

---

[1] See letter 107.
[2] i.e. Gerard.

150 *Sir Thomas Barrington, 16 June 1630* (*2645, f. 211*)

Madame   My care not to comitt any neglect in the charge I
received from you made me discharge your commaunds the next day
after I came home, from whence I sent since to performe your desyres
which you may perceive are executed by the inclosed, which saves me
the labor allso of relateing his messages. Only I add this, that my uncle
Sir Oliver Cromwell hath ben sick this spring of an ague but now is
well, praysed be God. Madame I am so confident in your resolutions
for a sodaine comming heather as that I will now saye no more, but
you must ever commaund what I can doe to give you content and
comfort, and so you shall, and especially whare I can best express it.
My wife offers you her dewtye and love, and I remaine (committing
us all to God)

           Your most dewtyfull and loving sonn   Thomas Barrington

Hatfield Broad Oak, June 16, 1630
My love and my wive's to my brother, sister and nephew etc.

Endorsed (*f. 212b*): To the honourable my verye good mother the Lady
Johan Barrington give [these] at Harrow on the Hill

151 *James Harrison, 17 June 1630* (*2645, f. 213*)

Good madame   It did not a litle greyve me to stay so litle while
with your ladiship and my other worthy freinds, but necessity lyeinge
upon me, seing my good neighbors could stay noe longer, and my selfe
was to be at home at the furthest towards the end of the weeke, I hope
your ladiship will pardon this fault in him who is truely and will
alwayes be at your service and command, if in any thinge there may
be use of him who is of so poore abilityes. Onely that which gyves me
comfort is the assurance of the truth of my affection and respect (as I
am much and many wayes bound) unto your good ladiship, if more
able to expresse them. After a wett and weary journey we came well
home blessed be God, where I found at the Priory all frends well and
glad to heare of your ladiship's good health and the rest of their frends,
but sory that I could gyve them noe more certenty of the distanc tyme
of your comeing to them, though they rest comfortably persuaded
that they shall shortly injoy you, a day longed for by many when ever
it be, as I hope it wilbe shortly. The lord guide your journey and
prosper it, and gyve you abundanc of comfort and blessing in it and
after it. I finde Mr Barrington much better then I left him, but yet not
so well as that he dares goe much abroad, but finds most ease in being

quiet within. Yet he feeds and sleeps well blessed be God, and I hope
the worst is past and that it was onely a great could taken which will
weare away. My Lady Lamplugh hath beene for some 10 dayes
reasonable well, but I finde that her minde is not so well setled as I
wishe it were, and as I hope by God's blessing it will in tyme be. It was
late and I was weary when I went to the Priory and the Berry[1]
yesternight, so as I had litle speech with them, and Sir William Meux
hastens this morning towards Oates and so for London, upon the
occasion I tould him for your ladiship.[2] And therfore with my oune
and my wyve's duty and service with all thankfullnes for all your
bounty to us, and this last favour of it to my wyfe, humbly craving
your prayers for us and for your litle godsonne, desyring that my
service and thankes may be remembered to the worthy knight and
lady, I take my leave, resting ready to attend your good ladiship in
your journey to us and promising alwayes to be at your ladiship's
comand and service
    James Harrison

Hatfeild, June 17, 1630

Endorsed (*f. 214b*): To my honorable good lady the Lady Johanna
Barrington at Harrow, Midlesex, geve these

152   *Sir Thomas Barrington, 29 June 1630*   (*2645, f. 215*)

Madame   My wife and my selfe are desyrous that you will
resolve upon owr affectionate indevors to be comfortable to you when
you are heear, and to make this appeear to you that no will shall be
wanting to make your contentments compleate. Meane while we shall
praye that your health make you the better able to keepe your word,
and shall be hartyly glad that it may please God to give us a happye
meeting. In the meane time, with both owr dewtyfull affections
tendred unto yow, I rest
    Your most obedient and loving sonne   Thomas Barrington

Hatfield Broad Oak, June 29, 1630

Endorsed (*f. 216b*): To my much honored and trewly honourable good
mother the Lady Johan Barrington give [these] at Harrow
The cherrytrees in the garden and orchard afford not store enough to

---

[1] The Bury House in Hatfield, home of Robert Barrington.
[2] Perhaps Meux's constant preoccupation, the search for a husband for his daughter.

loade one purposely to you, for of those few that have ben, the greater part is stolen. This my wife desyres you might know as [*torn away*] she would have sent you som if the boy had not s[topped] by the way, or could wel [have] caryed so many as could [be] worthy your acceptance.

153 *James Harrison, 29 June 1630* (*2645, f. 217*)

Good madame   I blesse the lord to heare of your health and that your resolution of comeing to us now drawne to a certenty, of the altering of which I hope there will fall out noe just cause. My trouble in my head I finde so to be renewed and increased upon the least occasion of rideinge that I feare I shall not be able to performe what I promised and truely purposed in wayteing upon your good ladiship in your journey. If I be not able I know you will hould me excused, my poore prayers shall wayte upon you and it, unto him who onely is able to make the wayes of his prosperous, that he would be pleased so to watch over you for good every way as you may have much experienc of his gracious presenc and we all much cause of thankfullnes. I beseech your good ladiship let me intreate the helpe of your prayers even in this particular, that it would please the lord to teach me to make a good use of this trouble that doth mak dull all my powers and much unfitt me for the dutyes of my calleinge. I desyre to rowle my self upon his promises and providence. If it may be an occasion of draweing me nearer to him, and of furthering my care for my owne and others spirituall good (which is the thinge I humbly and heartely desyre), I shall blesse his holy name, however it please him to dispose of my outward estate. Good madame I have much cause to bless God for your great and bounttifull love to me and myne (the lord recompenc it abundantly in the best thinges) and amongst others your favors for your willingenes to gyve me a longer tyme for some part of that which hath so much pleasured me; I hope you shall finde me carefull and faythfull though I be slow. My wyfe humbly thankes your good ladiship as for former so for your last expression of your love. Your litle sonne I blesse God thryves well, we pray your good ladiship to blesse him by praying for him. So with rememberanc of our dutyes I take my leave, resting alwayes

        at your ladiship's command   James Harison

Hatfeild, June 29, 1630

Endorsed (*f. 218b*): To my honorable good lady the Lady Johanna Barrington at Harrow in Midlesex geve these.

154 *Lady Elizabeth and Sir William Masham and Oliver St. John, n.d.,*
[*June 1630*]   (*2650, f. 304*)

Deare mother   I confes it did much afect me to part from you,
but the hope I have of injoying you at Hatfeeld shortly doth revive
my spirits againe, but especialy to thinck of our living together in
heven, worlde withowt end. I se daly more and more the vanity of all
erthly comforts; even the greatest of them all must leve us or we them
we know not how soone, therefore it is God's wonderfull mercy to give
you and yours an assuranc of those comforts that shall make us hapye
here and for ever. I am very glad to here my sister Lamplugh is
sumthing refreshed, God never casts downe but he raseis up againe. I
am sure you willbe much revived with the company of my cosin
Arthur Hildersham.[1] I shold have bin very glad if he had come while
I had bin with you. My nephewe Mewx was with me this morning
and I here he means to goe down with me. I dare not intreat him, but
if he goe of himself I will take the best care I can of him and I hope to
return him safe againe to his father. Thus with my humble duty and
humble thanks for all your favors to mee and mine, I rest
          Your dutyfull daughter   Elizabeth Masham

I beseech you to remember me to all my frinds with you.

Indeared mother   I must saye what my wife hath written,
though I could not so easely expresse it with the eyes, but my harte
and hand, as my selfe, is ever
          Yours in my dearest affection   William Masham

Thanks to you for all your love to me and myne, and our loves to all
our frends with you. We rejoice much in our hopes to see you at
Hatfield shortly, and pray for you.

Grandmother   My wife and my selfe remember our humble
dutie unto yow, to geather with our humble acknowledgment for your
large expressions of your noble favour
          Oliver St John

Endorsed (*f. 305b*): To my much honoured mother the Lady Barington
these be given

[1] See letter 35.

155 *Sir William Masham, n.d.,* [*July 1630*]   (*2650, f. 316*)

Deare mother   As the hope of your returne to us was alwayes pleasing, so now much more your approach, which revives our spirits that have bene longe deade in your absence. And we are the more glad that we shall injoye you with your health, which we shall all labor with God's blessing still to preserve to his glory and all our comforts.

A full vessell sounds litle, so a joyfull hart cannot express it selfe so well in wordes as actiones, wherin I hope to make good what this scantling of tyme and paper cannot, being very late at night. So with our humble dutyes I commit you to God['s] protection and safe conduct and rest

          Your observant sonne   William Masham

My coatch shall attend you at the daye appoynted, being glad that any thinge of myne maye do you service. We commend our best loves to my good brother and sister, not forgetting the rest.

Endorsed (*f. 317b*): To my much honoured mother the Lady Barrington these be given

156 *Robert Barrington, n.d.,* [*July 1630*]   (*2645, f. 164*)

Madam   Wee are heere joyfull for your resolution to come to this place where you are so much desired. My carte shalbe with you at the appointed day and, if it please God I continew to recover my health as I begin, I purpose to come and attend you. If I cannot I know you accept of my true desire. Your god sonn, who by me craves your blessing, hath ben at nurse Birde's aboute 14 daies and is (I thanke God) very well weaned; the cause why we have donn this is the findeing that my wive's milke was to hott. Soe with my owne and wive's humble service I committ you to the lord and am

          Your dutifull sonn   Robert Barrington

Endorsed (*f. 165b*): To the honourable my very loveing mother the Lady Johan Barrington at Harrow on the Hill give [these]

157 *William Hook,*[1] *6 July 1630*   (*2645, f. 219*)

Much honoured madame   It was my dutie to have presented your letters with mine, and I hoped to have done it, but that still I

----
[1] See letter 142.

wayted for an opportunity, which till now I found not, to send this approved messenger unto you, trusting in your ladiship's clemencie for a dispensation with such an omission of respect as you may deeme me guiltie of. Your first letter I receaved by Mr Tomelins at the end of the terme and your second about fort night after; in both of them ther's mention made of my wive's portion uncertaine. In the first your ladyship mentioneth an earnest prosecution of the matter by my wive's sister Marie;[1] in neither am I advised what to doe. To be at expences upon such uncerteinties unexpected I am not willing, desirous to reteine and improve what I may of your ladiship's bounty (thankefully receaved) least I should be utterly stript. Neither dare I acquaint any of my dearest friends or kindred, least for my proceedings without theyre profered help and counsell I should become an object either of derision or pittie among them, and I am loth to trie my patience upon either. I request nothing of your ladiship but pardon and prayers. I have well tasted of your munificence, endeavouring my best recompence in my tenderest care of your beloved niece, as I labour heerein to approve my selfe to the greate match maker of heaven, whom I have more surely enfeoffed with my selfe and myne. He is Levie's portion without quaestion, whom I humbly beseech for your ladiship's wellfare everie way, and in whom I remayne

Yours in all dutifull respects devoted   William Hooke

Upper Clatford this 6th of July, 1630

Endorsed (f. 220b): To his honourable and highly respected ladie the Ladie Johan Barrington these be given

158 *Thomas Saunders[2] to Sir Thomas Barrington, 6 July 1630*

(2645, f. 221)

Sir   The favour yow have shewed mee in the continued offer of my tithe, with protestation of your love, doth more praevaile with mee

---

[1] See letter 147.

[2] The problems arising from substantial landowners owing tithe dues to Lady Judith Barrington in Flamstead were exacerbated by her living away from the parish after her marriage to Sir Thomas Barrington, and made almost impossibly complicated by the links by marriage between the families of Saunders, Luke and of her first husband, Sir George Smith. Her husband's father Thomas Smith died in 1594. His wife Joan then married Sir John Luke who in turn, after her death, married the widow of John Saunders of Puttenham. Thomas Saunders of Beechwood was his son. The irascible Luke must thus have felt himself a patriarchal figure in a parish he could not entirely control. H. Chauncey, *Historical Antiquities of Hertfordshire* (1700), 568; Cussans, *Dacorum and Cashio Hundreds*, 356–8.

then either the guift of the thing it selfe or force could doe. It is not my nature to be vexatious although I want noe opportunity, as it seemes yow please to take notice, neither indeed can any man that way inclined (though having less of conveniencie then I) as experience doth daylie confirme. But in a word, my desires are to serve yow. I swallow my late loss[1], which would stick in another man's throat and labour to digest it, although yow may please to remember what a lease (and how hardly it) prevailed. For your offer of a lease for yeares, I humbly thanke yow and doe protest with out any manner of reservation that, as the case in praesent stands with me, it cannot be worth the money. I would with all my hart yow knew the full truth. My profitt shall ever perswade with mee, who know my ground will be the worse for having the strawe carried off it (and your tithes also will consequently doe soe too), and my ease tells mee rather this way of years then any other, as more certaine for mee. For the praesent I know not where to pick out a season for one plowe of all the ground I have for this weed (impregnable) coltfoot, we call it dunngleaves, which noe cost will cure but only long rest (as I have this year throughly experimented). And should I hope for profitt in future, my wife's jointure will defeat it, wherin 250 acres such as she shall find leye ground at my death, is to be soe continued during her time, soe that unless I should outlive her (vouchsafe I pray to see the indenture and I will shew yow it) that hope is lost. I could wish indeed (upon your offer of a lease for yeeres) I had not done what now I cannot recall, for certainly this course of lease had been more convenient both for yow and mee, which I leave to your judgement herafter to resolve. For your proposition of 2 and 4^S (it is the course of our parsons best read in the profitts, as masters Stubbing[2], Barber, Combs) and I hould it yett easier for mee then the lease at this rate, and I take it very thankfully as proceeding from your love and desire to deale with me some ways or other. My wheat this season is pretty good and (I cannot dissemble) worth the money, and truly I expected it would have been much better, for I bestowed extraordinary paines and cost which it seemed all winter to repaye mee, but now when it should come to the proofe it failes, as I perceive to my smart all poore wearied grounds will doe. My pease cropp is this yeare also exceeding badd. For your last offer of 20^d the acre for all my land, I doe beseech your comment upon it. Iff yow meane for all the land I plough, that is for my wheat, lent graine and fallow, it comes then to 20^d for lent corne and 10 groats wheat, the fallow which is alwaies a third part being given in,

---

[1] In 1628 Saunders had unsuccessfully claimed that his manor of Beechwood was tithe free. E.R.O., D/DBa E60.

[2] Perhaps Mark Stubbing, rector of Wheathampstead.

as it is in that of 2 and4ˢ. And this I understood to be your meaning, as being a good way of incouragement to me to plough the more by being dealt with cheaper then other men, and which will indeed be to yow the more profitt as my ground shall mende. [*f. 221b*] But if yow should by all my lands meane plowed lands together with pasture, leye and hedgreens, then is this last offer harder then both the former, which (I praesume) is not your will, who offer this last also as a wrench and as an act of favour, for the tithe of pasture is milke and calfe, that of leye wooll and lambe, that of hedgreens grass (which latter are by law discharged, as I am informed, if they bee noe bigger then will well serve the horses and plowe to turne upon), soe that a fift part of the valew of corne tiths these will not amount unto, though never soe duely paid according to custome usuall. And yow may please to remember that these smaller tiths are yett in Sir John Luke's hands. I therfore take the first to bee your meaning, although I durst not praesume, but beseech yow to be your owne commentator. For I build upon this, that all now offred proceeds meerly from your love, which noe mistaking of mine shall praejudice, as being neither lost nor misplaced, which I desire to express by assuring yow that upon your being pleased to write backe your will to mee some such course shalbe taken as shall give yow due satisfaction for the praesent, without putting yow upon the least inconvenience that I can praevent, and a resolution left in mee to subscribe to such conditions for the future as your selfe shall reasonably devise when either your commands or my opportunity shall call mee to await yow. For a busines of this nature and consisting of soe many parts as this doth is too bigg for the short life of a letter as this is, already I feare too longe. But longiori opus est mora quaestionem ut solvas quam ut proponas, and I crave your pardon, not omitting my wife's duty and mine to my noble ladie together with your selfe, whose

Humble servant is   Thomas Saunders

Beechwood, this 6th of Julie, 1630
Forgett not your promise made non obstante and find good hawking and my father and my selfe full gladd of yow.

[*No endorsement*]

159 *Sir John Luke*[1] *to Lady Judith Barrington, 23 October 1630*

(*2645, f. 222*)

Noble lady   I have bene importuned very much bie this bearer hereof, Nicholas Kilbie, my neighboure, to solicite and intreat you that Sir Thomas and you wilbe pleased to make him your baylife for the gatheringe up your rentes here in Hertfordshire. The man is reputed amongest us honest, besides hath a reasonable estate, a house and thyrtie acres of land. He offers, if it please you, to put you in good bond or securatie bie land for the faithfull performance of that trust and charge that you shall imploye him in. Besides this I knowe of my owne knowledge that he hath as good knowledge to make sale of underwoodes or timber as any man in this countrie, so as (if you have not disposed of the place already) I thinke you can not find a fitter man abought to fitt your turne better. I doe presume (that Davie[2] beinge dead) you will resume into your handes his twoe leases of Roe Ende and Margrett Streate, which if you doe, I doe entreat earnestlie Sir Thomas and your self that my sonn Mr Thomas Sanders may be your tenant for them. You shalbe sure to have your rent duely and truely paide, which is a good thinge in these dayes. I knowe for some causes you may have great helpe bie him to doe you good in your purchase of Roe Ende in findinge out that which will make it of more benifitt, but what it is in particular I cannot relate unto yow, but saith if it please you to have him come over unto you he will not faile (God willing) but waight uppon Sir Thomas and you to see if he can bargaine with you for the tythe of those twoe endshippes, and then he will geve you satisfaction in thother. I thanke you good madam in that it pleased you to send me word bie your servant Jhon Kendall, a privatt message, how you have been advertised that I have felled some trees out of Gatlie Springe. It is true I felled some twoe spires and one tree hardlie worthe a marke, which made but one length in borde and made but a dozen in all, and them I clapt unto the barne besides the bordes of twoe other trees which I bought of my sonn Sanders and have bestowed uppon the barnes. The twoe spiers I made studdes withall, wher the olde ones was decayed, and soe I hope I have geven you good account for the imployinge of them, besechinge you to have noe jealiouse opinion of me that I will ever abuse you or your sonnes in any thinge that I have any power in, but alwayes shalbe ready to doe you or them the best service I can as longe as I live, and not any waies to doe you harme, for I professe they are deare unto me, boeth

---

[1] See letter 158, n.l. Until at least 1614 Luke retained an interest in Lady Judith Barrington's estate of Annables through his first wife.

[2] Edward Davie, Lady Judith Barrington's bailiff in Hertfordshire. Eg. 2650, f. 222.

for your and ther father's sake and ther owne. And soe remembringe
my wife's and my service to you and your noble knight, I committ us
to God and remayne
        Your ladyshippe's ever to be commanded   John Luke

Flamsteed this 23 of October, 1630
I pray that our kind respectes may be remembred to mistris Jeane
Litton and mistris Barrington

Endorsed (f. 223b): To the honorable his noble frend the Lady Barrington at Hatfeild present these
[*In the hand of Lady Judith Barrington:*] Sir John Luke's letter to desire
Mr Sanders might hyer Roe End and Markett End tyth, and some
what of felling trees in Gately ground, 1630.

160   *Ezekiel Rogers, 1 November 1630*   (*2645, f. 224*)

Madam   Though I am now very unfitt to write, being weary
after the sabbath and having lately taken colde, yet to welcome you to
Hatfielde I have inforced my selfe to salute you in a fewe lines.
Hatfielde, I say, a place which may represent a greate sort of objects
and notions of no small importance, a place wherin you long injoyed
so many blessings. How many yeeres lived you there in peace? How
faire a posterity? What increase of outward things? A worthy husbande, and especially the gospell? Againe, a place also that may putt
you in minde of not a few changes. A whole generation (if not more)
of the ancienter sort worne out in your time, some of your posterity,
that deare companion of yours also gone, of whom every your walkes,
table, chamber, bed, tell you that David's place is empty, and himselfe
being gone before seemes to call upon you to prepare dayly to followe
him. I say to be allwayes ready, that when your master shall also
come, you may readily, cherfully wayte upon him. I speake not to
occasion wor[l]dly sorrowe or sadnes, but heavenly providence, and
therby joy too, for I hope that your olde disease of melancholy is
banished away by faith, as it is high time. Besides (but that I hasten)
I might adde much of Hatfielde: it may be there be some neighbours
of whom you have not yet taken, others to whom you have not yet
done, that good that God woulde have you doe and now sends you to
that ende for a time. But I must not now proceede; the lorde fill your
age with the fruites of faith and righteousnes and joy, which (with my
service) shalbe ever the prayer of
        Your ladyshipp's poore but faithfull well wisher
                                                Ezekiel Rogers

Rowley, November 1, 1630
My wive's service also. My daughter now waytes on my lady Constable.[1]

Endorsed (*f. 225b*): To the honourable the Lady Johan Barrington at Hatfielde Broadoke

161   *William Chantrell, 1 November 1630*   (*2645, f. 226*)

Noble ladie   I much joy to heare of your health and present settlement at your house in Essex where your comfortes (I hope) are and ever shalbe great and unspeakable. That glorious light of profession and conversation which was carried in the hand of worthy saynte departed may be by your good diversions and advice perpetuated to posteritie. Good madam, shewe your selfe a right true Barsheba to your Lemuel[2]; doe to yours as she to hers. Yow know in these dark and decaying tymes light will be comfortable, but a shining and burning light (as John was) very resplendent. Yow forgett not how God hath been honored in and by that your familie; I hope yow wilbe zelous that he may still abide in your tentes, and pitch his tabernacle about yow his Jacob.

Your plentifull and frequente instigations by your faithfull pastor shall not need any sharpeninge from me who as so dull my selfe, yet are my prayers for yow and yours that yow may dailie build up the house of Israell and be famous in Bethlehem.

I heare that Sir Thomas your sonne mindes to sell Cottingham in our cuntrey and so to dispose him of those profittes he hath amongest us. I pray God direct him, only I desire your ladishipe to be so mindfull of Gode's cause that the two parsonages which have been at the Christian dispose of his honorable predecessors be not infolded in the sale and they be come a pray to foxes, and made Aceldama[3], for beleive it madam, I know no better way how the pietie and blessed memorie of your house can be more blazoned then by honoring God in the worthy bestowinge of those ecclesiasticall endowmentes which he hath intrusted yow with.

I owe all that I have and what I may be in this world to yow and to that your royall progenies which make me the more willing to impart

---

[1] Sir William Constable of Flamborough had been created baronet at the same time as Sir Francis Barrington. Constable intended to accompany Rogers to New England in 1638, but in the event did not go. G.E.C., *Baronetage*, i. 44; Mather, 410–11.

[2] Bathsheba, mother of king Lemuel, taught him religious doctrine. Proverbs 31.

[3] Aceldama, 'the field of blood', was the name of the land bought with the money received and relinquished by Judas Iscariot.

this last clause to your consideration as the due obsarvaunce of him who is

Your ladishipe devoted servaunt William Chauntrell

Walkington, 1 November, 1630

Endorsed (*f. 227b*): To the noble ladie, Ladie Johana Barrington at Hatfeild Broad Oke in Essex give [these]

162 *Nathaniel Cotton and Edmund Nelle[1] to Lady Judith Barrington, 10 November 1630* (*2645, f. 228*)

Good madam My servis remembred unto you and to Sir Thomas, with my best desiers for the healthe and happines of you and yours. Thes lines are to certifie your ladishippe that goodman Nelle and my sellfe spake with goodwiffe Davis[2], which had gotten a letter written to your ladishippe, but wee refused to receve it, but caused the man which writte it to breake it open before hir face, and I coppied it out from his mouth verbatam, which I have heare insertid. Allso she brought your [keyes][3] which lye buried in the grownd as yet. Thus levinge to be anie furder trubellsomme to your ladishippe I sesse. From Harppendenn this tenth of November, 1630,

Your lovinge tennenttes to be commanded
Nathan Cotton Edmund Nelle

Thes tooe men of Cadington your ladishippe had not nottis of
William Maston . . . . . iij^{li} v^s ij^d
Edward Dearmer . . . . . iiij^{li} xix^s

[*f. 228b*] Worthy madam My servis remembred unto you and all your good howsholld, with my prayers unto God for you. Madam this is to give your ladieshippe to understande that sence you harde from me last I have founde a booke of my husborn's wharein I founde he had paide Mr Gudger for Edmund Nelle's rennte, the twentith of Januarie thirtie poundes and more he paid to Mr Gudger, in Junne last, thirtie poundes; as I trust in God I shall make it good to your ladieshippe when it shall please God I shall speake with your ladie-

---

[1] Nathaniel Cotton of Turners Hall and Edmund Neele of Ing's Place, both in Harpenden. V.C.H., *Herts.*, ii. 307, 308.

[2] Widow of Edward Davie, Lady Judith's bailiff. Letter 159.

[3] If keys, perhaps they were buried as a precaution against the plague referred to at the end of her letter.

shippe. I was in good hope wee shoulde have goone abroade at this time but it hath pleased God to take awaye one of our nursse children the daye before wee shoulde have goone abroade. Good madam I dooe most earnestlie intreate you to be pleased to have pacience with me and I hoppe in God when it shall please him to give me leave to gooe abroade, and that our towne be cleare againe, to give you good satisfacsion. I thinke your ladishippe hath binne misinformed against my husbornd and me, but if it please God when time shall serve I hoppe to prove a greate deale contrarie that I thinke you have binne towld of us. So once morre, good madam, I dooe intreate you to be favorubell unto me in this my greate destrese, as I trust your ladie-shippe will shew mercie unto me. So I and mine shall be bound to praye for you and yours. And so with a greved hart I take my leve, from Markatte Streete this tenth of November, 1630,

Your poore destresed nursse and servant to comand

Marie Davis

(*f. 229*) [*In hand of John Kendal:*]   Memorandum that uppon the agrement betweene Sir Thomas Barrington and Mary Davis the said Mary doth promiss to pay her lady day rent in due tyme and also twenty pownds of the debt which she oweth unto the saide Sir Thomas betwixt this and the feast of St. James next comeinge, which shalbe in the yeare of the lord 1631

Endorsed (*f. 229b*): To his much honored Ladie Judeth Barringtonn at hir howse in Hatfeeld Brodocke give this
Leve this at Mr Gudger's howse in Watling Strete at the signe of the bell, to be convaid acordinge to the derecksion
[*In hand of Lady Judith Barrington:*] Widdow Davis letter, November 1630

163   *Sir Francis Harris, [27 December 1630]*   (*2645, f. 230*)

Worthy lady and my honored aunte   The remembrance of my deere uncle (your deerest) his love and favors, together with yours towardes me, makes me to accounte my selfe in perpetuall obligatione in any acceptable services. But first give me leave good madame to tell yow newes that I dare saye (owte of your love) will please yow, which is that I thanck God (thoughe with difficultye and debate with my selfe) I have cast awaye all greife. Next, it being my fortune to be in

Suffolk where one Mr Garnishe[1], a gentleman of a worthy famely and my longe acquayntance, I brake with him touching his onely sonne and heier to feele him howe he stood affected to a propositione of marryage for my cosin Mewes, whoe imbraced it fryndly and with muche respect, in regarde of her honourable freinds deceised and your selfe liveing and the worthe of her parents. I felte him what he would setle on his sonne, and likewise joynter and present estate, and in truthe, being a very honest gentleman, dealt playnely and freely with mee, which was he would convaye better then 2,000^{li} land per annum and all other lands as God shall inhable him, being a forehanded manne, and for joynter he would give 400^{li} land per annum, and present mayntenance 300^{li} a yeere, which in my oppinnyond is fayre as theise tymes are; but in breife hee expects 2000^{li}, assuring me (as I knowe he faulters not) hee maye have a greater portione uppon theise termes. For the younge gentleman, he is a very proper talle manne, uppon my knowledge, of the age of 22, and hathe noe more sisters then two, wherof one is marryed, and his possibilityes are great by his uncle Sir John Wentford, whoe by the lawe is his next heier, I meane that knight dwelling neere Yarmothe[2]. In conclutione my service shall attend yow to morrowe if yow please, for a present answere is to bee made. And so I humbly rest

Your ladyship's ever loving nephew to command

Francis Herris

This present Monday, Saint Johns daye, Dunmoe[3]

Endorsed (*f. 231b*): To the right worshipfull his honored and honourable aunte the Ladye Joane Barringtone, theise

164   *Jane Hook[4], 28 December* [*1630*]   (*2645, f. 112*)

Good madam   My most humble duty remembred unto your ladyship, with many thankes for your kind leteres which I have receved, and I would have bene bould to retourned thankes but that I durst not send any leter to London in regard of the plauge that is

---

[1] Charles Garneys of Boyland, Norfolk. He married Elizabeth, eldest surviving daughter of John Wentworth of Darsham, Suffolk. W.C. Metcalfe, *Visitations of Suffolk* (Exeter, 1882), 175.

[2] Sir John Wentworth of Somerleyton, knighted 1603 and without issue in 1611. *Ibid.*

[3] The letter is endorsed in a 17th-century hand 'Sir Francis Herris Letters, December 26 1630'. The Feast of St John the Apostle, 27 Dec., fell on Monday in 1630.

[4] Lady Joan's neice Jane Whalley, now married to William Hook. See letter 142.

there[1], but I hade a full purpose to have writ by Mr Lashford, but your ladyship, he did send my urine to a docter at Salesbery whoes exceding glad to heare that your ladiship came so well to Hatfilde. I pray God continue your health and lengthen out the threed of your life as may be most for his glory and your comfort. It has pleased the lord these 18 or 19 weekes to visite me with an ague, two dayes well and one day ill, for some 7 weekes together, and since it has pleased God to alter the corse of it, that I injoyed but one good day and had two ill dayes together, and now God has graciously given me again tow good dayeis and but one ill, and has both shortened my fitte and mittigated his hand with a great deale of mercy. Oh that I hade such a hart as to be actually thankfull to such a good God. Mr Hook, whome I desire to blesse God for, with not forgetting my thankese to youe ladyship, he did send my urine to a docter at Salesbery whoes judgment was that I was falling dangerously sicke except I used some speedy course of phisick wich he would prescribe, and indeed I was so weak that I did not think to have lived thus long. I could nether eate nor scarce goe about the house without a stafe in my hand. Mr Hooke would nedes have me to Salesberry to lye at a freind's house of his and ther to take phisik, where I was all most 3 weekes, and never more kindly used of a stranger in all my life. She was so carfull for me when I was in my fittes to mak me thinges, and that I should not take could in my sweats, that I could not chuse but see the goodnes of God to me in it. Madam I could wishe with all my hart that my cosen Jone Mewix had no worse yoke fellow then God has given me. I am fully perswade then that you would be excedingly joyfull to think that two of your grande children were so hapyly bestode, for to say which was best you cold not tell. He often makes me thinke of Mr Barrington that was so carffull over his wife when she lay very weak; I thought that I shoulld never have seene the like, but now, blesed be God, he has dealt with me very graciously in that kind that now I have a helpe both for soule and body.

I think madam that I am with child, becase I have not had them but once which whas a mounth after I had bene here, which [if] it be soe, I desire earnestly that your ladyship would be pleased to be earnest [f. 112b] in your prayeres to God for me that he would prepare me and help mee to undergoe whatsoever he shall be pleased to exercise me with all, that I may indur his hand pasiently and meekly. Madam out of obedience to God's commandementes and for the satisfiing of myne one consience which has often cheked me, I shall be bould to crave an ernest request, beseeching you not to deny, and that is you would be pleased to forgive me my carlesnes and untowarnes

---

[1] Plague was reported on 5 and 19 Dec. Birch, ii. 84, 88; see also Shrewsbury, 357.

when I was your pore and unworthy servant, for I doe confes that I did much offend God in being carles of my caling towardes your ladyship. I thanke God that he has opennend mine eyes to see that it was a sin against his magesty, for the wich I ernestly desire mercy at his handes and lyk pardon from you. I know that time will com when as the devill and mine one conscience will acuse mee of thoughtes, much more of wordes and dedes, but I desir to do it my selfe and save them a labour, that so when death com the sting may be pluced out by vertu of Christ merrites. Good madam pray fo me that God would be pleased to afford me the inward comforts of his holy sperit, which is more worth then all the world be sides. Oh I know right well that time will com when I shall have speciall need of faith and pacience and depending upon his power. As yet I am but furnished but with a small measure, the lord, if it be his will, ad strength to weakenes. I beseech you for Christ sake remember me by nam in your ernest prayeres, that God would be please to fit me for the day of tryall and that I may not faint in the day of my affliccion. Oh my sines are great, both towardes heaven and earth, and are like to prevaile if God's mercyes doth not take place. I had never more ned of the prarres of God's saintes then now; I beseech you pray for me that God would forgive mine offences don to you.

I feare I have ben to trublesom and overbould with your ladyship with my scribled lins, but, hoping that you will be pleased to accept of them as from one who desires to do better, my pore prayere shall be to the allmighty to continu you still amongst his saintes and children. I remaine

Your pore and unworthy servant till death   Jane Hooke

Upper Clatford in Hampshier, Desember the 28 day

Endorsed (*f. 113b*): To the right honorable my very good lady the Lady Johanna Barrington at Hatfild give this

165   *Jane Hook, n.d., [January? 1631]*   (*2650, f. 282*)

Good madam   It doth much rejoyce my harte to heare that it hath pleased God to recover your ladyship of your great could, for the which I desire, as my duty bindes me unto, to give God most humble and harty thankes. Madam I would not have bene thus long ere I had retournd a leter of true thankefullnes had I not bene prevented by weakenese and sicknes, for when goodman King was gone to Hatfeld at that time Mr Hooke and I was so scard in the night (as we thought with theves) that Mr Hooke lost his voyce that I thought would never com againe and my selfe toke such a frite that I was fane to keepe my bed two dayes together and had those paines upon me as made me afraid that I should be delivered incontenently. But now it has pleased God to reveale unto us the author of our frite, which was our maide in letting in young fellowes in to the house at unseasonable howers to riot with them both with our beare and bread, indide we did little suspect her becase she came up to helpe us cry out theves. I thanke God that she is gon, for I have since her departur savid a peck a meale a weeke besideds otheres tinges.

Good madam, I give unto your ladiship most humble and harty thankes for so much linnin receved from you by Willan King. I did little thinke to have receved such a larg extent of your ladishipe's love, I confes that I com short of deserving any thing. Good madam, I be[s]ech you pray for me, for I am brout very low throughe the good hand of God; my ague dos yet contingu and begines to renew its strenght. Oh that it may please God to renew that inward grace of his holy sperit in me which is more worth than x thousand worldes. I most be faine to cut of before I am willing becase I am troubled with a greveous pane in my back. I am exceding glad to heare of your ladiship's health, I pray God of his mercy for to contingu it; my pore prayeres shall allwaies be for the same. I remaine

Your pore unworthy servant   Jane Hooke

Endorsed [*in the hand of William Hook*] (*f. 283b*): To the honourable and my much esteemed lady the Lady Johan Barrington at Hatfield Broad Oake thes be given

166 *Sir Thomas Eliot*[1]*, n.d.,* [*January 1631*]   (*2645, f. 232*)

Most noble lady   Understanding from my wife that hath latly visited you that your ladiship was pleased to acknowledge the re-membrance of soe meane a frend as my selfe (which is very rare upon the least obscuryty), I am bould yet a little further to entrude my selfe with thes my lines of loveing salutations and harty prayers for your ladiship, that togeather with this new yeare it may please God to renew many more comfortable and happy years unto you here upon earth, and in the end to reunite you to your beloved that is gone before into that presentes of happynes wher is fullnes of joy and pleasure for ever, this pilgrimag upon earth being but a passage to that better biding place, which might easily resolve us that all the comfortes or discomfortes of this life should no more affect us then a good lodging

---

[1] See letter 3.

or a bade should doe in our travels, which we are to change the next day, this I thanke God is partly my resolution in my latte uncomfortable lodginges, comforted yet withall to thinke that God can turne all for the best. My hoopes therfore I thanke God exceede my feare, to be yet once more able to recover some frendes and to shew my selfe thankefull for ther loves, and in the fierst ranke my greatest ambition is to enjoy still the love of your ladiship whose noble favours and loveing affections I have bine soe longe time acquainted withall and am engaged unto, desiring alsoe I may thus fare presume of noble Sir Thomas and his good lady to comend my service to ther commandes, as it shall please God any wayes to enable me therunto. With my best salutations alsoe to all other my good frends that are at this time happy with your ladiship's good company. And thus being streightened for time upon the sudden warning of the messenger, that I have scarce leysure to looke over my letter, I must comprehend all in my harty prayers to God that as a chosen and elect lady of his love you may be for ever happy in the same, resting

ever bound to the service of your ladiship   Thomas Eliot

My warning was soe short that I could not bethinke me of any newes, yet ther is some talke of two or three lordes and ladyes that they say are latly dead, as the countise of Barkshire and the Lord St John, that I thinke was alsoe an earle, and the Duke of Castelheaven that was the Lord Audley remaynes, as you have hard, comitted to the tower for many beastly propertyes of luciousnes[1]. In steed the far of newes I have sent your ladiship a merry tale that I once tooke from the mouth of a reverent devine, Doctor Gibson[2] that is now with God, and for his sake I have ever since keept it by me, and with all I have sent you to peruse an other paper that was given me of the abridgment of all that have dyed and ther diseases this last year in London, 1630, which thanks be to God is fare short of what was feared in the begining of the yeare.[3] The siknesse this last weeke at London was only foure or three.

Endorsed (*f. 233b*): To the honourable good lady the Lady Joane Barrington thes be given, Hatfield

[1] The Earle of Castlehaven had been moved to the Tower in December. Birch, ii. 86.
[2] Probably Abraham Gibson, D.D., d. 1629, who had been curate of Witham, vicar of Little Waldingfield in Suffolk and a preacher at the Temple church. Venn.
[3] 2645, f. 234 is a printed bill of mortality: *A generall Bill for this present yeere, ending the 16 of December 1630, according to the report made to the Kings most excellent Matie By the Company of Parish Clerks of London etc. . .*

167   *Thomas Bourchier,*[1] *20 January 1631*   *(2645, f. 235)*

Good madame   Tho of late motives to be frequente in present-
inge my service to your ladyship are so little enforcinge (that if I sholde
hearken to the whispers of my owne spirit I sholde for ever keep
silence) yet antient and undeserved favours doe justli challenge my
takinge everi opertunitie to expresse my gratefulnes for the same.

Madame I presume your experience (by reason of longe exercise) is
such that yow are able to speake pregnantli to whatsoever quiri your
poore wounded kinsman shall acquainte your ladyship with. I beseech
yow thincke not my ensuinge discourse springs from a desire to trye
my owne wit or an ichinge desire to be refreshed with your partes
(which I acknowledge are inferiour to few). Madame, of late I have
had such infinite sadnes springinge from feares of my union with
Christe, that truli I have scarce bin able to subsiste. My feares are not
about his faithfulnes, with whome I knowe there is no shadowe of
chainge, but they arise from secret doubtes of the truthe of grace
(without which all prophession does but aggravate condemnation). I
knowe the spirit of man onely knowes what's in man, experience tho
of God's dealing in strates gives no small lighte to another wounded.
Give me leave therefore humbli to supplicate your ladyship to sende
some balme to him whoe indeed does not a little langwish in the
inwarde man. Tho thus I complaine, (I blesse God) when I am at the
poynte of deathe I still hope, and indeed some tymes have such
refreshings, that the sweet thereof invites to truste tho God kill. I
cannot attribute these feares to any thinge more then to melancholli,
which is not a little fed by the wante of imployment. 'Tis just I
acknowledge with God that the sleighte esteem of the motions of God's
spirit and the sweet councell from your ladyship and your noble
branches, 'tis juste I say that I not yeildinge to so faire inducements
sholde now taste of the worke of my owne handes. Yow knowe tho
greate wounds by the skil of applyinge fit medicines are healed, yet
there remaines scarrs and at tymes aches: the same experience has the
soule, tho I am confident that that precious blood which some yeares
since I have applied does perfectli justifie me and in some measure by
its efficaci I am clensed, yet the thoughtes of wastinge my marrowe in
vaniti does manye tymes produce stronge assaultes. I confes 'tis the
weaknes of my faithe; I shall the better encounter and foyle strong
conflictes if when yow are before the throne of grace yow commende
my case to him whoe indeed can make a worme doe valiantli. Madam
I beseech yow pardon me that thus I fill your eares with complaintes,
if I were not confident that yow are a mother in Israel I wolde not

---

[1] Younger brother of Sir John Bourchier of Benningbrough. Table 1.

thus stuff my lines with riddles. I need not now make any other apologie for not salutinge those worthies with yow, the minde not beinge in frame is a faire excuse, tho scarce pleasinge. Madame, I knowe yow will enquire whether my wife be with childe. I dare not peremtarili averr she is, 'tis veri probable, tho, she is neare quickninge; I beseech yow helpe her bothe to bringe forthe and to be a meanes to enlarge his kingdome. Madame we bothe in all humiliti presente all due service and duty to your ladyship, not forgettinge all humble respecte to all with yow. If I may be so bolde I beseech yow commende me to Mr Harrison. Thus in haste I humbli reste, not a little longinge to receive a line from your ladyship. If yow see nothinge in me worthy your love, yet let the image of him yow so deareli love drawe something from yow. However, I am resolved whilste I breathe to remaine your dutyfull and obedient nephew in all fideliti to serve yow

Thomas Bourchier

Yorke this 20 of January, 1630

Endorsed (*f. 326b*): To the truli honourable my noble aunte the ladi Johan Barrington these at Hatfielde

168   *Oliver St. John, 23 January 1631*   (*2645, f. 237*)

Most deare and much honoured madame   I received your letter and therewith Sir Edward Altham's desyers of a peacable end of the things in difference betweene us[1]. The protestations to that purpose

---

[1] Lady Joan's letter to St. John, dated 22 Jan., has survived among the Manchester papers (Hunts. R.O., dd M48A, bundle 4). She wrote:-
'Good sonne   This day Sir Edward Altham beinge here had some speach with me about your buisines and makes protestations of his desire to have a peaceable end, and to that purpose intreated me to write unto yow to appoint a tyme of meetinge when your leisure will serve yow, at which tyme he would have my cosin Hildersham to be there to testifie what he knowes in that behalfe, and yow shall find him willinge to yeald to any thinge that shalbe thought fitt by my sonne Gerard and Sir Thomas Leventhorpe. I told him yow would not admitt of any other arbitrator but my sonne Gerard and he is now willinge therwith, and is desirous to have the meetinge betweene this and Candlemas, and therfore I pray you let me heare from yow what tyme you appoint that I may send them word accordingly. Thus wishing a good conclusion of this buisines, with my love remembred to all your good company, desiring God to blesse yow and your litle one, I rest
     Your assured lovinge grandmother   Johan Barrington'

made unto your ladyship have bin often heretofore made unto my selfe but nothing of performance hath ther uppon ensued. I doubt not but your ladyship's desyers are in this busines to leave the ways and meanes of persecution therof unto my selfe, which if your ladyship be pleased to doe I have fully signified my minde unto Sir Edward Altham in the answere to his generall propositions which your lady- ship may be pleased to see, they being in my lady Gerrard's hands. Concerning a day of meeting, I being to goe to London upon Mun- day next can appoynt none, but leave the matter wholly to Sir Gilbert Gerrard and the care of meeting to Sir Edward Altham, intending to begin a legall course as soone as I come up to London. But soe as if Sir Gilbert Gerrard and Sir Thomas Leventhorpe[1] can meete and make an award before candlemas, I will stand to it if Sir Edward doe signifie the like to Sir Gilbert Gerrard and will desist from any further pro- ceedings. Praysed be God my wife and your little goddaughter[2] are both in good health. We are glad to heare your ladyship is soe well after your watery voyage and presente our humble thankes to you for taking soe ill a jorny for us. And with my humble dutie I rest

Your ladyship's humble and obediente both son and servant

Oliver St. Johns

Oates, January 23, 1630

The signature only is Lady Joan's; the text is in the hand of Toby Bridge. This letter was kindly pointed out to me by Mr Christopher Thompson.

St. John's wife Joan was the only child of Lady Elizabeth Masham's first marriage to Sir James Altham, who died in 1610. Sir Edward was his younger brother. Sir James had left money in his mother's charge for his daughter when she should marry. A conflict of interests was almost inevitable. By July St. John had begun a suit in Chancery over the matter. The main issues raised during the course of the case (which was still under way in Feb. 1632) were the legality of Sir Edward Altham's title to the estates formerly held by his brother Sir James; the executorship by Elizabeth, mother of James and Edward, of the will of James; Sir Francis Barrington's administration of the wardship of Joan Altham and of the trust entered into between him and Sir James; the administration by Sir Francis, and later by Robert Barrington, of a loan of £200. Breach of promise by Sir Francis, mentioned in letter 231, was alleged in this last matter. Table 3; E.R.O., T/A 531/1: Altham MSS. I, f. 3; letters 171, 210, 231; P.R.O., C2 Chas. I S104/41.

[1] Mary Hautrey, in a letter to her sister Lady Altham the following July, described how Leventhorpe and Gerard had agreed to meet to attempt to settle the difference, but 'before ever they came to discuss of the differences they dispayred of ending them'. Sir Thomas Leventhorpe was Sir Edward Altham's wife's brother. Their grandmother was one of the daughters of Sir Henry Parker, thus providing a kinship link with the Barringtons, and the Leventhorpes were also related to the Franck family of Hatfield Broad Oak. E.R.O., T/P 195/16; T/A 531/1: Altham MSS. I, f. 3; pedigree 1.

[2] The St. John's child was born on 10 Jan. and baptised Joan at High Laver on the 27th. Lady Joan gave her plate worth more than £10. E.R.O., D/P 111/1/1 and D/DBa A15, ff. 17b, 18.

Endorsed (f. 238b): To the much honoured lady the Lady Johan Barrington at Hatfeild Priory these present

169   *Sir William Meux, n.d., [before 24 January 1631]*   *(2650, f. 324)*

Madam   I am very sensible of my Lady Barrington's care and paines concerning the match propounded for my daughter in Hampshire; an endevore of requitall shall by God's assistance never be wanting in me. As for an enquirye of his behaviour and parts, that long since hath bin performed on my parte and noe just exceptions that I can either finde or heare can be taken against him. The reason of the not proceeding was occasioned by my Lady Barrington in that she gave me an advertisement, as I remember, that the father would settl noe land uppon him, which made bothe her and my self the more colde in the business. Heerein I assure my self shee will cleere me and therefore I hope yow will not impute any carelessnes to me in this pointe. I have desired my lady to propounde the matter to the father by her freinde, whome if shee shall find to return such an answere as shall be reasonable, God willing I will make good what formerly I have promised. I confess I have more affection this way then the other, for growing in yeeres travaile will be unpleasing, and soe farr distant she may be as a lost childe unto me. I shall now humbly intreate yowr ladyship no sinister conceite may possess yow concerning my self, who have bin, and by God's help will be, as redy to doe yow service and as carefull of my children's good as yow yowr self shall desire. The allmighty preserve yow,
              Yowr assured loving son   William Meux

One thing I shall intreate yow, to acquainte my brother Masham with this business, and intreate him to enquire of my cosin White of the Midle Temple, of which house this gentlman is and chamberfellow to Sir William Lisle his eldest son of our country[1], as concerning his religion, which is moste easy for him to doe.

Endorsed (f. 325b): To his much honored mother the Lady Barrington att Hattfeild give these

---

[1] John Lisle, son and heir of Sir William Lisle of Wootton, Isle of Wight, was admitted to the Middle Temple 11 May 1626. V.C.H., *Hampshire*, v. 205; H. F. Macgeach and H. A. C. Sturgess, *Register of the Middle Temple* (1949), i. 117.

170   *Sir William Masham, 24 January [1631?]*   *(2650, f. 320)*

Madame   I was sorrye to parte with you in so ill weather, beinge
glad to heare you did so well after so bad a jornye. As touchinge your
letter, I shalbe willinge to doe any service to further a good match for
my good cosine Meuxe. The gentleman I know not, but as you desire
I will write to my cosine White by this bearer, whom I have appoynted
to call for my letter on Wensdaye morninge, for I knowe of no other
meanes to send to London this weeke, Pinchine being gon to London
this daye. And I presume by the returne of my sonne St John the
beginning of the next weeke I shall heare from my cosine White. So
with our humble dutyes and thanks for your last great favore to us
and ours, not forgetting all our frends with you, I commit you to God
and rest
                    Yours obliged   William Masham

Otes, January 24
My mother presents her best respects to you and all her frends with
you.

Endorsed (f. 321b): To my much honoured ladye and mother the Ladye
Barrington these be given

171   *Sir Edward Altham, 25 January 1631*   *(2645, f. 239)*

Honorable lady   In performance of my promise I sent to Sir
Thomas Leventhorp to prepare him agayne for that busines whearin
his paynes (togeither with the other noble genteleman's) had beene
formerly fruiteles. Hee is very willing to itterate his travayles and my
self very ready to doe all right; and when wee heare of Sir Gilbert's
returne wee shall adresse ower selves to give him and my nephew St.
John a nue meeting, assuering your ladiship that their shalbe noe
default in mee to cause the busines to succeed otherwise then in justice
and conscience it ought, my thoughts tending onely to peace besides
the unfayned desier I have to mayntayne love and amity with every
braunch of your honorable family, to which I have not heither to
beene an unrespective servant. And I doubt not but that my nephew
(thorough your ladiship's good counsell) will temper his heigh
thoughts with some correspondent respects, and (like a discreet gentel-
man) advise him well before he engageth him self into the wayes of
strife and unkindenes, seing he maye have his owne with love and
peace. And to gett more then his owne, I will not entertyane any such
thought of him as to imagine that hee thinketh him self soe powerfull,
or mee soe weake.

But to apply my selfe wheare I ought: your ladiship is the party with whome I am to treate concerning the mony left in my mother Altham's hands by your son and hirs (Sir James Altham) for the use of his daughter Joane (now my neec St. John), and your ladiship is shee with whome I am to deale (lett my nephew St. John frame what conceits hee pleaseth to himself). Interpose theirfore your wisdom and autority, I beseech you, and be pleased to make demand (and accept of) what you knowe or I knowe to be due, and by God's grace it shalbe faythfully and justly discharged to the uttermost of my mother's estate.

And soe presenting my service to your ladiship and all my honorable friends with you, I signe mee

Your ladishipp's humble son and servant

Edward Altham

Marke Hall, January 25, 1630

Endorsed (f. 240b): To the very honorable and his much honored lady the lady Joane Barrington present theise, Hatfeild

172 *Sir William Masham, 5 February* [1631]   *(2645, f. 241)*

Deare mother   Since my comminge to towne I mett with Sir John Bourchier, who hath propounded a good match for my cosine Mewxe, if you and her father shall approve it. The gentleman is Sir William Strickland of Yorkshire[1], a widdower of 32 yeares of age, having 4 daughters very yonge and a fayre estate betweene 1500^{li} per annum and 2000^{li} after his father death, aged betweene 60ty and 80ty yeares, and during his father's life but 300^{li} per annum for his present mayntaynance. My cosine gives a very good reporte of the gentleman, who desires to have a sight of her privatly, with out any notice till approbation, and therfore you shall doe well to keepe this very private and to acquainte Sir William Mewis with this proposition forth with, that so upon his answere you maye take some resolution. The mayne discouragment is the far distance from Sir William, yet other things maye make a mends. I praye let me know your mynd by the next, and I shalbe ready to doe you or yours any service that lyes in my powre. So with my humble dutye and service, best respects to all my frends with you, I commit you to God and rest yours obliged

William Masham

[1] Sir William Strickland of Boynton, whose first wife died in 1629. He married Lady Frances Finch, the eldest daughter of the Earl of Winchilsea, in May 1631. J.W. Clay, *Dugdale's Visitation of Yorkshire* (Exeter, 1917), iii. 124.

London, February 5
This daye Mr Allwaye argued in the exchequer for the kinge against
the gentlemen in poynt of knighthood and on Tusdaye the judges will
give judgment[1]. Ther is no other newes stirringe.

Endorsed (f. 242b): To my much honoured ladye and mother the Ladye
Barrington these be given

173 *Oliver St. John, 6 February 1631* (*2645, f. 243*)

Most deare and honoured madam   Sir John Bourchier, Sir
William Masham and my selfe had last night some speech of a husband
for my cozen Meux.[2] It was occasioned by Sir John's nomination of
one Sir William Strickland, heretofore my fellow puple, though long
since. His age is about 33 or 34 yeares, hee's a widdower and hath 4
children, but all daughters, he hath a verry good report, his estate is
voyced to be above 1500[li] per annum, but lyeth in Yorkshier. I am
bould to advertise your ladyship of these things to the intent that if Sir
John Bourchier should not doe it (to whome I have sent this messenger
to that purpose) that your ladiship might have the larg time to advise
thereuppon, and in the meane time, with out making the cause therof
knowne, I thinke I shall have some opportunities of better informing
you concerning the gentleman's personall worth and estate. And with
my humble dutie to your ladyship and service to all my worthy good
freinds with you, I rest
      Your ladyship's in all dutie and service   Oliver St John

Lincolnes Inn, 6[to] February, 1630

Endorsed (f. 145b): To the honourable lady the Lady Barrington the
elder att Hatfeild Priorie these

[1] Mead wrote to Stuteville on 30 Jan: 'Yesterday was the day ... appointed to decide
the pleas against ... fining for knighthood'. Birch, ii. 93.
[2] That the question of a husband for Joan Meux remained open seems largely to have
been due to her father's wish to have her settled near him. Sir Gilbert Gerard was to
criticise this attitude in May 1631 (see letter 184); on 4 April Meux had written to Lady
Joan as follows:–
'Madam   The truth is that I have bin carefull in the pursuite of a mach for my
daughter in Dorsettsheer, neere unto me, but itt pleaseth God that my desires take
not effect. I shall now make enquirye once more betweene this and the terme, when
(God Willing) I will bee with yowr ladyshipp and give yow such assurance of my
love to my childe as that yow shall have noe cause of dislike. I confess I like not the
distance of place proposed by yowr ladyship but yet I must submitt my self to him
whoe governs all things, and shall allwaies remaine most thanckfull for yowr love
and care. Soe leaving yow to the tuition of the highest I rest yowr assured loving son,
      William Meux.'
E.R.O., D/DBa F30/4.

174   *John Masters*[1], *to Lady Joan Barrington and others, 14 March 1631*
(2645, f. 245)

Right worshipfull   My good lady Barrington and Sir Thomas
Barrington with Mr Roberte Barrington and my good lady Lampleath, and to the right worshipfull Sir Gilberte Gerrett and his good
lady and to Sir William Massome and his good lady, with all the rest
of the gentlemen and gentleweomen in all your families, grace and
peace be multiplied in our lord Jesus Christ to yow all. Right worshipfull and welbeloved I knowe not how sufficiently to stile yow, nor yet
how to greet yow as yow deserve at my hands, nor yet as your
worthines requires, but haveing so much experience of takeing in good
part my rudenes in speakeing, I make bold to trouble yow in writing.
But your great kindnesse and respect of mee, that am so unworthie,
makes mee to muse how I should in any measure requite it, but I
knowe not how to doe it, but I pray yow to accept of the acknowledgment of all your kindnesse by way of thankfulnes. And because yow
desired mee to write of this country and said yow would beleeve
what I should write, I would faine graunte your desire therein; and
because I could not write before I had some experience of the country
I thought it fitt to deferre it untill now. The country is very good,
and fitt to receive lords and ladies, if there were more good houses,
both for good land and good water, and for good creatures to hunt
and to hawke, and for fowling and fisheing, and more also our
natures to refresh in. And if yow or any of yours will come here, I
knowe yow might have good cheere, but because the right worshipfull Sir Richard Saltonstall hath putt mee in place to oversee his
great family[2], with his worthy sonne, and that his busines being so
great as it is, I cannot write so large as I woulde, for besides his great
family hee hath many cattle and kyne and horse and swine and some
goats and poultry. Hee hath also much building at his owne house,
and fenceing, ploweing and planteing, and also to helpe build the
new citty, and first for a house for God to dwell in. These thinges will
require my best dilligence, because that Sir Richard will be long
absent, and therefore seeing that hee is now come over to advise with
the wise, to advance the glory of God in planteing the gospell here,
and to helpe forward those that intend the good of this country,

---

[1] John Masters was admitted as a freeman of Watertown, Massachusetts in 1631 and
early on protested at the admission of unworthy members to the church. He died in
1639. C.H. Pope, *The Pioneers of Massachusetts*, (Boston, 1900), 305; *Winthrop's Journal*
(ed. J.K. Horner, New York, 1908), i, 83; *Transactions* Colonial Society of Massachusetts,
viii (1906), 129; *New England Historical and Genealogical Register*, ii (Boston, 1848), 180.
This letter is also printed in *New England Hist. and Gen. Reg.*, xli (1937), 69–70.

[2] Saltonstall, one of the principal undertakers of the Massachusetts Bay Company to
go out to the colony, left on 30 March 1631. *D.N.B.*

therefore I pray yow to conferre with him of the same, for I have made bold to acquaint him with the acquaintance of your worships. And then Sir Richard will enforme yow of all the particulars that can be sayd of this country, so much of it also as will bring over my lady Lampleath and Sir George her husband, and some others of my good Sir Francys Barrington's lineage, that I may lay my selfe downe at their feet to doe them some service, for that extraordinary love and kindnesse and respect that I received from my good Sir Francys and my good lady, which I feare I shall never be able to requite.

I am unwilling to take off my hand from writeing in paper, but if I could write yow any better matter; but I hope hereafter to answere your letters, which will make mee much more all your debtors. My God and my lord and your God blesse yow all and yours with all heavenly blessings and heavenly graces, untill wee all meet in heaven in our places. Amen.

Your friend in all service, till death end   John Masters

Watertowne, neare Charles river, New Englande, March 14th, 1630

Endorsed (*f. 246b*): To the right worshipful Lady Barrington at Hatfield Broadway, or to Sir William Marsome at Oates in Essex, these be presented, in England

175   *Alban Plumtree*[1] *to Lady Judith Barrington, n.d.*, [*March? 1631*]
(*2645, f. 247*)

Noble lady   I am importuned (if my intreaties may any whil prevaile) that you would bee pleased to make Captaine Sanders a lease of Beachwood tythes for so much rent as you two ar agreed on by the year, which is so much as it is worth or can bee, for hee is resolved to sow but 60 acres of wheat at a season, and his wife (if heedy) is bound not to exceed. My request therefore (if there bee any thing in it) that hee may have a lease for reason which hee promiseth to give to the utter most, which wilbee a meanes of avoiding troubles and of confirming frendship. Concerning my businesses, I shall not need to write any thinge: I referre the relation thereof to Mr Smith. I have sent you a byll of your hand for the receipt of 80[li] which of late by chaunce I found, not thinking I had any. I thinke veryly it is paid; I received at London some 40 or 50[li], I know not of whom I received the rest. Ned Davie was wont to be very strict in demaunding bondes and bylles, but I knowing you to be very just and much more circum-

---

[1] Perhaps the man of this name who was later schoolmaster at St Albans. V.C.H., *Herts.*, ii 65.

spect and of a better memorie then my self, leav it wholly to your consideration, knowing yow have a care to satisfie your own conscience. And so with many thankes for your kinde tokens to my wife and mee, with the remembrance of our service and dutie to noble Sir Thomas Barrington and your ladiship etc., I end and rest

Your ladyship's poor and faithful servant   Alban Plumtree

Endorsed (f. 248b): To my honourable lady the Lady Judith Barrington at Hatfeild

176   *Alban Plumtree to Lady Judith Barrington, 4 April 1631 (2645, f. 249)*

Worthy madam   I desire to know whether you have so agreed with Captaine Sanders for your tithes as that you shall not need any of my barnes, but that I may freely dispose of them without any prejudice to you.

I have some occasion of mony at this time; if it please you that the widow Davie[1] may help mee to ten poundes, shee is content to pay it mee.

There is no covenant between us of paying mee use for such monies you have of mine. It is a gaine I never approoved of in my judgment nor practise, I desire therefore for the peace of my conscience and for the preventing of further losses, to take a lease of Roe End tithes according to that proportion that I was to pay for Mr Cullam's lease of 30^{li} per annum, which for 2 yeares amounted to 250^{li}. Not that I would any way wronge the widow, I would rather doe her good, only shee should turne tenant to mee and pay mee that rent shee payeth to your ladyshipp, unles I agreed with her to take the tith into my own handes, which I thinke shee will not be unwilling to doe. This is a very reasonable bargain and therefore agreeable to that you have often promised. I am not apt to plead my own cause, neither shall I need to alledge reasons that may move you to shew mee favour which, when I behold, I shall more valew then any gaine, and rejoyce more in your goodnes then in your goodes. This saith hee that is and alwayes hath been

Your ladysship's faithful servant   Alban Plumtree

April 4, 1631

Endorsed (f. 250b): To my honourable lady the Lady Judith Barrington at Barrington Halle

[1] See letter 162.

177   *Lady Mary Eliot[1], n.d., [April 1631]*   *(2645, f. 251)*

Much honnored ladye mother   The goodness and mercifullnes
of your dispositon moves me now in gratt and hauvye burden that lies
on me to flye deare ladye to you as my best and most hoopfull friend
to doe me good. My humbell request and sutt is that you would be
pleased soe fare to condesend as to furnish me with five pound[2], for
the which token of your love I shall ever rest bound to you and whiles
I live acknowledge the same with all thankfullnes. Pardon my
bouldnes I humbelly besaech you that ever remaines
          Your faithfull lover and daughter to command   M. Eliot

Endorsed (f. 252b): To the honnorabell and my verye good ladye the
Ladye Barrington give these

178   *Sir Gilbert Gerard, 19 April 1631*   *(2645, f. 253)*

Good madam   I now thinke the time very long sithence we
heard how your self with the rest of our good friendes with you doe,
therfore I have sent this bearer for that purpose, which I should have
done sooner, but that I did expect dayly either to have seene some of
your company or to have heard from your ladyship, but you have bine
so full of great company that your poore friendes at Harrow it seemes
now forgotten. But my comfort is that you are in health, otherwise ill
newes would soone come unto us. My wife now begines to looke bigg
upon us and wisheth your company heere, which if shee may not be so
hapy to have shee doubts not of your praiers. I must now also pray to
bee excused for not visiting you, being lame of my old legg, but you
have furnished mee with so good a surgion that I hope by the blessing
of God upon her labor I shall be shortly upon my leggs againe, and
the sooner if you please to bestow upon us some of your white [sutar]
cloth. So for the present I rest your dutifull sonn
          G. Gerard

19 April, 1631

Endorsed (f. 254): To my honourable good mother the Lady Barrington
these be given.

> [1] See letter 3.
> [2] Payment of £5 to Lady Eliot is recorded for the week of 20 April 1631. So large an
> amount was not paid to her at any other time during the years covered by the account
> book. E.R.O., D/DBa A15, f. 20.

179   *Thomas Saunders[1] to Sir Thomas Barrington, 20 April 1631*

(*2645, f. 255*)

Sir   I am ready (according to your commaunds) to subscribe to
your manner of tything at 2ˢ and 4ˢ for my mannour of Beechwood,
and upon the warning or alteration upon consent therin expressed.
Beseeching yow to (faverably) excuse my not retuerning my service to
yow subscribed under mye hand till this time, for I have had a letter
ready written ever since, butt wanted the opportunity of a messenger.
I praesent my humble service to your selfe and my ladye praying yow
both to pardon my brevity at this time, the reasons be pleased to
accept from the relation of your servant John Kendall, to whose report
I referr my selfe in this, as in some other particulars, who am
          By yow to be comaunded while   Thomas Saunders

Aprill the 20th, 1631

Endorsed (f. 256b): To my most honoured freind Sir Thomas Barrington knight and barronett praesent this

[*In hand of Lady Judith Barrington*:] Mr Saunder's letter that he would
pay us 4ˢ and 2ˢ an aker for Beechwood tythe, 1631

180   *Sir Gilbert Gerard, 25 April 1631*   (*2645, f. 257*)

Good madam   I resceived the last weeke from your ladyship a
summons to give a meeting to the rest of our friendes at Otes about
my brother Lamplugh his busines[2]. I was very sory I could not doe it,
for noe man would be more willing to take any paines to put a good
issue unto his troubles then my selfe, but madam it is so that I have
not stirred out of my owne doores sithence my brother Lamplugh
went from us saving on Sundaies to the church in my coach, neither
could I goe to the sessions this last weeke although I had much busines
there, being detained by my lame legg for the recovery whereof I have
this last weeke taken some phisick and doe thinke I shalbe advised to
enter into a course of phisick, having this day sent unto my doctors.

---

[1] See letter 158.

[2] Sir George Lamplugh had married Lady Joan's daughter Ruth, but, although there
were children, the couple were estranged by 1626 and Ruth was being taken care of by
her parents. Lamplugh had projects in Ireland. In June 1626 he tried to persuade Sir
Francis Barrington to influence archbishop Ussher of Armagh on his behalf and to send
Ruth into Ireland with Mrs Ussher. Sir Francis refused to do anything until Lamplugh
could demonstrate that he had better prospects. In April 1627, using Ezekiel Rogers as
an intermediary, Lamplugh again tried unsuccessfully to effect a reconciliation with his
wife. Ruth remained with her mother after Sir Francis died. Lamplugh died in 1633.
Eg. 2644, ff. 236, 251; Introduction 19; *T.E.A.S.*, n.s.ii. 28.

But I hope my absence was noe impediment unto there meeting, there being so many good friendes so well able to determine of such a matter, and I should bee gladd to heare that all things were well setled unto my brother and sister's mutuell comfort. Madam, I being now by God's hand sequestred from busines of the world, I desire to imploy my selfe so that I may be the better prepared for another world, and if it please God instead of the use of my leggs to doe him service heere on earth, to give mee the wings of true devotion to raise up my meditations unto a better life, I shall account my self abundantly recompensed. And if wee would rightly consider of it, when God either by sicknes or age or other infirmitie doth give us our writt of discharge from our worldly affaires, if he continue our sences, and give us hintes to bestow our time in his spirituell servise, we have more cause of joy then sorrow for it. That I may die thus I desire you to pray for your dutifull sonne

G. Gerard

25 April, 1631

Endorsed (*f. 258b*): To my honourable good mother the Lady Johan Barrington these

181 *Sir Gilbert Gerard, 29 April 1631* (*2645, f. 259*)

Good madam   I have perused my brother Lamplugh's propositions, which I resceived from you. They were not strange unto mee, therefore I needed not long for to advise upon them, and I likewise persceive by him that there is noe hope to persuade any of you to lay downe any mony, so that now there is noe more to bee considered but whither you will give way to the sale of Sigeson[1] unto a stranger, he depositing upon the sale 1500^{li}, according to the agreement, for the use of my sister, and this it seemes you all agree unto, neither doe I discent if it can bee done. His desire, therefore is [that] he may have a wrighting under my sister and her freindes handes testifying thus much, with out which noe body will treet with him about it, and that I hold to be a reasonable request and shalbe readie to signe when I see my sister's hand unto it with your owne who are her cheifest friend. And this is all that can for the present be said in that busines. Now good madam for our selves, my wife begines to grow bigg and being deprived of her old midwife shee wisheth shee might be so hapy to see you heare in whose company she had much comfort when you were

---

[1] Kirkby Sigston in the North Riding of Yorkshire, a Lamplugh property from 1570. By 1641 it was in the hands of Benjamin Tiffin (see letter 211). V.C.H., *Yorks., North Riding*, i (1914), 406.

with her the last time. It doth please God that it fales out at such a time that the seeson of the yeere doth invite you, and I doubt not but the jorny would doe you much good, and heere are many good friendes would joy much to see you heere. My wife would have wrighten herselfe but her belly is so bigg shee cannot, and shee would likewise be glad of your company to have your advise and heelpe in her surgery with mee, for I must acknowledge you were the best surgion that ever I mett withall, and by your meanes I was last cured. I hope these notions will persuade you to come unto us, which if you shalbe pleased to doe you shall engage us ever and binde me in perticular to bee

    Your dutifull sonne   G. Gerard

Flambardes, 29 April, 1631

Endorsed (*f. 260b*): To my honourable good mother the Lady Johan Barrington these be given at Hatfield

182 *Sir Thomas Barrington, n.d., [before 14 May 1631]*   (*2645, f. 263*)

Madame   Thare cannot be that toe often occasions should be offred, nor I weary of imbraceing every such happy meanes of tending my dewty and service unto you, and trewly he that treades or troules over London stones cannot but heear the eccho of newes from theire very sound, loude enough to reflect it to Hatfeild every moment. This day hath ascertayned the Lord Castlehaven his suffring upon Saterday next;[1] to prepare him the better he hath caused his coffin to be sett at his doore. His continewed bestillyty hath (for ought I heear) ben the cheifest cause that hath drawen his peears to theire verdit, and that rather then the perticular facts he was araigned for according to the proofes, but the point of law the judges tooke upon them selves and so satisfyed the jurye. The peace in Italy is thought to be concluded. In France things rest in a suspended ballance still. In Germany Sweden prospers; his takeing of Franckford is assured by a strategem, for the toune had 6,000 in garison. Sweden finding it strong, retyres, the toune all fell upon the reare of the armye, Sweden's horss fell instantly between them and the toune, cutt the garison of and tooke all the passages, and so broke in the toune and toke it.[2] Now for knights, one boute and so I kiss your hands: Sir Edward Allin hath payd 160^{li},[3] the

---

[1] Castlehaven was executed on Tower Hill, 14 May 1631. Birch, ii 118, 120.

[2] The newsbook of 9 May reported the taking of Frankfurt with the slaughter of 6,000 of the garrison. The news was confirmed in the book for 16 May. Dahl, 228, 229.

[3] An exchequer teller's bill survives for £80 paid by Sir Edward Allen of Hatfield Peverel, Essex, on 28 April 1631. E.R.O., D/DHt Z33.

lord Kingston 3000^{li}, the lord[s] sitt fowr dayes every weeke and take 2000^{li} every day. And I had rather bid your ladyship good night then say any more at this time but that I am ever your most dewtyfull sonn
    Thomas Barrington

Endorsed (*f. 264b*): To the honourable my most respected mother the Lady Barrington att Hattfeild these be given

183 *Sir Thomas Barrington, 13 May 1631*   (*2645, f. 262*)

Madame   If your scribe had a pen of steele and a hand of brass he could not write words enough to me to equall or counterballance the last, which (though only two) yet coming from your owne hand they are more to me then a volume from your amanuensis, which yet are beyond all other expressions because pened from your comaunds. I assure yow, madam, no busines can be more serious to me then the performeing of the dewes of dewty to your selfe and tharefor it is time spare that is spent upon other imployments, that which relates to you is my most proper worke. But now your child, and my neice, after her pleasures taken in being mistress of house and servants (wharein she hath contemplated the happynes of a maried life), is retourning to yow, and well knowing her abilytye of perfecting all newes I shall by her make the more unpollished tender of myne. This day the lord Faukeland's busines was heard in the Star Chamber, whare a deepe censure is to pass on one accusing him of the unjust condemnation of one in Ireland for the gaine of his personall estate, wharein the chief justice of Ireland is brought on the stage allso.[1] The mariage of Sir G. Allington is pronounced voyde in the High Comission and he fined 10,000^{li} for his incestuous match and bound in 20,000^{li} never heear-[a]fter to accompany with her againe; an excellent example.[2] The rest I leave till the next commer, only now assuring yow to make as much hast to settle my occasions as I can possibly doe, wharein Smithe's delay hinders me, who knowes that I can not doe any thing in my mother Gobert's busines for my children's portions[3] untill I have the

---

[1] Falkland had been lord deputy in Ireland until recalled in 1629. His son Lucius Cary, Viscount Falkland, sat in the Short and Long Parliaments for the Barrington borough of Newtown, Isle of Wight. *D.N.B.*

[2] He had married his neice. Birch, ii 113 (letter of 13 May) and 119 (20 May).

[3] John Gobert, the father of Sir Thomas Barrington's first wife, died in 1625, but the terms of his will had still not been properly carried out when his widow died in 1635, and the settlement of the estate between the families of his daughters was in dispute for much longer. P.R.O., P.C.C., 50 Sadler; will of Lucy Gobert, E.R.O., D/DBa F15; Eg. 2644, ff. 213, 219, 255 and 2646, f. 93.

leases that he must bring to London, which he hard Mr Rigby, my mother's counsell, say unto me; I beseich yow hasten him, for on my credit this is no excuse, for my desyre and my poore wive's is to be with yow, I assure yow, as soone as we can possiblye, God permitting. We are glad and [*f. 261b*] desyre God to continew your health, and for my honest and beloved playe fellow, I joye in her grunttles, for upon experience I have found that the more before the less behind; yet God send her well and God send us a joyfull meeting, that we congratulate owr tulipps and slash oute the old smock into biggers, for the little 'haunse in kelder' (ask Hawte this in English). I shall pray for my brother Everard's health, that he may gett som more fine boyes for a fayreing at St James.[1] And now my dewty to you, my love hartyly commended to my deear playe fellow, my good affection to my sister Lamplugh and the rest, sisters, brothers, freinds, children, I comitt us all to God and rest

Your most dewtyfull and as loving sonn

Thomas Barrington

London, May 13, 1631

I have sent yow papers from my nephew St Johns which are not to appeear allmost to any one. I beseich [you] lett me crave them at my retourne, which shall be ere long, by the blessing of God.

Endorsed (*f. 262b*): To the honourable my very loving mother the lady Johan Barrington give [these]

184 *Sir Gilbert Gerard, 23 May 1631* (*2645, f. 265*)

Good madam   My wife and I are both much bound unto you for your love and desire to heare from us. I thanke God shee is as well as a woeman in her case may bee, growing unwieldy and full of paines, and would have bine gladd if shee might have enjoied your company at this time. Shee wishes her selfe with you that shee might begg some cloutes of you, being destitute her selfe, and if you could spare her a paire of old sheetes you might doe her a pleasure.[2] For my self, I thanke God I am recovered of my lame legg by the healpe of a good chyrurgion of your breeding, who hath taken so much paines with mee and care of mee during my lamenes that I must intreat you to give her thankes for it. I doe assure you shee dressed mee so neatly and

---

[1] All this must be a reference to his sister Joan Everard's pregnancy.

[2] Perhaps an apologetic reference to the 'popish' custom of using a special sheet for lying in. Cf. W.H. Frere and C.E. Douglas, *Puritan Manifestoes* (1954), 28–9.

so tenderly that I cannot tell whither I tooke more pleasure and contentment in her paines with mee or sorrow for my paines of it. I am yet tender and dare not pull on a boote, otherwise I would visite upon you, but I doubt now I shall not see you at Hatfield untill my wife bee well up againe, for which we desire the continuance of your praiers. For my brother Lamplugh, I saw him not sithence he went unto you last, neither doe I know what he intendes or can doe, except he had some friend would disburse some mony for him, which I feere he hath not. For my neece Mewx busines, I wish all good successe unto it, and doe thinke you have done very well to send unto her about it, and if he stand upon the distance of the place (if otherwise the match be fitting) he is much to blame.[1] I am sorry my sister Everard is not well. I pray present my servise unto her and unto our disconsolate sister, who must labor to beare with patience what God sees good to lay upon her. And I wish all her friendes were as sensible of her afflictions as I am; if they were I hope wee should bring it unto some good issue quickly, for I thinke we ought all to take it to hart, and to bend all our endeavours to comfort her in using the meanes to bring them togither, for which my [prayer] and paines shall goe with the forwardest, but alone I am able to doe noething. I thanke you for the good newes of my little ones; I pray God blesse them and make them his servants, and amongst them I desire Jugg may be serviseable and dutifull unto your ladyship unto whom shee is so much bound, and me for her. And so good madam, with our thankes for all your love and our praiers for the continuance of your health and hapenes, I rest

          Your dutifull sonne   G. Gerard

Flambards, 23 May, 1631

Endorsed (f. 266b): To my honourable good mother the Lady Johan Barrington at Hatfield Brodoke in Essex these be given

185 *James Necton[2] to Sir Thomas Barrington, 30 May 1631 (2645, f. 267)*

Sir   I have caused the letter you left with me to bee delivered at Lambeth. And I was 5 or 6 tymes at Lincolnes Inn to have spoken with Mr Scott about the business of your fine at the assisses, but it

---

[1] See letter 173, n.1.

[2] Of the parish of St Botolph without Aldersgate, London. Necton was related to the Hatfield family of Hewett. He acted as agent in London for the Barringtons on a number of matters. T.C. Dale, *Inhabitants of London in 1638* (1931); Eg. 2644, f. 226.

should seeme Mr Scott was gone downe into the countrye the same daye you your selfe went downe, for I could not meet with him. I have sett your business forward with Mr Eden, and I have delivered unto him an abstract of all the landes in particular whereof the revercion is in the crowne,[1] which abstract I made out of the evidence which you left with me and out of the last office which I drewe my selfe for you two yeeres since,[2] soe that Mr Eden is now very well satisfyed for all the severall particulars of the landes which you are to pass, except it bee for your mannor, or rather royaltye, of Hanguest Freindless in Yorkesheire. For the valewes of all the other mannors and landes are sett downe in the offices particularly by them selves, but the valew of Hanguest Freindless is joyned with the mannor of Aldboroughe together at the rate of 4^{li} per annum. Now the mannor of Aldboroughe you have not, for it is past awaye longe since, but I thinke wee shall finde out a course to helpe it by setting downe a proportionable valew uppon it severally. I think I shall soe carry the matter with Mr Eden that you shall not paye much above 4 yeeres valewe for your fine. If you desire to have the patent it selfe (which is your best course) and not a duplicat, then you must name two of your frendes who are constantlye resyant at London to bee the patentees, bycause they maye bee readye at hand to seale the conveyances to such other persons whoe are allso to pass estates in this patent. Mr Eden him selfe hath offred me to bee one of the patentees, which if hee will performe, then you neede to name but one other. Mr Eden prayeth you to supplye him with 25^{li} as soone as you maye towards the charge of passing the booke. [f. 276b] One thing more I am to remember you of, that you procure some man of creditt to make oathe before one of the barons of the eschequer of the number of the issues remayning yett alive, whoe are inheritable to the estate tayle, wherein you shall not neede to bee soe precise to sett downe all, but any convenient number. When Mr Eden hath drawen the booke I will peruse it and conferr it with my recordes of the offices found, both for the particularitye of the landes to pass in the same and concerning the severall valewes thereof. And soe, remembring myne and my wief's service unto you and your good ladye and the rest of our good frendes there with you, I take leave of you for this tyme and commend you to the protection of allmightye God

Your very loveing frende at commandment   James Necton

---

[1] The formal grant of the reversion of the Barrington manors was issued on 15 June 1632. P.R.O., Exchequer, Chas. I, no. 160.

[2] The inquisition *post mortem* on the death of Sir Francis Barrington, dated 29 Nov. 1629. E.R.O., D/DHt T70/5.

Alldersgate Streate, the 30th of Maye, 1631

Endorsed (*f. 268b*): To my muche honored frende Sir Thomas Barrington knight and barronett at Hatefeild Brode Oake in the countye of
Essex give [these]
[*In hand of John Kendal:*] Mr Necton's letter about the taking the
remaynders out of the crowne, 1631

186   *Sir Thomas Barrington, 14 June 1631*   (*2645, f. 269*)

Madame   Among all my freinds and occasions, which make me
allmost not my selfe in London, yet still I retayne the memory of my
dewty to yow and the meritt of your love is ever before me, no more
either of them to be layed by then my hand from my arme; nor can
that poore hand (your servant) be (by all that ocean of busines which
I have hear) kept from breakeing through to this corner of time found
out to serve you in. This sweet month of May (lately past) hath
brought forth nothing, allmost, that may be called new but the beau-
teous fruites of the earth, which are heear so plentifull as with yow.
This present moneth hath disposed 3 of the hirarcky to theire last
home and called for som new actors to the stage; owr prayers to God
are and ought to be that the next scene may be better performed,
especially by those that shall be destined to so large a part as the
northerne see.[1] We heear of Morton, and wish him;[2] the other two
bishops whose course is runn are Elye and Worchester (as I take it). I
heear the king's shipps are all to be vewed to morrow where (if busines
has not ben my cheife care, and my retourne as soone as I can to yow
my labor) I had intreatyes enough to have ben, and am yet solicited
so much as that I hardly know my owne strength. Madame, I have
sent yow som hartychokes, the best present of this season in my
judgment, and tender yow my prayers and begg yours for me and
myne, your most dewtyfull and loving sonn
        Thomas Barrington

June 14, 1631, London, Alld[ersgate] Street
Your busines I am so proude to be imployed in that you shall need to
[no] spurr to so free a solicitor, nor can any many be so carefull as he

---

[1] Samuel Harsnett, archbishop of York, died 25 May 1631. *D.N.B.*

[2] Harsnett was succeeded by Richard Neile. Thomas Morton moved from Lichfield
to become bishop of Durham in 1632. Both of the livings owned by the Barringtons
were in the diocese of York. *D.N.B.*; Introduction, 13.

that gloryes in well doeing and yet makes dewty and love his neather
and upper storye.

Endorsed (*f. 270b*): To the honorable my very good mother the lady
Johan Barrington

187 *Sir Thomas Barrington, 20 June 1631*   (*2645, f. 271*)

Madame   My brother being my meanes of tendering theise to
you might well make me thinke that what I wright to yow as newes is
no more then a breviate of his store, but I will rather express my selfe
in needless labors then blame my selfe for silence towards yow. The
latest newes at the court is that the Duke of Saxony hath declared him
selfe against the emperor and the rest of the princes of that union,[1]
confidently pretending not to lay downe theire joynt sword untill that
catholique force renounce theire confederate indevors against that
adverss partye, so that now the drumm beates in London dayly and
forces increase. The peace in Italy depends upon som tounes surrendr-
ing which are not yet yeelded up. The intelligence from Holland is
that the States, with his excellency, found Bruges toe well fortifyed for
an assault or a leager and the Spanish forces resolved to give him
battell (being within a dayes march) before he could worke into the
ground, whereupon a counsell was called and som (that speake most
favorably) say the prince his retrayte was not made untill a summ of
mony was given by the toune and som dorpps made contributors. But
the contrary part speake loude dishonor of retraytes next unto flight,
1000 men lost and cutt of in the reare withoute once turneing theire
faces. The midle sort (which is the trew intelligence) say that the
prince made such modest hast as that he forgott 100 fyrelocks that
were sent forth upon service and lost them all but som number of two
that swamm for theire lives. The sea of Yorke stands yet all cold for
want of an ecclessiastical hawnch to fill that chaire; we looke on
Lincolne and Coventry, being both on the way northward, but
London, in roweing, hath watermen that looke contrary to theire
pretences.

And now madame, for my selfe, give me leave to assure yow that I
make all the hast that I can possiblye, not leaveing my necessary
busynes by the way. Your freinds heear are all well, God be praysed,
and I every hower indevoring to be at home with yow, in the meane
time and ever pray for God's blessing on us all and remayne
     Your most dewtyfull sonn   Thomas Barrington

[1] Reported in the newsbook of 25 June. Dahl, 231.

196   BARRINGTON LETTERS

Middle Temple, June 20th, 1631

Endorsed (*f. 272b*): To my honourable good mother the lady Johan Barrington give [these]

188   *Sir Gilbert Gerard, 20 June 1631*   (*2645, f. 273*)

Good madam   My wife desires your advise unto this poore man for a child of his that hath lately a swelling falen into the codds[1] cleere like a bladder of water. My wife doth remember yow cured a child at Kingston of such a disease. This poore man makes a journy of purpose unto your ladyship for your heelpe heerein, which I doe assure my selfe you will most willingly afford him[2]. Upon Satterday my cozen Whally was heere and brought me a letter from you which was to the same purpose I resceived another from yow, accordingly I have given order unto my cozen Brewster for the sueing of the suit, thoughe I doe not like Mr John Whallie's[3] unwillingnes to answere the bill, for the more he is falsly accused in the bill the more willing should he be to acquite himselfe by his answere upon his oath, that his innocentie might be recorded as well as his accustion is. My wife is yet a foote and waites God's hower, and desires your praiers. So with my humble duty in hast I rest

        Your dutifull sonne   G. Gerard

20 Junii, 1631

Endorsed (*f. 274b*): To my honourable good mother the Lady Johan Barrington at Hatfield Broadoke be these given

189   *Sir Thomas Barrington, 24 June 1631*   (*2645, f. 275*)

Madame   My dewty and love contends but for meanes and oportunytye to express them selves, which when I have, no sonn shall appeear ever more willing to doe that which he ought then my selfe,

---

[1] Cod: testicle.

[2] There was an enduring tradition of practical medical help being given by gentlewomen to people of lower social position. I. Pinchbeck and M. Hewett, *Children in English Society* (1969), i. 29. *Cf.* the character of Lady Bountiful in Farquhar's *The Beaux Stratagem*, 'an old, civil country Gentlewoman, that cures her neighbours of all distempers'.

[3] Perhaps the son of Edward Whalley, second son of Richard Whalley. Noble, ii. 153; Table 2.

God willing, to you, and trewly it is my joy when I can be inabled to performe any acceptable service unto yow. For your busines at Clavering, I hope the advice I sent yow will serve your desyres fully, and what ellse you commaund, or I can imagine may any way bestead yow, shall be donn as far as my poore abylyty extends ever.

The newes heear is that the king of Sweden hath neear upon 200,000 men in the feild, and the Marquis of Hambleton gathers his forces dayly, the king haveing written new letters to the lords lieftenants in all countyes to assist to theire uttmost, and 14^d by the day is heear payd every volunteer, and the Marquess his tents are up in Islington feilds. The Scottish are still in prison, none knowes why as yet[1]. The king of Sweden hath taken an other towne, where his owne sword had the honor of brave heroe and the trophy of his enymyes blood on the poynt. The Duke of Saxony and the princes have drawen theire swords on the protestant part[2]. I am in hast and must now rest for this time and committ us all to God and be ever

      Your most dewtyfull son and as loving

                            Thomas Barrington

Aldersgate Street, London, June 24th, 1631

Endorsed (*f. 276b*): To my honourable good mother the Lady Johan Barrington at Hattfeild give [these]

190   *Mary Long,*[3] *29 June 1631*   (*2645, f. 277*)

Honorabell lady   I must confesse I may seeme guilty of neglect and ingratitude in omitting to present my service thus long or to expresse my thankefullnes for your many undeserved favors, yett I hope your ladyshipp will hold mee excused who by reason of my many crosses have had all my purposes diverted from their proposed ends. I doe and shall ever acknowledge my selfe bounde unto you and your family for the best part of my education, whereby in my many dis-

---

[1] Hamilton had first attempted to raise troops in Scotland in March 1631. He had little success, partly because he was accused of treasonable intentions. When he returned to London action was begun against his accusers, and, with royal approval, he again set about raising forces. His expedition sailed on 16 July. Birch, ii. 125, 127; Gardiner, vii. 182-3.

[2] The decision of the Duke of Saxony and the protestant German princes was reported in the newsbook of 25 June 1631. Dahl, 231.

[3] William Long of Stratton married Mary, daughter of Thomas Lovibond (d. 1618) of Whippingham, Isle of Wight. F.T. Colby, *Visitation of Somerset 1623* (Harl. Soc. xi. 1876), 70; V.C.H., *Hampshire*, v. 200.

tresses I have since receaved much comfort, which makes mee bold to present one of my owne daughters to serve your selfe or any of yours whensoever you shalbee pleased to accept. I hope your ladyshipp will pardon the boldnes of her who dayly praieth for the prousperous estat of you and your family and will ever continew to bee

        Your ladyship's humble servant   Mary Long

Stratton uppon Fosse in Somerset, June 29, 1631

Endorsed (*f. 278b*): To my [*torn away*] Lady [*torn*] Joan Barrington bee these given

191   *Sir Gilbert Gerard, 4 July 1631*   (*2645, f. 279*)

Good madam   I thanke God for it, your daughter doth yet continue in health and groweth strong a pace and was never better of any child, God make us both thankfull for it.[1] Wee doubt not but wee fare the better for your praiers and the rest of our good friendes, and God doth dayly give us good experience that it is not in vaine to serve him and put our trust in him, who doth manifest him self to be a God so readie to heere us. I wish these experimentes may so strengthen our faith in his promises that wee may therby be prepared for greater trialls, even for the last and greatest, that we may be readie and willing to cast our selves into the armes of his mercy when he shall please to call us out of this world; for as he doth not faile us in the way neither will he in the end. God preserve you and keepe you and in his good time give us a hapy meeting either heere or in a better world. So in hast for the present I rest

        Your dutifull sone   G. Gerard

4 Julij, 1631

Endorsed (*f. 280b*): To my honourable good mother the Lady Johan Barrington at Hatfield these be given

192   *Ezekiel Rogers, 26 July 1631*   (*2645, f. 281*)

Madam   This messenger going from us I coulde not chuse but salute your ladyshipp with two or three lines, not only to returne my humble thankes to you all for my kinde intertainement and to lett you

---

[1] The Gerards' daughter Katherine was baptised 6 July 1631. Hewlett, i. 200.

knowe that I returned safely (thankes be to God) but that I might lett you knowe also that I woulde not omitt ay occasion wherby I might shewe my mindfullnes of you. I was not a little sory that I was urged to spende so short a time with you, and that in that little time we had no more conference, especially not knowing whither we shall meete againe or no. I woulde wish you to begge of God on your knees that gift of free, ready and frequent opening of your hart and cases[1], and in speciall to practise it with your reverende pastor, though to others too, as you have opportunity. And I beseech you, not only by your prayers and example, but advise, to helpe forwarde your sonne and daughter. Forgett not that your time cannot be long and therfore be a good huswife in plying your worke. Among other thinges which my hast made me forgett, one was to begge of you a token to your cousen Thomas Bourchier his wife, a worthy gentlewoman. I pray if you please to sende one, lett it be directed to me to deliver to her. So (having short warning of this messenger's going) I committ you to the goverment and protection of God, and with my service rest your ladyshipp's to commande in the lord. I beseech you to excuse my not writing to Sir Thomas and my lady in this hast, with my service to them all

Ezekiel Rogers

Rowly, July 26, 1631

Endorsed (*f. 282b*): To the honourable the Lady Johan Barrington at Hatfielde Broadoke

193   *Sir Gilbert Gerard,* [*9*] *August* [*1631*]   (*2646, f. 36*)

Good madam   I would have sent my boy purposely to have seene you an Satterday but that the constable is so busy this harvest I was forced send my men to conveigh this woeman unto the place from whence she came, and from thence whither you please. Madam, now you have bine yeared and daied at Hatfeld your friendes heere have little hope to see you heere againe, because if you were let a stray you were forfeited. Madam, to leave jesting, my wife remembers her duty unto you and desires to be so much bound unto you as privatly to enquire for her concerning one Mrs Browne that is skilfull in musick and in takeing yong woemen; she hath lived in Mrs Scott's house, if you thinke her fitt for my wife for her daughters, shee may have her. I pray be pleased to informe us of her as you can with conveniencie.

[1] See letter 111, n.1.

God keepe you and continue you long to the comfort of many of your childrens' childrens' children, which is a blessing now, and therfore by you not to be forgotten. So with my dutie and my wife's, and both our thankes, I rest your dutifull sonn

G. G.

[9] August, [1631]

Endorsed (*f. 37b*): To my honourable good mother the Lady Johan Barrington these be given

194 *Joan St John, 9 August 1631*   (*2645, f. 283*)

Deare grandmother   That you may se my former want of right-ing no neclect or forgetfullnes of you I shall not omet any ocation wherin I may express my dutie and thankfulness for yowr many larg and reall expressions of love to me and mine. I had presented you with a letter before now but that it pleased God to aflict me with the toothach. I was in so much pain for almost a weeke that no medison would do me good but I was forced to draw it, which I did, and now I thank God am perfictly well. I thought my husband and my selfe should have seen you at Hatfeild before this time but that my husband is not yet returned from my Lord of Bedford's, wher he hath bin above a weeke. Dear grandmother, I dare not be to bold in righting for fear I should bringe the ruine into my teeth againe, therfor I besheech you pardon my brevity and to except of thes scribled lines from her who ever disiers to be

Your afectinat and obedient grantchild to comand

Joan St John

Harow the 9° of August, 1631

Endorsed (*f. 284b*): To the much honoured ladie the Ladie Johan Barrington at Hatfeild present thes

195 *Sir Gilbert Gerard, 25 August 1631*   (*2645, f. 285*)

Madam   I have brought your daughter into Essex to waite upon you, but hearing that you are so full of greate company wee have forborne to come unto you untill wee heare that the coast is cleare. I have sent this bearer to see how you and my brother and sister doe, and purpose, God willing, to bee with you this weeke if you bee not to full of company. I doubt not but you have heard the good newes, but it may be you have not seene it, therfore I have sent you these bookes.[1] So with remembrance of my servyce and duty, I rest

Your dutifull sonne   G. Gerard

Otes, 25 August, 1631

Endorsed (f. 286b): To my honourable good mother the Lady Johan Barrington at Hatfield these be given

196   *Sir Gilbert Gerard, 11 September 1631*   (*2645, f. 287*)

Good madam   Had not this bearer occasion of his master's to draw him to Hatfield I would have sent one purposely to have seene how your great toe dooth, and I hope to heere by him that you are againe at libertie. If not yet, I am gladd your paine is so farre from your hart, and yet not so farre but that it is a messenger to put you in mind of mortalitie. God would have us alwaies mindfule of our later end, and not to passe by any oportunitie of preparing our selves for that great day whereof I doe assure my selfe you are ever mindfull, yet my dutie compells me to neglect noe occation to expresse my love unto you, and amongst all the evidences of God's love unto us there can be none greater than to love his saints because they are so. Madam I humbly thanke you for your love unto mee and mine when wee were with you, espetialy for your great love unto my daughter; God make her truly thankfull unto you for it. I thanke God we came all well to Harrow on Satterday. And so committing you to the protection of the almighty I rest your dutifull sonne

G. Gerard

11 September, 1631

Endorsed (f. 288b): To my honourable good mother the Lady Johan Barrington at Hatfield these be given

197   *Sir Thomas Barrington, [11] September 1631*   (*2645, f. 289*)

Madame   I am sorye to remember that I left yow no better at ease, and shall not fayle to pray to God for your perfect recovery,

---

[1] The newsbook of 20 Aug., reporting Gustav Adolf's defeat of Pappenheim at Magdeburg, was issued in two parts. Dahl, 234, 235.

which I hope will be had after this alteration of weather, your suffering
being only an exterior payne which coms by humors dispersed with
the change of the season, which will retyre againe and soone leave yow
as theay found yow (at ease I hope), God willing. I have no newes to
send you but that the Polish embassador, being horssed by the king to
hunt in the forest of Walltham, lost himselfe and was not easyly found
but that he was as greate as a kingdom.[1] All this company tender yow
theire service and love and I remayne

      Your most dewtifull sonn   Thomas Barrington

Harrow, September [11], 1631

Endorsed (f. 289b): To the honourable my very good mother the lady
Johana Barrington

198   *Sir Gilbert Gerard, 19 September 1631*   *(2645, f. 290)*

Good madam   Your letter bearing date the twelf of September
came not unto my handes untill yesterday when I came from church,
so that wee could not returne you an answere sooner. Wee are all
gladd to heare of your good recovery, and it is noe small cordiall unto
my wife that God is pleased to use her as an instrument of conveighing
any comfort unto you. She will by my brother send you word how the
salve is to bee used. I am much bound unto you that you are pleased
to accept in good part my poore desires of your hapines. I know you
are fare better able to advise your selfe, yet my love inforceth me in all
things to advance your good and espetialy in that which is most
permanent, for in comparison there of all other things are not to be
named; therefore Doctor Sibbs[2] taught us well this weeke to advise
seriously with ourselves what is that thing that our hartes doe desire,
and if upon triall wee find not our hartes doe desire, and if upon triall
wee find not our hartes willing to part with all to purchase that priceles
pearle in the gospell, he could not assure us of any comfort of our
estate. This lesson he did with much ernestnes presse upon us. But my
paper puts mee in mind to end, so committing you to God's holy
protection I rest your dutifull sonne

                G. Gerard

19 September, 1631

   [1] The arrival of the ambassador was reported (more politely) by Pory in his letter to
Puckering of 8 Sept. Birch, ii. 127.
   [2] Richard Sibbes was still preacher at Grays Inn at this time. *D.N.B.*

Endorsed (*f. 291b*): To my honourable good mother the Lady Johan
Barrington at Hatfield these be given

199   *Sir William Masham, n.d., [3 October 1631]*   (*2645, f. 315*)

Deare mother   As your sadnisse hath bene a greate greife to us,
so we are glad of any good occasion to cheare you up, which is the best
newes that came this many daye to England and I have sent it
hereinclosed. It came post from Prauge to the kinge and is generally
reported to be true.[1] I sent it you this daye being a fit daye to rejoice
in the workes of God, amongst which the deliverance of his church is
an espetiall worke. The last newes was that Tillye had made great
spoyle in Saxony, wherby he intended to diverte the kinge of Swede
and the duke of Saxony from falling upon Bavaria, which now I hope
theye will when theye have freed Saxony of Tillye's forces. Thus we
see man's extremity is God's oportunitye. I praye acquainte my brother Barrington with this inclosed and give him thanks for the paper
he sent me. If he can, I would intreat him to leave with you the
presentment of the grand jury this last assises touching purv[e]yance
and the copye of the last commission and instruction touching knighthood;[2] I will returne them safe to him againe. So, with our humble
dutyes and prayers for your health and comfort, I committ you to the
God of consolation, and rest
        Your obliged   William Masham

We hope to see you shortly, in the meane tyme I praye be merry.

Endorsed (*f. 316b*): To my much honoured mother the lady Barrington
these be given

200   *Sir Gilbert Gerard, 10 October 1631*   (*2645, f. 297*)

Good Madam   I purposed this day to have sent my boy unto
you to see you and to bring us newes how your ladyship and your little
remaining company doe, but this bearer having a purpose to tender
his service unto you I shall spare my boy untill another time. I was
sory to persceive by your last letter that after your freedome from the

[1] 'A letter newly received from Prague' is announced in the news book for 3 Oct.
1631. Dahl, 240.
[2] The collection of knighthood fines had been proceeding during the summer of 1631.
Gardiner, vii. 167; see also letter 182.

goute you have some other affliction befalne you, but I hope by this time yow are freed from it or find it swete unto you, for although noe affliction be for the present pleasing, yet all God's children have ever found them of great use, and have found more good in them then in all the pleasures of this world, otherwise God would not make them the portion of his dearest children. They be God's rodds to drive into way when we erre, and to weane us from the world which we all love to well. And if Christ our head had his part we that [are] his members cannot escape; they be the meanes to cause us to looke into our waies, and most needfull in these times when it is a rare thing to meete with any that loves us so well as to tell us wherein wee doe amisse. I doubt not good madam of your experience heerin. I pray God to sanctifie all his dealing with you. So in hast I humbly rest

   Your dutefull sonne   G. Gerard

10 October, 1631

Endorsed (*f. 298b*): To my honourable good mother the Lady Johan Barrington these be given

201 *Sir Thomas Barrington, 12 October 1631*   (*2645, f. 299*)

Madame   My Lord of Warwick his present occasions doe instantly importune him to use the hand of his freind for the payment of som monyes whare he is very unwilling his honor showld be questioned in publique and as unwilling to use any straunger for the procureing thareof. You know my bond and word unto yow tyes me to doe nothing in this kind with out your knowledg and allowance.[1] If yow shall be therefor pleased to give way heearunto, and by this bearer's retourne to signify your pleasuer, I doe assure yow it will much accomodate my lord. And yow shall see that my counter securytye is so honorable and full as that there is no possibillytye of prejudice to accru to me by it or to myne, neither doth my lord intend to be indepted to any man beyond midsomer next, when my young lord willbe of age. Thus in great haste I comit you to God and rest

   Your most dewtyfull and loving sonn

            Thomas Barrington

London, October 12, 1631

---

[1] Sir Thomas's promise to his mother 'not to be bounde with any man' was well remembered; it was quoted by his steward John Kendal in a law suit in 1646, two years after Sir Thomas died. E.R.O., D/DBa L34.

My lord makes over his personall estate unto me for securytye, but it must not be knowen to anyone.

Endorsed (*f. 300b*): To my honourable good mother the Lady Johan Barrington give [these] at Hatfield

202   *Robert, Earl of Warwick,*[1] *n.d.,* [*October 1631*]   (*2645, f. 301*)

Good madame   I have desired a curtesy of your son my cousin, wherin I pray you beleeve so well of me I would not for a world doe it that he might receive the least prejudice, for I will amply secuer him. Neyther would I desier it but with your consent. You know me so well as I hope I shall easily obtaine it, I will only tell you I love you and all yours and will ever rest
        Your faithfull frend to serve you   Warwick

Endorsed (*f. 302b*): To my worthy cousin my Lady Barrington at Hatfild

203   *Sir Gilbert Gerard, 13 October 1631*   (*2645, f. 305*)

Good madam   I must begg your pardon for a fault which I have made against my will. The last night while wee were at praiers this inclosed letter was brought unto mee, I, never looking on the superscription, did open it and found by the contents it was to you, which being as they are I am not sorry that I have opened it, because it may a little trouble you. My cozen Brewster being with mee, wee two have considered what wilbe best for you to doe and we thinke you shall doe well to send Toby unto him and lett him know that although, as you are executrix unto your husband he may sue you upon his bond, yet he should not doe well in so doing because you have noe interest in the house, the lease whereof went unto your sone's wife as executrix unto her husband,[2] and shee either yet continues his tenant or hath put him in a man that is suffitient to doe it, and therfore he shall not need to trouble you, which if he doe you must bee forced to fly into the chancery for releefe and sue both him, your daughter and the present

---

[1] Robert Rich, 2nd Earl of Warwick, the leader of the opposition group in Essex in the 1630s, parliamentary admiral in the civil war. There was a long association between the Riches and the Barringtons. *D.N.B.*; Introduction, 1, 4, 8.

[2] This can be presumed to refer to the wife of Lady Joan's son Francis. Lady Joan's will, made in 1641, includes a bequest to Francis, the son of her dead son Francis Barrington. P.R.O., P.C.C. wills, 151 Evelyn; letter 136.

tenant, and you doubt not but my Lord Keeper in this case will releeve you, which I thinke he will doe. But in this case relie not on my advise, but send unto my nephew St John who can informe you what is fittest to bee done. You may likewise send unto the tenant to wish him to repaire the house, and you may send unto Higham to know what securitie he hath from the tenant for the paiment of the rent and reparations, but I suspect it may be there plott to cause the landlord to wright this letter unto you to see what they can gett from you. Madam, if in this or any thing other I may serve you I wilbe readie to doe what you direct, upon warrant from you, if you send unto mee. I purpose God willing to be at London on Friday and at my nephew St John's you shall heere of mee. God keepe you ever,

      Your dutifull sonne   G. Gerard

13 Octobre, 1631

Endorsed (*f. 306b*): To my honourable good mother the Lady Johan Barrington at Hatfield these be given

204   *Sir Francis Harris*, [*October? 1631*]   (*2645, f. 331*)

My honored aunte   My noble cosin Sir William Mewx was not a lytle glad to heere of your ladyship's good healthe and his dawfter her hope of recoverie,[1] and please God, as by the inclosed[2] I conceive will appeare. He entertayned my propositione for my alye his sonne and daufter very kindlye, and will the next weeke or the weeke following, by God's grace, come to London and so to yow, to give a fatherly assistance for the preferment of them, professing nothing in this worlde cane joye him more then to see them well bestowed in marryage. And for your grandchilde his sonne, he seconded his command to him by me by his letter, that he should not sturre from his uncle Sir Thomas Barrington any wheather, but to be gided and rewled by him, which I trust he will most gladly (and like a respective nephew) imbrace. I have sent yow madam (because I harde yow once saye yow loved forryne newes) a new boke, and could Mr Scott have stayed but an ower longer yow had received likewise the weekely currant, but if it please yow to command Pinchesone to calle at Mr Goodyer's next weeke, yow shall have such newes as is sturring, and

---

[1] The account book has payments for an apothecary's bill for Joan Meux and for women to care for her over some weeks on 19 Oct. and 23 Nov. E.R.O., D/DBa A15, ff.21b, 23, 23b.

[2] Letter 205.

so contynew to send unto yow, weekely, unles I receive contradictione. Thus with my best wishes for the contynewance of your ladyship's helthe and happynes, I humbly rest, your ladyship's ever to dispose of
Francis Herris

From Mr Charneck's my lodgeing in Grayes In Lane, neere the gate, my Lord Mayor's daye, 1631

Endorsed (*f. 332b*): To the honourable ladie my honored aunt the Ladie Barrington these

205   *Sir William Meux, 20 October 1631*   (*2645, f. 307*)

Madam   I have received yowr letters by Sir Francis Harris, wherein appeareth yowr greate care and love to my daughter, of whoes recovery (thancks be unto the author of all helth and good) I perswade my self there is good hopes. My prayers shall not be wanting for the restoring her to perfect helth, and my endevors shall be to the uttermost to give her contentment. I intend to be with yow (God willing) about the feast of All Saints, when I shall express my self further by God's assistance. In the meane time I leave yow to the allmighty and rest yowr assured loving son
William Meux

Kingston the xxth of October, 1631
Concerning the business Sir Francis Harris hath propounded, I must take som time to consider.
I am soe much bound unto yow for your many favor as that I know not how to make a sufficient acknowledgment.

Endorsed (*f. 308b*): To my honorable mother the Lady Barrington att Hattfeilde give these

206   *Sir Thomas Barrington, n.d., [October 1631]*   (*2650, f. 192*)

Madame   Yow see I have obayed your commaund in takeing Mr Rogers along with me, hopeing that it hath not putt any inconvenience upon yow; neither was it in my thoughts to take him of my selfe before I was mooved on his behalfe, but I have as soone as I retourned from the Wight sent him to wayte upon yow, hopeing that he shall find yow in as good health as I desyre, recovered of your sadnes, which I wish had not ben so indiscreetly occasioned; and in truth I well may wish it, for upon my honest word that busines was not digested with me under 3 dayes travell, for which time my spleane perplexed me intill I sett it in tune againe, I thanke God, so that I now see that the best way to have a comfortable life is both for yow and me to be where we may lead a life in quiet and where we lye not under the eye of malignancye. I thanke God I can and doe desyre my freinds advices, but thare is an envyous aspect and an indevor to deprave that nothing but reproch can satisfye; I desyre to heear of any fault, but doe not desyre to live where people search and hunt after faults, but my hart goes with yours and my desyres are constant to enjoy yow with me whatsoever I beare and wheresoever, I thanke God. [*f. 191b*] My wife and I tender owr dewtyes and harty prayers for your good health, and will expedite owr retourne unto yow as soone as we with any possible convenience can in respect of owr busines, which will of necessyty stay us a while by the way in London, being first allso in respect unto owr good brother Wallop, owr nephew and neices, to spend som time heear with them, but desyre yow to conster us aright, as we are confident yow will. We have a charge to present my brother Sir H. Wallop[1] his love to yow and the service and thankes of all my neices for yowr kind respect and love to them. And thus I comit us all to God and remayne faythfully

   Your most obedient and loving sonn Thomas Barrington

My love and my wive's to owr brothers and sisters, with Mr Harrison and all that love us hartyly.

Endorsed (*f. 192b*): To my much respected and honourable good mother the Lady Johanna Barrington give [these] at Hatfeild Broad-oke in Essex

207 *Lady Judith Barrington, 21 October* [*1631*]   (*2650, f. 160*)

Madam Whear I owe so much unfained respects my thinks my husband's letter cannot say enough for me without some few expressions of my owen. I am full fraught with large relations of our traveiles, wherin we have been merchant venturers, but it wilbe to teadious for a letter. On Thursday next we are resolved to resist all inportunities heer (which think a week's stay to litle a time for 4 year's absence)

---

[1] Sir Henry Wallop, of Farleigh Wallop, Hampshire, was Lady Judith Barrington's brother-in-law. In 1632 his daughter Bridget married Sir Henry Worsley of Appeldur-combe in the Isle of Wight. Wallop was later a member of the Long Parliament and his son one of the regicides. Keeler, 376–8.

and intend to be for London for a week, in which time I hope what I can doe with my Lady Weston wilbe effected, and with my Lady Worsley, who stayed a week longer in the country to have seen me then her great affaires at coort aboute the haven could well permitt, and so the second day after I came into the Island she was constrained to goe for London. I begin to think I [*f. 160b*] longe now untell I am with you againe, that I may rejoyce as well at the sight as now at the news that you are so well that you come into the parlor againe. My prayers shall not be behinde anies that you may longe to all our comforts enjoye your health. And so desiring if you have any service to command me whilst I am in London that I may next week heer from you at Mrs Necton's whear we intend God willing the later end of the week, I humbly take my leave ever resting

Your faithfully loving daughter ever to command

Judith Barrington

Farly, this 21 of October

Be pleased to receave all my neece's, your daughter's and Sir Henri's and my nephew Meux services, and I desire to have mine to my sister Masham, my sister Everett, my sister Lamplugh, my neece Meux and my neece Jug Gerett.

Endorsed (*f. 161b*): To the honorable and my most respected mother the Lady Barrington this at Hatfeld

208 *Sir Gilbert Gerard, 25 October* [*1631*] (*2650, f. 247*)

Good madam   You shall by this bearer heare that your sonne and daughter are safly come back unto Farly, and by him I must likewise returne you many thankes for your kind intreatie at my late being with you, and espetialy that you were plesed to give me leave to speake freely unto you in that busines whereof wee had so much conference. Good madam, as I wished you then, so againe lett mee earnestly intreate you to bee advised by those that love you best. I know you are wise, yet in businesse that concernes our owne particulars wee are all to seeke, and madam this now is noe privat thing, and except you shew your selfe to be well satisfied and to thinke that there was cause of complaint, it wilbe an occation to make others more bitter, and what inconveniencie may come thereof you cannot foresee. The more it spreades the more it will grieve good people and the more scandall will grow thereby, and there wilbe some that are noe friendes unto religion wilbe readie upon this occation to taxe all religious people as the sensorius ones. Therefore I beseech you good madam, as you desire to avoid scandall, as you desire to advance the gospell, stopp this inconvenience. It shalbe your glory to passe by offences, and as you have hitherto laboured to further religion, suffer no disgrace as neare as you can to fall upon the meanest of God's children, although he have sliped yet assure your selfe it was in love. I will conclude as your selfe did when I left you, consult, advise and give sentence, and the God of Heven direct you in it,

   Your dutifull sonne   G.G.

25 October

Endorsed (*f. 248b*): To my honourable good mother the Lady Johan Barrington these at Hatfield

209 *Sir William Masham, 28 October 1631*   (*2645, f. 309*)

Madame   Your late renewed favors challenge no lesse from me then a renewinge of all thanks unto you to whom I owe more then my selfe; and the more I strive to paye this debt still the more I ame obliged in dutye, which cannot be expressed better then in my faythfull respects to your soule in promotinge your spirituall good, which is most deare unto me. It is the common faulte of frends to prefere the outward before the inward man, but it is my desire and prayer (with St John's for [Gazer]) that you maye prosper as your soule prospers: the soule's health is the foundation, and therfore must needs be the proportion, of the bodye's health. The soule beinge the more excellent, our care must excell for that more noble parte; and as it hath beene my desier, so lately my indeviour in my free expressions touchinge that late passage, wherein I doubt not but as you approve your harte to God, so you desire the approbation of good men; and what lyes in me shall not be wantinge in this as in all other occasions. Your kind intertaynment of faythfull councellors (which I was glad to see) makes waye for this; and you cannot doe better then to follow the advise of that faythfull frend we left with you, which maye save me labor in that kinde at this tyme. [*f. 309b*] The forraine newes continues still very good: that the kinge of Sueede hath defeated Attringer and Fuger's[1] armye and hath slayne most of them, which if it be true, the Emperor hath no army left in Germanye.[2] And the kinge of Swede

---

[1] Johann von Aldringen, imperial general, and Otto von Fugger.

[2] An inaccurate account of the battle of Breitenfeld was given in the newsbook of 20 Oct. The next newsbook did not appear until 29 Oct. More details of the battle are given in the succeeding letters. Dahl, pp. 182–3.

hath taken in againe Wirt[e]mbergh, which revolted, and divers other free cityes and states and hath layed great somes upon them for the mayntaynance of his armye. And it is reported that Rosticke[1] in Pomerania is taken by the king of Sweden's forces, so that now the emperor hath no footing there. It is thought now the kinge intends Bavaria, which his soldiers long for and call for, seing a rich country and unfortefyed, the duke presuming much formerly upon his Tillye. We have noe domesticke newes, only some whispers a Parliament. When the booke of newes comes forth I will send it you; as yet I cannot heare of any this weeke. So with remembrance of my humble dutye to you and of you to God in my dayly prayers, I commit you to the safe preserver of Israell, and rest

      Yours obliged in all dutye   William Masham

London, October 28, 1631
I pray remember me to all my frends with you. My sonne St John and daughter are well and present there dutyes to you.

Endorsed (*f. 310b*): To my much honoured mother the ladye Barrington these be given

210   *Oliver St. John, n.d., [28? October 1631]*   (*2645, f. 311*)

Most honoured Madam   Your servant Tobie was with us this morning, by whome I heare your feared trowble concerning your London howse is like to be blowne over. Sir Edward Altham hath put in his answere to my bill with all those falce imputacions uppon Sir Francis Barrington which when time comes I hope to cleare and to vindicate his unspotted sinceritie.[2] We are all heare, praysed be God, in good health and should be impaciente of my Lady Masham's being from us if she weare not with your ladyship in your presente eb of companie. The news your ladyship hath heard of Tillie's defeate and death is true; some popish newsmungers would have him yet alive,[3] which falls out to be his nephew, but he is deade. Mr. Noy[4] of our howse is king's atturny, the last atturny cheife justice of the comon pleas, and the chief justice of the comon pleas is removed to the king's

---

[1] The taking of Rostock (by Tott on 6 Sept.) was reported by Beaulieu in a letter of 2 Nov. Birch, ii. 138; Roberts, ii. 517.

[2] See letter 168.

[3] *Cf.* Gresley to Puckering, 27 Oct.: 'our papists will not by any means believe that Tilly is dead'. Birch, ii. 138.

[4] William Noye was appointed attorney general, 27 Oct. 1631. *D.N.B.*

bench. And with my owne and my wives most unfayned service and-dutie, I rest

        Your servant to my poore power   Oliver St. John

Endorsed (*f. 312b*): To the honourable lady the Lady Barrington the elder att Hatfeilde Broadoke these

211   *Sir William Masham, n.d.,* [*October/November 1631*]   (*2645, f. 325*)

Deare mother   I must give you great thanks for your greate care of my wife in my absence; this reciprocation of love is a great confirmation therof and incryment of our dutifull affections to you. I cannot requit your love better then by relation of our occurrents here, which is only a confirmation of the former good newes in the mayne overthrow by one Mr Casuell whoe brought a letter to our kinge from the kinge of Sweeden on sabbath night last, which it seemes was pleasinge newes to him, for he knighted him presentlye.[1] He came from the king's campe seaven dayes after the battell wherein he served, and sayes that then Tillye was not deade but mortally wounded, as appeared by the confession of one of his surgions that was then taken prisoner, and relates that Tyllye himself was overtaken prisoner and held so for 3 houres, though unknowne, but rescued againe by 6 of his gard that had an eye after him. It maye be by this tyme he is deade or taken, the kinge pursuing so hard after him; howsoever he is not like to make any opposition this yeare. I have sent you here inclosed the currant, which I would have sent the last weeke if I could have got it before Pinchine went away, but it seemes it came out after his departure.

It was reported that Sir George Lamplugh was deade,[2] but Mr Tyffine tells me he was lately well and is gon after Mr Vauhan into Ireland who hath deceived him (as he sayd) of a horse. Mr Tyffine is desirous to deale with my sister for her joynture and therfore I cannot put any great confidence in his relation. It were good the truth were [known]; I will learne what I can. So, with my humble dutye and love to all my frends with you, I commit you to the safe preserver of Israell and rest your obliged

        William Masham

---

[1] The arrival and knighting of Caswell on Sunday 30 Oct. 1631 was reported in a letter of 2 Nov. Details of the news that he brought were published in the coranto of 9 Nov. Birch, ii. 138; Dahl, 245.

[2] See letters 180, 181, 184.

My sonne St John and daughter present theyre dutyes to you.

Endorsed (*f. 326b*): To my much honoured ladye and mother the Ladye Barrington these be given

212 *Robert Barrington, n.d., [5 November 1631]* (*2645, f. 321*)

Madam   Intending to come home this weeke, and being prevented by busines, I have made bould to acquainte you with that litle newes that I heare, which it may be also you may have had from the handes of some other. Yesterday morneing, very early, the queene was delivered of a daughter which was presently christned; we had both bells and bonfires for joy.[1] I heare that the childe is weake, sure it is the queene comes before hir tyme, for I heard certeynly the nurse was not provided. I have not tyme this morneing to enquire the certeynty. Heere is arrived at court the duke of Vendome, who is the king of France his base brother. He hath ben all this summer in the Low Countryes with the Prince of Orringe. The certeyntie of the newes concerning the king of Sweden came to court but this day seanight by a gentleman who was sent from the king to our king with letters.[2] In breife, Tilly sent two messages to the king dareing him to fight, but he returned this answer: tell that ould dog that he shall not appointe me when to fight, but I will make him fight when I see cause. But it seemes that Tilly drew all his forces into the feild and tooke both the advante of winde and of a hill, yet the king was resolved to fight with him especially knowing that there were other forces redy to joyne with him. The duke of Saxon and the king brought up both their armies together, the one on one hand the other on the other. But after some houre fight, the battle grew so hot that the duke with his forces ran quite out of the feild and was not seen in 2 dayes after. The king being thus lefte made good the fight and he and Tillye's army came soe neere that they were within pistoll shott. Being soe neere, upon the word given by the king his musketeirs all kneeled downe and laid their musketts upon each others shoulders and soe shott of on a sudden so many shott that they made a greate slaughter and the king with his horse soe seconded it that Tilly was routed and his whole army slaughtered. The next day the king with his horse brought in 4000 prisoners. The 3rd day he made to Hall after Tilly, who was not [*f. 321b*] to be found, but his surgeon said he was desperately wounded.

[1] Princess Mary, born at St. James's in the early hours of Friday 4 Nov. 1631 and baptized later that day by William Laud, bishop of London. *D.N.B.*
[2] See leter 211, n.1.

The most certeyne report is that he is liveing and about the rayseing of an armie; he lost 30,000 men. The king is now I beleeve within a few miles of the Palatinate; he hath sent to the king to desire him to aide his brother and sister and he will by Gode's help rediliver their inheritance to them. The gentleman who brought the newes was knighted. Thus in extreame hast, being to goe to church, I must desire you wilbe pleased to pardon my abrupt conclusion, and soe, committing you to the Lord, I rest

      Your most dutifull sonn   Robert Barrington

I beseech you excuse me to my wife by your letter, for truly I have no tyme. I stay in towne and doe not goe to Harrow as I intended. Winchester removes to Yorke certeynly, and Morton to Durram, Durram to Winchester.[1] Bangor is dead and the doctor at Hakney[2] hath his place. London removes not.

I cannot but desire both you and all Gode's people to observe the wonderfull deliverance which the Lord wrought for his church in that great victory, for wheras we heard what advantage the king of Sweden had by the winde and by a strategem of powder, there was no such thing, for Tilly had all manner of advantages, especially when Saxon was fled; and it's certeyne the king had of his 20,000 men but 8000 that did him any service to purpose, and by them was the victory wrought. The Lord shewes us that we should not trust in meanes but in him, to him therfore let us returne the honor of the day.

[*In margin*] I beseech you pardon all slipps for I cannot reade over my letter.

Endorsed (*f. 322b*): To my honourable good mother the Lady Johan Barrington at Hatfeild Broadoke these

213   *Lady Judith Barrington, n.d.*, [*5 November 1631*]   (*2645, f. 319*)

Madam   I have onely time to thank you for the favour of your lines which welcomed me to London as I lighted. We came late, our horses tyred, and your sonne gone by 6 a clock this morning to the coort to some lords, being the first of 3 in the bill for sheriff. We ware secure that our intended parly with my lord tresurer would have for this time delayed itt, but I heer he is not our frend in itt. Sir Henry

---

[1] See letter 186, n.2.

[2] David Dolben, not formally elected to the bishopric of Bangor until 18 Nov. *D.N.B.*

Appleton and my brother Masham are the others.[1] We had great bon fyers and ringing last night for the queen's deliverance of a daughter the night before aboute 2 of the clock being at 11 at a playe, and yesterday morne it was christened, being weak. The queen's base brother, the Duke of Vandome, is come; a brave gentleman, he hath brought the remainder of the queen's portion, being 150,000ˡⁱ. It's doubted Tilly is not dead, but the victory is great. The earle of Midlesex is called upon now for his fine layed on him at his fall, which he had promise at that time to be forgiven, it's 80,000ˡⁱ; it seems it's longe of some disgracefull words he lately cast out upon the duke's memory.[2] I must not only beg pardon for your sonne's not writing now, but for my owen hasty scribbling: the porter stayeth. My brother Meux is at Harrow, come of purpose aboute his daughter business, liking the propositions heatherto. [f. 319b] Sir Henry,[3] my nephew and neece Anne are come to London with us, who all remember thear service to you; you guess at thear jorney. When that business is somewhat setled I shall think longe to waite upon you, which I guess wilbe at the late end of next week or the begining of that following; in the mean while I shalbe happy in any of your imployments. And soe with all affectionate service to you, my sister Masham, my sister Lamplugh, who I thank for her care of Lucy, I rest

   Your most respectively lovinge daughter

               Judith Barrington

Saterday
I have made bould to send you the book of news. Your 2 daughters tendor thear best services to you.

Endorsed (f. 320b): To my much honored mother the Lady Barrington at [*cut away*]

214 *Sir William Masham, n.d., [5/6 November 1631]* (*2645, f. 317*)

Madame   I cannot let passe this bearer without some advisoes, though but litle hath happened since my last: only the kinge of

---

[1] Sir Henry Appleton of South Benfleet, Essex. Lady Judith had written to Dorchester (an undated letter) of her fears that her husband might be nominated for sheriff, attributing the danger to 'unfriendly neighbours' taking advantage of his neglect of public business. P.R.O., S.P. 16/205/83; Introduction, 10.

[2] The crown did not reopen enquiries into Cranfield's gains as a minister until 1632, although he brought a suit against the heirs of Buckingham in 1631. M. Prestwich, *Cranfield* (Oxford, 1966), 493–4, 497.

[3] Sir Henry Wallop. Letters 206, 214.

Sueeden still proceeds prosperously in the prosecution of his victorye, having taken Francford an emperiall toune (as is reported) a place of great consequence and within 2 dayes jornye of the Palatinate, which it seemes now he maynly intends after the suppressinge of Attringer and Fuger's forces and those of Lurronie[1] wherof 7 or 8 companye he hath lately cut of, and I hope by this hath met with the rest, which he labors to hinder from joyning with those other of Attringer and Fuger. We heare no certaine newes of Tyllye, it is like theye will conceale his death if he be deade. The papists reporte that he is 50,000 stronge and that the emperor hath the kinge of Sweden in a trapp, beinge in the harte of Germanye. I perseive now he is master of the feild he can safely make his waye out. I hope by this you have reade his letter which I trust will worke well. I gave my sonne St John the copye, and intended to send it you by this bearer if he had not prevented me. The duke Vendoma, the queene's brother, is come over to visit her; and this Fridaye morninge she was delivered of a daughter, a fortnight (as some saye) before her tyme. The child beinge weake was christened Mary presently. My brother and I stand still in the bill of 3 and Sir Henrye Apleton with us; wee shall not know who wilbe sherife till sabbath be past. So with my humble service to you and best love to my sister Lamplug and the rest of my frends with you, not forgetting you in my dayly prayers as I desire to be remembred of you, I commit you to the good blessing of God and rest

      Your obliged   William Masham

It is reported that the Duke of Bavaria hath made a leauge of offensive and defensive against the house of Austria.

My brother Barrington came to London this Fridaye night, with Sir Henry Wallope and a great companye.

The booke of newes is not yet come forth for this weeke.

Endorsed (f. 318b): To my much honoured mother the Lady Barrington these be given

215 *Sir Thomas Barrington, n.d.,* [*7 November 1631*]   (*2645, f. 323*)

Madame   My wife and I in one joynct petition humbly beseich

---

[1] Perhaps Charles of Lorraine, who in Sept. was marching to join Tilly, is meant (Masham's writing, as ever, is far from clear). Aldringen's and Lorraine's forces were jointly the subject of a report in the newsbook of 10 Nov. Roberts, ii. 548; Dahl, 246.

yow not to thinke that we either make busines, stay upon slight occasions, or defer owr coming to yow longer then of necessytye we must, and withall intreate yow to be comfortable unto your selfe and to have either my sister Masham, sister Everard, or som cheearfull body with yow. I know yow by my selfe, for allthough I desyre not to [be] unacquainted with private and inward sorrowes of spirit, which end in joyes inexpressive, yet God keepe me from those unnecessary sadnesses of mind and disquiets of hart which make me for my part unfitt for all dewtyes to God, man and my selfe. I speake my cleear thoughts; had I not taken my journy when I did, to carry me from the inquisition of owr examiners and from the dej[e]ctednes that the continewall renewing thereof did urge upon me, I was in a fayre (or fowle) way to a dangerous feaver, and so ill was I that I protest I durst not have taken a journy had not my judgment tould me that [*f. 323b*] I had no other outward meanes left to preserve my selfe. And God, I thanke him, vouchsafed me the good effects of my health, which did dayly and sensibly accompany me in my voyage, I prayse God. I say no more untill I waite upon yow of this, but in truth, in truth, somewhat must be don to alter the miserable condition of distraction that we are falling into thare, or else we must begg of yow to attend yow else where and perswade yow that we may in[j]oye some little comfort else whare. For in owr present condition we are worse then the poorest servant, since all owr actions are more by so much inquired into, and that with so eager desyres and solicitous indevors, to find out faults and to lay upon us blames.[1]

But my passionate apprehension of theise mischifes makes me all-together forget my selfe; God guide us aright, I [*f. 324*] pray God. The newes of the toune is of a parliament, but not beleived yet. Swede prospers, God be praysed; the Lord Craven is goeing over with 300 of his owne charge and 1000 for the king of Sweden. In Fraunce things goe ill still in relation to the king and Monsieur but well for Swede and God's church, for the emperor sent 200 of the Lorainers to Mounsieur whom Mounsieur Le Force [has] put to the sword, so that the French king, who intended to have ayded the duke of Baveir against the Swede, is now as ernest against the emperor, so that he is in a greate straight now. The report is that Tilly hath recovered 30,000 again, but such as are fresh and rawe and unexercised men. I for my part escaped this yeear's office very narrowly, coming to towne but one day before the pricking and being first in the bill, but I prayse God my Lord Chamberlain, my Lord Holland and my Lord Dor-

---

[1] *Cf.* Masham's comments to Lady Joan 'I praye be merry' (letter 199) and on her 'kind intertaynment of faythfull councellors' (209) in Oct.

chester did express a greate deale of particular love to me.[1] I am called
to diner and my paper put of the table to give place to meate; I
therefor comit us all to God, with my blessing, and his to all myne;
and I shall ever be your ladyship's most dewtyfull and loving sonn
            Thomas Barrington

Endorsed (*f. 324b*): To the honourable my very good mother the Lady
Joane Barrington at Hatfeild Broadoke give [these]

216   *Sir William Masham, n.d.*, [*November 1631*]   (*2645, f. 313*)

Madame   I hope you received my last by Mr. Carpenter; we
have litle newes since, only this (which is very good if true), that
Papenhaime that went to releive Magdenburgh[2] is slayne and his
forces cut off, so that now for certaine the citye is taken, which is of
great consequence to the King of Swede because it commands the
Oder in those partes. It is reported that the kinge of France wilbe
seperated from his queen upon a nullitye, and that the king and his
greate favorite the cardinall are very sicke. Since his peecing with the
kinge of Sweede ther is some suspition of some ill measure towards
them. The kinge of Sweede's forces are dayly augmented, and he
together with the protestant princes wilbe able to bring 100,000 into
the feild the next springe. My lord Rich is come out of France and he
sayd the kinge and cardinall are well and that the kinge of Spayne
will make Mounsier generall of his great armye, which I can hardly
beleeve. I have sent you this week's curranto and I hope the next will
make things more certaine. So, with our dutyes and thanks for your
kind letters, I rest your obliged
            William Masham

I pray present our services to my sisters and loves to all.

[1] Sir John Mead, a minor gentleman, served as sheriff of Essex for 1631-2. By 9 Nov.
it was reported that the king was angry 'that the best men in the shires be not put into
the bill'. The rumour of a parliament has particular significance, for as well as undertaking onerous duties, particularly in collecting taxation, a sheriff could not sit in
parliament during his term of office. E.R.O., Q/SR 277; Colvin, 183; Birch, ii. 140.

[2] The newsbook of 19 Nov. 1631 reported Swedish moves against Magdeburg. Pappenheim broke through the Swedish blockage and relieved the town on 4 Jan. 1632. He
was not killed until the battle of Lützen, in Nov. 1632. The alliance between Sweden and
France, negotiated by Richelieu, had been concluded at the treaty of Bärwalde, Jan.
1631. Dahl, 247; Roberts, ii. 690, 768.

Endorsed (f. 314b): To my much honoured mother the Lady Barrington these be given Hatfeild

217   *Sir John Luke*[1] *to Lady Judith Barrington, 22 November 1631*
(2645, f. 333)

Honorable lady   Since I was last with you I have much pondered of the busines that I was bold to treat with your ladyshipp concerninge my sonn Sanders, and I have not lost time as opportunitie could fitt but to deale with my sonne, whoe I find very willinge to obtaine your ladyshippe's favor and love and not to have any varience or contention with you, and the rather that such truely is his meaninge he with all his hart desires that you should have the benefite of the tieth of his grownd before any other whosoever, and therefore to prevent all futer differences he offers to geve your ladyshipp twentie poundes a yeare for the corne tieth of all kindes and will pay me iiij[li] a yeare duringe my lease for the privie tiethes. And truely madam I thinke ther is no man will geve more, nay scarce soe much. I am hartely glad he hath made so faire an offer, and if it please you good madam to accept of this (as I hope you will) I shall take a great deale of joy and comfort in it, and wilbe very thankfull unto you for it whensoever it shall please God we meete againe. And I hope you shall herein doe your sonn a great good (that if it please God he comes to enjoy it and live a neare neighbour); it will be a great meanes to encrease and unite a great deale of love betwixt them, all which I hartely desire out of a reall affection, and it shalbe alwaies my sincere prayers unto almighty to blesse the same, they ar soe neare and deare unto me. In this cloze of my letter I make it my humble suite that in your favour I may soe prevaile as you wilbe pleased to accept of this offer, and I shall account it as a great favor done to me. And soe remembringe my humble and respective service to you and your noble knight, I committ us to the protection of the almightie and remaine
Your ever true affected servant   John Luke

Flamsteed xxij[th] of November, 1631
My wief praies me to present hir service to Sir Thomas Barrington and your noble self with hir due respectes to mistris Jeane Lytton and myne not to be forgotten.

Endorsed (f. 334b): To the honorable my deare frend the Lady Judith

[1] See letters 158, 159.

Barrington at Mr Necton's house in Aldersgate Street present these with respect

[*In the hand of Lady Judith Barrington:*] 1631, Sir John Luke's letter of offringe 24¹ a yeer rent for Beechwood tythe

218   *Sir William Masham, 26 November 1631*   *(2645, f. 335)*

Madame   I ame sorrye my cold would not suffer me to visite you this daye, we have therfore sent this bearer to bringe us good tidinges of your good health, and to let you know some ill of my wife, who was yonge with child and hath mis carryed this daye. It is the greater greife to us, having bene thus longe without; I praye God sanctefye this affliction to us, and prepare us by this for greater. It is his mercye that he hath given us any children, and that he hath continued them unto us with his blessing upon them. We knowe not the cause of this, unlesse it were her last jornye to Hatfeild, and yet she was very well since, only some what ill of her throate. So craving your good prayers for us and good use of all, with our humble dutyes, I commit you to God and rest
      Your obedient sonne   William Masham

Otes, November 26, 1631
My wife is now some what better then she was. I praye let me know by this bearer when my brother Barrington returnes. We will send for my cosine Gouge when we can with any conveniencye, being sorrye she proves not fit for that service which we much desired.

Endorsed (f. 336b): To my much honoured mother the Lady Barrington

219   *Sir Gilbert Gerard, 28 November 1631*   *(2645, f. 339)*

Good madam   At my being in London this last weeke I understood that Doctor Twist hath accepted that my Lord of Warwicke's living lately falen in Northamtonsheire, and my lord hath used meanes to procure Doctor Twist's living at Newbery for Mr Wright his chaplin, which if he doe Mr Wright's living wilbe in his dispose, which is at

Banson not farre from you.[1] I heare the value of it is about a hundred pounds by the yeare. I presume my cozen Hooke would not exchange for that and leave Clatford because Clatford is better, but if your ladiship have so good an opinion of this bearer as to move my lord to bestow Mr Wright's living upon one that you shall commend unto him, in performance of his promise unto you, if I am not much mistaken in the man I doubt not but if my lord bestow it upon him he shall find him both an honest man and a learned and a wise man, and that both my lord and the people shall have much cause to give you thankes for him. Now madam, because it is uncertaine whither my lord may have alreadie disposed of it, if you please to wright I thinke you should doe well to conseale his name untill you know my lorde's pleasure, and to wright only that you will nominate unto him a worthy man and such a one as his lordship shall well aprove of. Madame I doe not this because I am weary of Mr Sudbry, for I expect not such another, but I thinke him an able and fitt man to doe good service in his church, and I shall ever preferre the publique good of the church before my owne private, and I doubt not but if my lord have not alredie disposed of it he will performe his promise unto you, and the rather in regard of the last curtesy you did him. And if this be gone, you shall at least procure a promise of the next that shall fall, and have it in wrighting. Thus not doubting of your redines to doe so good a worke, and somewhat the rather at my request, I committ you and the issue of this busines unto the wise disposing of the almighty and will ever rest

Your dutifull sonne   Gilbert Gerrard

Flambards, 28 November, 1631

[1] William Twisse was recalled from Heidelberg, where in 1613 he was chaplain to Elizabeth of Bohemia, and became rector of Newbury in 1620. He eventually decided not to accept Warwick's offer, which was of the living of Benefield in Northamptonshire. William Wright was rector of Benefield 1632–1658. However, Sir Gilbert's candidate was not appointed to Barnston. The living went in May 1632 to John Beadle, a stalwart Essex puritan, previously rector of Little Leighs, near Chelmsford, and later author of *The Journal or Diary of a Thoughtful Christian* (1656), a work dedicated to the Earl of Warwick. *D.N.B.*, *s.vv.* Twisse, Beadle; Venn; Smith, 362.

An undated letter from Warwick to Lady Joan (Eg. 2645, f. 303) also concerns Beadle:–
'Madame   I received a letter from your ladyship concerning Mr Bedell's remove, which ther is noe such thing. If ther had I had soner taken your recomendation then all the bishops in this kingdome. Thus with my best love to you I rest
Your ladyship's to serve you   Warwicke'

This letter appears to be related not to Beadle's move to Barnston, but rather to a threat to him from the ecclesiastical authorities, either earlier at Little Leighs (see Smith, 41) or once he was settled at Barnston.

Your daughter remembers her duty unto you.

Endorsed (*f. 340b*): To the lady Johan Barrington at Hatfield in Essex be these given

220 *Joan St. John, n.d.,* [*December 1631*] (*2650, f. 343*)

Deare grandmother   My husband and my selfe humbly thank you for your kind remembrance of us in sending such great daintis; they are not so plentifull at Hatfeild as thay are hard to com by in London, wher is no greater dantis then a country capon. If my ocations would have given leave I should have bin glad to have sene Hatfeild this Christid wher I fear my husband wil be som part of the time, which will much truble me to have so long absent. I hope my unckle Altham wil not be so tedious in his examinations as we fear; I am sory thes diferences should be amongst frinds, but I am suer for my husband's part he hath sought al means to end it with peace though my unkle falcly accuses him with the contrary.[1] Dear grandmother here is litle nuss stiring but what the booke relats which my husband sent you last week; as soun as any more coms out you shal have it. Thus, with my owne an husband's humble duty, I disier ever to remain yours

      Joan St. John

Endorsed (*f. 344b*): To my much honoured grandmother the Ladie Barrington at Hatfeild thes

221 *Joan St. John, n.d.,* [*December 1631*] (*2650, f. 339b*)

Deare grandmother   I cannot but return you second thanks for your dainty capons, which with other good frinds I have tasted of but never eate better. I am sory to reseve so much and am no way able to requit. My husband comands me to tel you there shal be a parlament; you may beleve it for it cam from my Lord Treseure who told it my Lord Bedford of a sertain. Whither it be cause of joy or sorow, the sucses will shew. I heer also for sertain that Suffolk House is taken up

---

[1] Joan's uncle Sir Edward Altham had delayed the law suit over her inheritance by attempting to introduce new witnesses. See letter 231.

for the queen mother, who coms over.[1] I have sent you the book of nus with a map which is new printed. Deare grandmother I cannot be larg, being cald to my litle one which is il, but I hope it is only teeth. Thus with my duty to your self I remain

Your granchil to be comanded   Joan St John

Endorsed (*f. 340*): To my honourable grandmother the Ladie Barrington at Hatfeild thes

222   *Sir Gilbert Gerard, 21 December 1631*   (*2645, f. 341*)

Good madam   This bearer having occation to come into Essex I have taken this oportunitie of presenting my service unto you and desire by him to heare how your ladiship and all the rest of your good company doe. My wife would have wrighten but desires to bee excused, having so many things to doe now at this time. I was this day at London where is noe newes. My neece St John her little one hath bine very ill but this was prettily amended, which I presume my nephew wilbe gladd to heere. So with my humble duty remembred, with my thankes for all your love unto me and mine, espetialy unto my daughter with you, I take my leave and will rest

Your dutifull sone   Gilbert Gerard

Flambards, 21 December, 1631
My wife remembers her dutie unto you and hath sent your ladyship a [small sage?] leafe which she praies you to accept in good part.

Endorsed (*f. 342b*): To my honourable good mother the Lady Johan Barrington these be given

223   *Sir Gilbert Gerard, 23 December 1631*   (*2645, f. 343*)

Good madam   I am in a dilemma and know not which way to turne my selfe. On the one side I am unwilling to adventure my sone such an unseasonable jorny, on the other I dare not deny my brother lest he should take it unkindly, yet at the last to satesfy my brother I have intreated this bearer Mr Hide to accompany my boy, who was

---

[1] Pory had this rumour of the impending arrival of Henrietta Maria's mother, Marie de Medicis, on 14 Dec. 1631. By 21 Dec. her journey was thought less likely and she did not in fact come to England until 1638. Birch, ii. 153, 157; Gardiner, vii. 185-6 and viii. 379-80.

desierose to find an opertunitie to waite on your ladiship, yet could not conveniently have gone at this time. I praye thanke him for his paines in undertaking the jorny and importune him to stay with you as long as you can; he wilbe ernest to come away. I desire Gilbert should come back on the Munday after twelf day at the farthest. In the meane time, I pray doe mee the favour as to chide him if he be unmannerly or disorderly, or commend the care of him unto his godmother, unto whom I have noe leisure to wright. So with my harty praiers for your health and hapines I rest

Your dutifull sonne   G. Gerard

Flambards, 23 December, 1631

Endorsed (*f. 344b*): To my honourable good mother the Lady Johan Barrington these be given

224   *Sir Gilbert Gerard, 16 [January] 1632*   (*2646, f. 1*)

Good madam   Your man Isack made such hast home, either unto you or your maide Jugg, that he would scarce give mee time to wright unto you.[1] Now this bearer being desirouse to see his friendes at Hatfild that he may shew himself how proper a man he is growne I must not let him passe without a testimoniall, and all that I can say for him is that I hope he is as honest as I found him, and if he be so that is all. I shalbe gladd that he prove himself so by his behaviour during his aboad with you, which I have given him leave to be as long as hee please, so that he be at home on Satterday night. I thanke God your daughter and all myne heere are well. You must pardon my wife for not wrighting at this time, being taken up in the entertaining a great lady who is come unto her this night, but by the next messenger you shall not faile but heare from her. There is noe newes at London but what you may find in the Swedish inteligencer or the last new currant. I did expect to have heard from you before I wright this letter but my boy is not yet come. So with my thanks unto your good ladyship for all your love I rest

Your dutifull sonn   G. Gerard
16 [January] 1631

Endorsed (*f. 2b*): To my honourable good mother the Lady Johan Barrington at Hatfield these

---

[1] Lady Joan's servant Isaac Ewers married her maid Joan Smith in 1632. Introduction, 18.

225 *Sir Gilbert Gerard, 27 January 1632*   *(2645, f. 337)*

Good madam   My wife having occation to send this bearer unto
you, I should be much to blame if I should neglect this duty which I
know you accept so well of from your poore friendes who have noe
better meanes of expressing there thankfulnes, which I have good
cause to doe by all meanes, being so many waies indebted unto you
for your many favours unto me and mine espetialy for your love and
bounty unto my daughter Joane, who is much bound unto you for
your care of her.[1] I was very gladd to see your good report of her in
your last letter, I pray God shee may still prosper in the best things,
which shalbe more comfort unto mee then any thing in this world. I
shalbe gladd to heare by this bearer of your good health. Wee have
noe newes to impart unto you, so with our praiers for your hapines I
rest your dutifull sonne
        Gilbert Gerard

Flambards, 27 January, 1631

Endorsed (f. 338b): To my honourable mother the Lady Johan Barrington at Hatfield in Essex present these

226 *Ezekiel Rogers, 28 January 1632*   *(2646, f. 3)*

Madam   Though I have within these fewe dayes bene very ill
and feverish by a greate colde, yet I dare not wholly omitt such a
messenger as this is. We are exhorted to doe good while we have time;
now it were presumption in me to thinke that I am like to have much
time to write to you, or you to be written to. Oh madam, if we be wise
to followe harde the matter of assurance it will be no discomfort to
thinke our time to be short; yea it wilbe an inconveivable joy to thinke
that it [is] so neere. I hope you growe dayly more skillfull in packing
up and abridging your thoughts about the worlde, and inlarging both
hart and time in higher meditations. Truly I thanke God I have
somwhat fixed my minde (since my being in the south) about providing for chaunge and I blesse God I finde some more comfort therin,
and hope of more assurance comming, then ever I had. Which I tell
you for your incouragement, that if you sett to it still in good earnest
the lorde will come with it ere you be aware. And I confesse to you, I
see straite is the way, and I feare many professors will come short; I
beseech you therfore, sett upon this matter with a fresh assault. Adde

[1] See Introduction, 19.

to the rules which I have sometime given you this, to labour throughly to understande the covenant of grace, both on God's part and ours, that then in frequent meditation you may reflect and say with my soule, if this be to beleeve, then I beleeve; if this be the chaunge required, then it is in me; and then, if God's covenant be unchangeable, I am well. But alas I am not able now to inlarge my selfe as I desire; the lord supply all to you. So with my service I comitt you to him and rest

   Your ladyshipp's to command   Ezekiel Rogers

I much advise you to seeke helpe by the communion of the saintes.

Rowly, January 28, 1631

Endorsed (*f. 4b*): To the honourable the lady Johan Barrington at Hatfielde Broadoke give [these]

227 *Sir William Masham, 3 February 1632*   (*2646, f. 5*)

February 3, 1631
Deare Mother   Beinge come safe to London I thought it my dutye to let you knowe the same and howe well we founde all thinges here. Litle Jug[1] (God be praysed) is well amended, only here coughe doeth trouble here some tymes. My wife was much trobled with sad thoughts of her and finding her so well beyond expectation, it did much affecte us with joye; we shall now make the more hast to you. In the meane tyme I must give you an accounte of that litle newes which I have gathered since my comminge up. The mayne I have sent you hereinclosed, which is the grounde of that breach which we heard of betwixte the Pope and his cardinalls, and (as I conceive) this hath put the kinge of France upon some highe tearmes with the kinge of Swede in the behalfe of the catholike bishopps and the Duke of Bavaria and others of the catholike league, the particulars wherof I understand you have by a copye of letter, from my sonne St John. And I heare that the king of Suede made as rounde an answer and would receive no law from him, but at last, upon the arriving of a second embassador from the king of France that spake milde language, both kings were well peaced againe; and I hope theye will concurr well together, at least till the king of France hath attained his owne ends. The kinge of Bohemia is gon up to the Palatinate with good respects from the states: they have sent with him 2,500 horses at theyre owne chardge, besids 800 carabins which are his owne garde, and have given him 1500ˡⁱ to

---

[1] Joan, first child of Lady Elizabeth Masham's daughter Joan and of Oliver St John.

beare his chardges. The prince of Oringe presented him with 8 leane blacke coatch horses. And I hope he is safely come by this tyme to his owne, but as yet we have noe certainty of it. It is reported that Heidleburg is taken. I sent you the last corranto[1] by my brother Roberte; by the next you shall heare more. So with our humble dutyes to you and loves to our good sisters and the rest of our frends with you, I rest your obliged

William Masham

Endorsed (*f. 6b*): To my honourable good ladye and mother the Ladye Barrington these be given

228 *Sir William Masham, 7 February* [*1632*]   (*2646, f. 7*)

Maddame   Havinge this opportunitye I thought good to let you know the good newes of this towne, which is lately come from Sweeden by letters to Sir Thomas Roe[2] which were presented to the kinge on Saterdaye last. The particulars as yet are not knowne, only in generall that the king of Sweeden hath given a great blowe to Tillye's armye and thereupon hath taken some townes of great consequence from the emperor, which is thought will shake the empire. The tyme is observable, which was shortly after the conclusion of our league with Spayne, so that the emperor and Tillye are much affected not only naturally, but superstitiously with some feare, upon this occasion and a former predixion that the emperor should overcome till God overcame him, meaninge Sued, which is Deus backward, which is latyne for God as my brother Barrington can tell you, to whom I praye imparte these. And now I ame in this greate subject of God's workes of justice upon his enimyes, I cannot omitt a strange example of his judgment upon a gentleman of Grays Inne, Mr Pennington,[3] who in his health usinge much that excration of the divill take him, now in his sicknesse was much trobled with the presentation of a black dogge, sutable to his master, and at last found deade much torne and distorted, his eyes clawed out (as some thinke) by the divill. This Mr Dr Sibbs[4] told me at my brother Prine's chamber on sabboth daye last, where we dyned

---

[1] Dated 30 Jan. None of Masham's own items of foreign news are listed on the title page of the newsbook. Dahl, 257.

[2] The letter from Oxenstierna to Roe is mentioned by Gresley, 26 Jan. 1632. Birch, ii. 166.

[3] There were two of this name in Grays Inn, William, admitted November 1617 and John, son and heir of John Pennington of Chigwell, admitted 1624. J. Foster, *Register of Admissions to Grays Inn* (1869).

[4] Richard Sibbes, preacher at Grays Inn, 1617–1635. *D.N.B.*

together and where you were kindly remembred. I hope I shall heare from you shortly touching my cosine Mewex, to whome I wish well and should be glad to doe her anye service in this kinde; I praye let me know your mynde by the next. So with my humble service to you and best respects to my good brother and sister, not forgetting the rest of my frends with you, I rest

      Your obliged   William Masham

London, February 7

Endorsed (f. 8b): To my much honored Lady and mother the Lady Barrington these be given

229   *Nathaniel Cotton[1] to John Kendal, 8 February 1632*   *(2646, f. 9)*

Lovinge frinde Mr Kindall   I was with my Ladie Lucke this present morninge and spake to hir conserninge a composicion for those thinges that are past and which shee alltogether regecktes not fearinge a sapena. Then I moufed hir that no more wast might be made if it please God to determine Ser John['s] liffe, certifinge hir that my Ladie Barington had writte unto me to compounde for anie thinge that might be convenint for the howse which was in my Ladie Lucke power to take awaye, which mosion shee was willyinge to intertayne, and promesed that nothinge shoulde more be lernd untill Mr Sanders come from London, for shee hopped that Sir John was in no present danger of death but think that he will never gooe abrode more. My ladie named the frutte trees, the glase of the windowes and the wanscotte to be agreede for. I praye certifie my Ladie Barington so much and wright whatt I should dooe in itt. My ladie hath bought Mr Fordom's howse and hath remoufed som rosses and som small plan trees, but promeseth that no more shall be taken up till farder treattey. Thus for the present in hast I seas. From Hemsteed, this viij[th] day of February, 1631

      Your frend   Nathaniel Cotton

Endorsed (f. 10b): To his lovinge frinde John Kindall, servaunt unto Sir Thomas Barrington at his lodginge in Holborn neare Chansere Lane end give this

---

[1] See letter 162.

230   *Sir William Meux, 10 February 1632*   *(2646, f. 11)*

Madam   You have bin informed that my nephew St John had
conference with Mr Bacon, whome I have scene, and one that noe
way can be excepted against save only in the estate. What his mother
may be drawne unto I know not, but were itt that she woulde be
respondent to my reasonabl demaundes I should thinck itt time mis-
pent to enquire els where. I have acquainted my nephew with the
other motion of Cambridge shire; the gentlman he knowes well, and
further tells me that he is of good repute in the house, of a good famyly
and withall a good husband, his father and grandfather bothe of them
men of note in theire country for theire well deservinge. What to doe
in this case I am doubtfull, and before I enter the lists I desire som
conference with yowr ladyship, to whose judgment I shall willingly
submitt my self. In the meane time humbly desiring the allmighty to
direct me, as in all other things, soe particularly in this, I leave yow to
his safe keeping and rest yowr assured loving son
          William Meux

Holborn the 10th of February, 1631

Endorsed (f. 12b): To his much honored mother the Lady Barrington
give these

231   *Oliver St. John, 28 February 1632*   *(2646, f. 13)*

Much honoured madam   I am much bound to your ladyship
that you are pleased to take into your thoughts my busienes with Sir
Edward Altham.[1] We met att my lord of Warwicke's last terme wherin
I clearly freede my selfe from any contentiouse or unfreindly carriage
of the busienes and proved the contrarie in himselfe togeather with his
manifest breach of promise in some things, but we are come to noe
ende. He desyred last terme to have a new commission for examining
of wittnesses and made oath that he had 12 wittnesses still to examine,
and now the time is come and I have offred him the carriage of the
commission but his clarke that deales for him seemes as though Sir
Edward now would have noe commission.[2] All is still to make delays,
but I will prevente them as well as I may. He stands much uppon Sir
Frances' breach of promise, and lays much fault uppon my wive's

[1] See letter 168.
[2] St John's copy of his letter to Altham of 24 Feb. offering the carriage of a new
commission is in Hunts. R.O., dd. M48A, bundle 4.

freinds as though they only put me upon this sute, as if I had not discression enough my selfe to know whether I had just cause of sute or not. I have mad bould to present your ladyship with the last currant, and with my humble service to your ladyship I rest

    Your humble and much obliged servant

                                                Oliver St. Johns

Holborne, 28 February, 1631

Endorsed (*f. 14b*): To the honourable and much honoured lady the Lady Johan Barrington at Hatfeilde Priorie these

232   *Sir Gilbert Gerard, n.d.,* [*March 1632*]   (*2650, f. 245*)

Good madam   I must now confesse I have bine to long silent, having forborne to send during my nephew his sicknes. God be praised that he is so well againe and that it spread noe further. I thanke God your daughter and all mine are well heere at home, only Charles hurt his knee with a fall, which troubles my wife because it seemed a small matter and did heale up, but breakes out againe and lookes faire yet much coruption comes from it, and yet shee cannot see whence it proceedes. Shee desires your advise in it. My sone Francis is also sick of an ague which hath brought him very low, and I have removed him from his master's unto my brother William's house, and would willingly have him home to see if our aier will doe him any good, but I feare it may hurt him being so weeke. God dispose of him as shalbee most for his glory. I was yesterday at London where is noe English newes but very good out of Germany, there being very lately a strong towne of good importance taken in. The king of France hath signed all the articles desired by the king of Sweden unto his full content, and whereas the king of Denmarke was in treaty with the king of Spaine it is broken of, and [*illegible*] also attended. The Palsgrave is exceding freindly entertained by the king of Sweden and is in person to besieg Hieldeberg and the king of Sweden Frankendale.[1]

    Your dutifull sone   G.G.

Endorsed (*f. 246b*): To my honourable good mother the Lady Johan Barrington these be given at Hatfield

---

[1] The newsbook of 15 March 1632 reported that Frankendal was besieged by Gustav Adolf and Heidelberg by the king of Bohemia. Dahl, 263.

233 *Adam Harsnett,*[1] *22 March* [1632]   (*2650, f. 274*)

Noble and worthy lady   My humble service remembred, I received by the hands of this barer such a pledge of your love as I know
not which way to expresse my thankfullnes but by acknowled[g]ing
my selfe a debtor unto your ladyship, and bound to doe you what
service my poor abillitie will extend unto.[2] The respect which I have
found with your ladyship ever sithence I have been knowne unto your
ladyship tyed me to that service and to better, if better I be able to
performe. If any comfort may acrew unto your afflicted soule, or if I
have added but one cubit unto your spirituall growth, I shall think
my paines happily bestowed, my weake service highly blessed, and my
poore self richly honoured and rewarded. So soone as the lord shall
give me leave and libertie I shall make bold to visit your ladyship and
your worthy children. Ah good madam, how rich, how happy are
you? If the lord loved you not, he would never thus highly have
honoured you as to make you the good wife of so noble and honorable
a husband, to be the loving and deer mother of so many hopefull and
gracious children. Madam (God knowes) I flatter you not, but my
desyre is to comfort your heart in these your aged dayes and to stirre
you up to greater thankfullnes unto God, who hath heaped upon you
so many rich favours and is still fitting you for greater. Goe on (good
madam) in your holy course and labour every day to grow into neerer
acquaintance with the lord, that so you may finish your course with
joye, and in the end receive that crowne of glory which is prepared for
you. Thus I commend you to the grace of God, and shall ever rest
        Your ladyship's remembrancer   Adam Harsnett

Cranham, March 22

Endorsed (*f. 275b*): To the honorable and worthy lady my good friend
the Lady Johan Barrington at Hatfeild Pryorie give [these]

234 *Sir Gilbert Gerard, 10 April 1632*   (*2646, f. 15*)

Good madam   This bearer having occation to come in[to] Essex
is desieruse to tender his service unto you, by whom I shall rejoice to

[1] Moderate puritan writer; vicar of Hutton and rector of Cranham, both in Essex.
D.N.B.
[2] Lady Joan's account book has 48s. 4d 'paid for a Bowle for Mr. Harsenett' under 15
Feb. 1632. Harsnett's *A Cordiall for the Afflicted*, dedicated to Lady Joan and to Lady
Mary Eden, was entered at Stationers' Hall in Sept. 1631 and published in 1632.
E.R.O., D/DBa A15, f. 26.

heare of your health and hapines which wee now also howerly expect and long for by our late messenger that went to visit his master but is not yet returned. I thanke God your daughter with all our little ones heere continue in health, and to morrow I send a litter for my sonne Francis who yet hath his ague. The last newes I heerd of him was that upon a vomitt given him he brought up a great worme which I hope may occation his recovery, but he continues very weake. I doubt not but amongst the rest of your grandchildren you doe remember him in your praiers, for which as all other your favours I am bound to be

    Your most dutifull sonne   G. Gerard

Flambards, 10 April, 1632

Endorsed (*f. 16b*): To my honourable good mother the Lady Johan Barrington these be given

235   *Sir William Masham, 17 April 1632*   (*2644, f. 199*)

Madame   As I was comminge to see you this morninge my brother Mewis came and so I was inforced to put of my intended visit till another tyme, which wilbe shortly. My wife and my daughter have bene very ill of theyre eyes ever since I wrote last to you, or else theye had bene with you before this tyme. Theye desire much some of my sister Everard's water for the eyes. If she hath none at Hatfeild theye would intreate her to send for it and they will paye the messenger. So with our humble dutyes I commit you to God and rest

    Your observant sonne   William Masham

Otes, April 17, 1632
Theye desire also to know how to applye the water to the eyes. I praye present our best respects to my sister Evered and my sister Lamplugh. We long to be with you now you are alone, yet not alone with so good company.

Endorsed (*f. 200b*): To my honourable lady and mother the Ladye Barrington these be given

236   *Sir Thomas Barrington, 18 April 1632*   (*2646, f. 19*)

Madame   That horss I rode upon yesterday I have more thankes to give his master then him, who tyred me with desperate stumbling, which I hope he learned not of his owner; but if the beast could

understand as well as he, I should pray yow to chide him.[1] He has
kept me within, so that I could as yet com by no more newes then I
had from my honest sweet Charles who came to see me, I thanke him;
neither is thare any com over (as yet) more then my letters declared
unto yow, only that your freinds in London are well, thankes be to
God. Owr busines I have not yet entered into and therefor cannot as
yet any way account to yow for it. By the next I hope, God willing, I
shall be enabled to satisfye yow much better, meane while in greate
hast, with my wife's, my owne and sister's dewtyes to yow, I comitt all
to God and am ever

> Your most dewtyfull and loving sonn

> Thomas Barrington

London, Holborne, Aprill 18, 1632
I pray yow tell my neice Johan Gerard that I will remember her booke
and commend me to my sisters, and I pray yow tell my sister Everard
I desyre her to remember her charge of my house and to tutor the
boyes well, whom I pray God bless and send us well to meet.

Endorsed (*f. 20b*): To the honourable my very good mother the Lady
Johana Barrington give [these]

237 *Sir Thomas Barrington, April 1632* (*2646, f. 17*)

Madame   My indisposition of body, by reson of a very greate
cold, hath denyd me that exquisite accomplishment for intelligence,
occasioned by a retyred house keepeing (till within this two daye),
which I did both intend and desyre to tender unto yow; but what my
freinds have made myne I shall heearby offer yow. The entrance on
the threshold presents yow (tragically) sadd discourse, but shall conclude (comically) with a more pleaseing subject. My cozen Robert
Cromwell, sonn of Sir Philip, bound with an atorney, is (upon his
master's death) imprisoned and questioned for poysoning of him,
which we hope he will be cleear from in the close; I pray God he
may.[2] The king of Swede hath lately taken Auseburg[3] by assault and
it is sayd by som that Count Hoorne was then slayne (but hoped
better). The brave king made an oration to his souldiers before theay

---

[1] See letter 239.

[2] Robert, 5th son of Sir Philip Cromwell, born 1613, 'was tried, convicted, and
executed in London, for poisoning his master, an attorney'. Noble, i. 35. But *cf.* letter
248 where his reprieve is reported.

[3] Gustav entered Augsburg 14 April 1632 and this was reported in the newsbook of
24 April. Roberts, ii. 702; Dahl, 267.

went into the country of Baveir, inciteing them to obedience and vallor, promiseing them greate bootyes, which don he demaunded if none were unpayd and threatned to caseear every officer that had defaulced dew payment; the companyes exprest them selves generally satisfyed, whereupon he gave them all 2s a peice in all 4000^{li}. The proceeding thare is blessed: the Duke of Bavaria offers to make peace upon any termes, the queen of Sweden is sayd to be with child againe, and allthough Tylly and the emperor have greate forces in nomber yet theay are rawe and young, not dareing to see the king of Swede's face, thankes be to God. The Spanish fleet is assured lost to the nomber of 27 sayle and 3000 mariners, which is more then all the rest [f. 17b] unto the Spaniard, not to be recovered in an age of tyme by them. Thankes be to God for the weakening of his and owr enemyes.

Women are crewell this yeear,[1] Saturne raynes with strong influ- ence: an other wife hath given her husband a potion of melted lead, but it was because he came home drunke; of a badd act, no very bad example to our Hatfeild birds and now the plummer is at worke thare theay may the rather feare the alehouse. Thus in the forme I have made my selfe master of my preface, allthough in the substance I have sayd nothing; but must be somed up in favor of being accounted

Yowr most dewtyfull and loving sonn

Thomas Barrington

My wife and sisters offer theire dewtyes unto yow; my Lady Warwick hath sent for my wife to goe to the court with her even now else she had written to yow, and had it not ben for my wrighting I had gone with them. Thus I pray God bless us and send us a happy meeting, I pray God.

Holborne, London, Aprill, 1632

Endorsed (f. 18b): To the honourable the Lady Johan Barrington give [these]

238   *Lady Judith Barrington, n.d.*, [23 April 1632]   (2646, f. 21)

Madam   My lady Sey the widdow is now dangerously sick of the small pox. The Earle of Bedford in Lent last maried one of his daughters to the lord of Doncaster[2] against his father the Earl of

---

[1] See letters 239 and 241.

[2] James Hay, Lord Doncaster, married Margaret, 3rd daughter of Francis, 4th Earl of Bedford, 21 March 1632, being then, as here, styled 'Lord of Doncaster'. G.E.C., *Peerage*.

Carlile's liking, but the grandfather, the earle of Norwitch, hath setled on the yongue lord upon his marriage all his owen lands, being 4,000^{li} a year. The other of the Earl of Bedford's daughter, it seemes, is to marry the Earl of Bristow's sonne this returne[1] from travaile, thear being setled a private affection between the yongue couple. The Lady North lyeth dangerously sick and Sir Dudly is to marry one of Sir Charls Montague's daughters that hath 10,000^{li}; her sister maried Sir Christopher Hatton. For Mr Perin, I think if you give him after the rate of 3^{li} a peece it wilbe faire; that is the most I will give him, but I rather think 50s shalbe my rate. I have not worss a great while then last night and this day, therfore I pray pardon my abrupt writing which my duty hath a litle more put me upon then my discretion now; your sonne hath a great deale of news for you. And soe with my best prayers for your health I rest

   Your most respective and lovinge daughter

                                          Judith Barrington

Your daughter Lucy with her duty longes to be now at home with you quickly, before she forgett her coort relation of St. George's feast[2] whear she attended the kinge all daye and can tell brave storis. My aunt Hamden is well. I beseech you my service to my sister Everet, my sister Lampluch and my 2 neeces. I am glad honest Toby is so soon quitt of his ague.

Endorsed (f. 22b): For the Lady Barrington

239 *Sir Thomas Barrington, n.d., [April 1632]*   *(2645, f. 327)*

Madame   Newes coms so uncertaynely and slowly to hand as that the materialls for the structure of intelligence doe much fayle me, yow must therefor pardon your servant if his house be not raysed so many storyes as he desyres, nor lett not your expectation exceed his power. What my eares with carefull indevor have made myne I heear offer yow, desyreing yow to accept it with the same respect that I doe, even probable enough to be contraryed before it gett a roote of truth; when coming from so remote distance the portage may well alter the first originall. It is sayed by letters from Holland, both from the queen of Bohemia and others, which was delivered to owr king when my wife was at court, which he thanked God for, that the king of Sweden hath

___

[1] Illness evidently led Lady Judith to this imprecision.
[2] Grand-daughter is meant. St George's day is 23 April. Table 3.

lately beaten Tilly oute of his trenches, slayne Alstringer[1] and 2 other greate commaunders, taken the ordinance and baggage. But som others say that only Tylly fledd with out the greate loss; som others say that thare were 6000, som 9000 slayne, and the whole routed. What yet to fix upon for a certaynety no man knowes, but the least suerly is a greate matter of blessing and an assured testimony of God's mighty hand with the king of Swede, when the Duke of Baveir is reported fledd into Italy. The booty of Ausburg[2] was greate, for though the Fulcers (which are the bankers) conveyed away a greate treasuer to anticipate the king, yet he found enough in the gleanings after his trashing to pay his army for 3 months. That brave king tutors the king of Bohemia in his discipline for warr exquisitely, and concurrence betweene them is exceeding fayre and amicable; thankes be to God. We shall very shortly know the truth [f. 327b] of the king's last action, but all in generall thinke that the Swede and Bohemia have all Germany in theire graspe; praysed be God.

At London men and theire wives still make dolorous catastrophes of theire jarrings: an other woman hath poysened her husband and at last one husband is found so barbarous as to poyson his wife, which he did suer to keepe the women's sex from so extreme former shame, and so sett mariage in credit againe when the termes were made a little alike. And to make this the better on the women's side, or fowler on the men's, Sir Robert Howard hath converted his extremyty of loving lust into as foule a disguise of inhumanyty as he hath putt upon his long kept mistress the Lady Purbeck her fayre face, which (upon a jar between them) he hath made as many crosses upon with his unkind knife as he could find attractive beautyes in her severall features; an unheard of fer[oc]city, which though to her is justice from God, yet from him, the cause of all her shame and suffrings, most unmanly and salvage, trewly. I abhorr to thinke on it. She is com to London from Wales for cure.[3] Once more to retourne to the king that hath turned the wheele of Christendom with so swift a motion, the brave Swede: it is sayed he is so strong in his body (answarable to his mind) as that he is able to over graspe most men in an army upon equall termes. Your freinds, my wife excepted, are well, God be thanked. And my desyres to begg your commaund towards my children makes me so much the

---

[1] Aldringen had been wounded when Gustav Adolf successfully crossed the Lech on 14 April 1632. Roberts, ii. 703.

[2] For the taking of Augsburg see letter 237, n. 2.

[3] Sir Robert Howard, younger son of Lord Treasurer Suffolk, had long lived in adultery with Lady Purbeck, the wife of John Villiers, Viscount Purbeck, the brother of the 1st Duke of Buckingham. Their liaison survived even the open displeasure of Charles I and Laud in 1636, when they fled to France. Gardiner, viii. 144-6.

longer in troubling yow: and that requested, I comit us all to God and am your most dewtyfull and loving sonn

    Thomas Barrington

[*f. 328*] I beseich yow offer my love and service to my good sisters, and my blessing give I pray yow unto all ower children. And I beseich yow, lett my nephew Meux know I answar for my heavy head, that if it were the cause of his horse's stumbling so often, without all doubt then his head must needes be extreamly light, else his horss could never have caryed him so suer. It is my humor to answar him, whatsoever he sees in myne; and when he coms to London I have provided before hand Holborne and Hide Parke to be at his service to reconsile him.[1]

The Duke of Anioulin hath a very grate army at Callis and the Duke of Chevereux is com to him with an other army, which are pretended both for Artoys, but England is not feareless if theay see with theire best and most provident eyes; but I hope we shall be blessed by God. Sir Edward Coke hath his papers seased by reson of a report that he is aboute a booke concerning magna charta and is likely to incurr som trouble.[2]

Mr Ward hath time given him untill Lammas by our bishopp.[3] So I once againe comitt us all to God.

Endorsed (*f. 328b*): For my honourable mother the Lady Barrington

240 *Sir Thomas Barrington, n.d.,* [*April 1632*]   (*2645, f. 330*)

Madame   The newes groes not by accresion, but by vegitation; that greate king liveing in groth and groeing in his life of warr and victorye. Yesterday newes came that the Hague hath made bonfyres for the joyes of his conquest, reports of Tyllye's being slayne, of Allstringer slayne and Duke of Bavary taken prisoner and 2 other greate commaunders, of a generall defeate of the whole armye twice as great as that of Lipsich. But yet we have no certaynty, which amuses all men. It's sayed that the archdutches her armye is defeated in the lower Pallatinate by the Rinegrave, a brave soldier though a litle olde

---

[1] See letter 236.

[2] Order had been given by Charles I in 1631, when Coke was ill, for his papers to be seized at his death. Though he did not die until 1634, the papers were then impounded. Gardiner, vii. 359-360.

[3] Nathaniel Ward, puritan divine and rector of Stondon Massey in Essex, had been presented at Laud's visitation in the late summer of 1631 and was finally deprived of his living, for refusing to subscribe to the 39 articles, in 1633. Smith, 44, 47.

man. The French king sends forces, it's sayed, to the king of Swede and turnes other forces, it's thought, upon Artoyse and Dunkerke. The papists now interpret the prophesies of the Revelation concerning Antechrist upon the king of Swede, and say he shall continew the 3 yeears etc., but I hope God hath raysed him to sitt thare in that stead, but not as that man-beast, I know, but the destroyer of that monster by God's blessing, or the preface to that greate worke. Thus thankeing yow for my children and glad theay are all so well, praying for God's blessing upon your selfe then and us all, I remayne

    Your most dewtyfull and loving sonn

                               Thomas Barrington

London, this Saterday
Letters yesterday came from Hambrogh, Norinburg, the Hage to confirme this victory. All conclude that the kinge is master of the feeld.[1] My bounden duty remembred.

[*f. 329b*] My little Reinegrave (sayth my wife), haveing notice that the archdutchess her army was in the lower Psaltz, came downe to them and cutt of theire men and thay say count John de Nassau is slayne.

The proceed is thus: count John de Nassau marching up the Psaltz with 12000 men, the chauncellor Oxensterne with the Reinegrave cutt him and men in peices.

The next stepp is heear: the duke of Freidland assaulted a toune in Bohemia and putt the garison of Scotts and English, being 800, to the sword; count Thorne, heearing of this, came and blocked up the toune with his forces and the Freidlanders that were in it, who offers to surrender the toune, and Thorne denyes to take it but by force. All this was undertaken when Tilly was so strong in Bavaria, which made them hope that the resistance thare, being likely to be so strong upon the king of Swede and at the same time such fyre and sword by the archduchess her armye and the duke of Freidland in Bohemia, that this joynct force would have disquieted and diverted the good and great kings of Swede and Bohemia. But God hath turned theire devices into a trapp that hath caught them selves; thankes be to God. This was theire prime, theire cheife device; it is overthrowen (good, very good) and the enemy sayes he may be emperor when he will. The archduches is in greate perill to be lost by the French forces that are supposed to be that way, which causes our merchants, the factors, not to send over no more goods till theay see this feare overpast. There are

---

[1] A detailed report of Gustav Adolf's success appeared in the newsbook of 28 April 1632. Dahl, 268.

20,000 men a-leveling in Pickerdye for to sett against the archduches. And Sir Robert Howard sayth he never did cutt my Lady Purbeck's nose.[1] All this was dictated by word and word by my wife, Sir John Dingly and Mistress Jane my sister.[2]

[*No endorsement*]

241 *Lady Judith Barrington, n.d., [April/May 1632]* (*2645, f. 347*)

Madam My desire to tendor my service to you makes me venture on my dulnes thus-farr, which did perswade me to have made my excuse, for in truth I have been much out of tune ever since I came and I finde almost all my frends sick or a dyeng; the ayre is so bad this year, which may some what plead for our sickly household at Hatfeeld of late. Heer is litle news stirring, much expected the later end of this week: I heer the kinge hath taken 2 tounes more in Bavaria and that at Bruxells, by one [that] came lately from thence, they drink the kinge [of] Sweden's health though an enemy. This day was the poor woman burnt in Smythfeeld that poysoned her husband, which is wondred at the crewelty, sence thear was so much cause of mercy to her; I doubt not but you have heard the story of Mr Pickering. And soe, being not very well, I hast to rendor my selfe
    Your most lovinge and respective daughter to serve you
                                                    Judith Barrington

Friday the [*blank*]
I beseech you remember my service to my sisters and neeces. I am sorry to heer Toby hath gott an ague.

Endorsed (*f. 348b*): To my much honored mother the Lady Barrington, this

242 *Sir Thomas Barrington, 3 May 1632* (*2646, f. 23*)

Madame All that is com within my spheare since my last attended yow I shall now offer to your hand. The new king of Transillvania[3] hath taken up armes on the king of Swede his partye, and he is

---

[1] See letter 239.
[2] Jane Lytton.
[3] George Rákóczy, who was in direct negotiation with Gustav early in 1632, Roberts, ii. 573.

a brave prince. The king of Swede haveing lately an embassador in Muscovye who negotiated for the stopp of corne for his master his use, which the State's agents had indevored to gett, the agents gave som private ill words of the king of Swede whereupon the king's embassador made meanes to have them committed, and tould them if theay behaved not them selves better theay should be hanged. The French king's embassador and the king of Swede's, contending for place, sent unto theire master's; the brave king sent this answar, that his embassador should give way nor place to no king's embassador in the world so long as he hath his sword in his hand, which I wish may prosper by the blessing of God, to which I comit yow and us all with all myne

Your most dewtifull and loving sonn

Thomas Barrington

London, May 3rd, 1632

Endorsed (*f. 24b*): To the honorable my very good mother the Ladye Johanna Barrington give [these] at Hatfield in Essex

243 *Sir Gilbert Gerard, 10 May 1632*   (*2646, f. 25*)

Madam   I sent you word by my last that during your time of solitarynes in absence of your company I would visit your ladyship if you did not forbidd mee. I resceived noe answere from you and thearfore might take that for a forbidding, but I dare not nor will not, but thought if possibly I can to waite on you, although I heare you have very good company, but if my occations will not permitt mee I beseech you (if you please) to give my daughter leave to come and see her mother these holidaies. My brother Masham will apoint his coach to meete him halfe way and I will send him my coach so farre, and I pray you to be pleased to gett her conveighed unto Otes against the time my brother Masham shall apoint his coach to come, which he is not yet resolved on. I doe expect my brother Robert and my sister, who may come in the coach with Jugg[1] if they so plese. I am now in hast and rest

Your dutifull sonn   Gilbert Gerard

Flambards, 10 May 1632

Endorsed (*f. 26b*): To my honourable good mother the Lady Johan Barington these

[1] Joan Gerard.

244 *Sir Thomas Barrington, 15 May 1632*   *(2646, f. 27)*

Madame   What soever I can find gratious in your eye shall be
my joy to offer unto yow. The happy relations of theise newer times
have of late ministred much matter of comfort and my desyre shall
never be to make my selfe a delight in hard tydings, but to rejoyce
when mesages of peace to God's church and good to those that love
and feare him in the generall or perticular, are putt into my mouth or
hand. Yet lett it not dismay yow if I, in telling truth, lett yow know
that Ameleck may a little seeme to prevaile, that Moses his hands may
be againe more zealously and carefull supported; som Cananites must
remaine yet to keep us from securytye and make us seek unto and to
relye on God, who I hope will lett us see him still in this good worke.

The latest newes is that the king of Sweden, sitting doune and
intrenching before Ingolstadt whare the duke of Bavaria was at that
time allso intrenched, the towers of the toune gave the canon of the
enemye that advantage as that the greate shott raked along the king
his trenches and did much mischeife, in so much as that the king his
horss was slayne under him by a cannon shott, and the marquis of
Turlaugh and Baden slayen and Saxon Wymar is reported hurte, the
undaunted king mounted his ordinance against the towers of the
towne, which soone after were by him beaten downe, after which he
advaunces to the assault of the duke his trenches, and drives him by
force oute, and forces all the oute workes of the towne and makes him
selfe master of them, gets the [*f. 27b*] bridg and advances to the gates
and missed the toune at the assault very narrowly; then being at a
stand, he sent diverse troopes after the Duke of Bavaria.[1] What since
is done must be wayted for. The Spaniards have taken Spier in the
Pallatinate and make much havock thare, but Bavaria once gotten in,
theay will be made fly quickly, I hope. Meane while the confederacye
groes strong between the French and the States; the French king
comms downe to Callis whare he hath a greate power. My owne
busines depends on such an uncertayne ballance as gives me yet no
leave. Resolve yow or my selfe, so soone as I can I will. Meane while
I humblye desire your prayers for that and us all, and for your
grandchild John and all our comfortable meeting by God's blessing,
to which I committ us all and remayne

          Your most dewtyfull and loving sonn

                                                    Thomas Barrington

Holborn, London, May 15, 1632

---

[1] The attempt on Ingolstadt was not reported in the newsbooks until 16 May.
Maximilian of Bavaria left the town on 21 April. Dahl, 272; Roberts, ii. 704.

Endorsed (f. 28b): For the Lady Johan Barrington

245   *Lady Judith Barrington, n.d., [May 1632]*   *(2646, f. 29)*

Madam   I humbly thank you for the the favour of your last lines. Although I have litle to saye now, yett I cannot chuse but acknoledge itt and lett you know I am very glad to heer you are soe well that you now come doune into the parlor. You have made a good exchange with your maides since you are all so well pleased, especially if Elsibeth hould in health. I am glad to heer Gobert is soe well, for Mr Perin made us halfe afraide of him. Lucie hath gott the toothacke, her face is sweld, but I keep her warme and this night she hath slept well. The small poxe is so much heer that we wish our selves with you, for it increaseth and makes us affraide to goe abroad, so that soone as your sonne's park[1] busines is over we shall hast to you, which yett goeth on butt sloely and crossly. I hope you will commande all thinges at home to give you contentment; I am never better pleased then when I heer you are. And thus begging your blessinge with my prayers for your health, I committ you to the almighty
        Your most obedient daughter to serve you
                                                        Judith Barrington

Wensday
[f. 29b] For certaine I heer Ingolstat is taken[2] with the loss of 12,000 men and the duke of Bavaria mad, olde Tilly found enbalmed ready to be buried at the toune's takeing and yongue Tilly dead.

Endorsed (same folio): To my much honored mother the lady Barrington this

246   *Sir Thomas Barrington, 21 May 1632*   *(2646, f. 32)*

Madame   My troubles were lately increased by the feares apprehended of my poore daughter Lucye her sicknes, who was in a violent feaver for allmost 3 dayes, and we, fearing the worst of theise times, remooved owr lodging, leaveing her very neear and carefully attended with two keepers and two phisitians, whose meanes used God hath ben pleased so to bless as that she is now resonablye well amended, I prayse God. I have in my occasions had such interruptions and delayes

---

[1] Carisbrooke Park in the Isle of Wight. Introduction, 4, 5.
[2] See letter 244, n.1. Tilly had died at Ingolstadt on 20 April. Roberts, ii. 701.

as that my patience and best judgment have ben extended to theire best how to demeane my selfe. Wearye we are all of London, and more weary of owr busines so full of vexations, troubles and difficultyes, but I hope that gratious and good God who hath heatherto protected me, and raysed me freinds beyond and besydes my expectation, will bring me oute of this laberinth with peace and comfort. I must waite his leisuer and will hasten all I may by his favor and good blessing, desyring the prayers of your selfe and all my good freinds for his assistance in theise difficultyes, wherein that greatenes which now rayses it selfe up against more then one in theire perticular estates, with the heighth of pride as if all must and ought to stoope to an eye and prostrate to a word and, which is worst, doth labor to take all collaterall advantages to wring men [*f. 32b*] oute of theire owne, or else punish them by theire owne, but that God uphoulds and defends those who trust in him, emong whom I hope ever to have a portion and lott, for his sake who hath purchased it for all that love his first and second appeearing.

We have no certaintye of much newes, but yet som thare is. The king of Sweden after his takeing of Ingolstadt, heearing that the Bavarian and the Walestine armye endevored to joyne and were upon theire march to that end, he providently hastned a timely prevention of the uniteing of so huge and potent a bodye, and not being able to overtake the Bavarians with his foote, comaundes his fourelegged forces by theire takeing somwhat larger and swifter stepps to gaine ground of them, which theay did execute with such speed and spirit as that with in a short time those missives were mingled with the Duke of Bavaria his reare, whereupon the body of his army was compelled to faces aboute; and yet still the Swedish horss behaved them selves so stoutely as that theay kept them sufficiently in worke untill the king's infantrye came up, who once added theay cutt the duke's armye wholy of, and whither for him selfe he is fled no man heears yet more. The generall Banier[1] before Stode in Todd (that careless and bestiall man) his roome, who cared not for men's lives but suffred single combat [*f. 33*] even before the army and sayed the Scotish men must lett oute one and others hott blood, and suffre 1200 Scottish and English to be cutt of neear Stode, a salvage beast, my very bowell yearne against such crewell inhumanitye – whether he be executed (as he deserves) or only displaced, I yet hear not, but he hath made me so passionate I have allmost forgotten to wright sence – Banier in this traitor (or most unworthy at the least) Todd his roome, beinge before Stode, your freind Papinheim indevored to breake oute and to force his passage through the Swede's army under Banieir, but theay were beaten in to

[1] Johan Banér.

Stode againe, and Papenheim lost 1000 of his men in the service, God
be thanked.[1] Oxinsterne hath (it's confidently spoken) taken Frankin-
dale and the king hastens to incounter with the Spanish and emperiall
forces; God send him good succes I pray God. The French king is
retyred from Callis with his armye into Loraine and it is thought he
only came to settle a governour in Callis and to secure it against
Mounseiur. Thare is a greate embassadour newly com to the court
oute of Fraunce and som (that I beleive not) say assistance is craved
for Dunkerke against the French and Dutch, and that for reson of
state we have cause to feare Dunkerke more in so neear a neighbour's
hand as the French or Dutch, but this is but ayre. I hope I see no
realytye nor probabillytye in it. The Dunkerkers I am assured [*f. 33b*]
have taken 3 of owr shipps; I spake my selfe with a merchant, one of
the owners. The feofees for byeing in of impropriations are questioned
and how theay will speed is yet unknowen; the grounds I yet forbeare.
Thus with my prayers and humblest dewtye and most obliged thankes
for your love and care to and of me my selfe and myne, I rest, comitting
us all to God

      Your most obedient and loving sonn

                        Thomas Barrington

Holborne, London, May 21, 1632

[*No endorsement*]

247   *Lady Judith Barrington,* [*22 May 1632*]   (*2646, f. 30*)

Madam   I confess ceariously it troubles me much that I cannot
now attend you at Hatfeeld now. My husband business goeth very
sloely forwards and crosly, soe that it perplexeth us much; I pray God
send us a good end of itt. He thinks my being at hand to speak with
the lady of Holland sometimes may advantage him much. He is
resolved one way or other to end itt quickly, for he fears ells itt maye
worke him more mischeife, so that to morrow morninge he goeth to
Greenwithe to the coort and if he can dispatche in any time we shalbe
at Harrow to morrow night to spend the hollidayes thear, and then
heather againe to attend the conclusion. Thear is very great cause of
fear of the small poxe, every whear heer. Yesterday your cosen Crom-

---

[1] The action at Stade (there called Stoad) is reported in the newsbook of 4 May 1632.
The unpopular Tott was in fact severely defeated by Pappenheim 16–18 April, and
relinquished his command at the end of May. Dahl, 269; Roberts, ii. 687, 721–3.

well's tryall was heard;[1] the probabilities are foule but he is likely to finde great frendes. This week Mr Atturney fined the cittie 1,500 markes for not prosecuting the law against those that wear Doctor Lamb's death.[2] Thear wear last week some 40ty honest people sent to prison by the bishop, pretending they wear at a conventicle in Black Fryers, they founde them at prayers not exercise [but onely pretending their being thear was but to stay untell the church doares wear open *struck through*]. Heer is much speach of the bravery of a porter that hath taken a brave house and hath his coach and 4 horses. The Lord Mayor examined him how he gott that wealth; he answerd nothing. Then the lords of the counsell gott out of him that he being the Pope's brother, borne in Essex, goodman Linge's sonnes, was maintained by him and tempted much to have come over to him. These 2 brothers being ship boyes to a French pirate the porter gott meanes to come againe into England, but the other being a witty boy was sould to a coortier in Paris who, travelling to Florence, thear bestowed his boy of a great man who when he dyed tooke such affection to this boy that changeing his name to his owne, left his estate to him and so in time grew [*f. 30b*] a Florentine, a cardinall and now pope, and the grethest linguest for the Latine that ever was.

I had thus farr written on Thursday last, thinking that day to have sent Smyth doune to have waited on you, but Lucy falling extream sick made me stay him, fearing it might have prooved the small poxe or messells, which I did verilye expect; but I bless God, not sparing for speedy attendance with docter Alston and Doctor Foxe daily coming to her,[3] she is now mended so well of her feavour that we hope to have her abroad the later end of this week. And I hope the end of next week we shall waite upon you, for it troubles me much thus longe to leave you. I beseech you rendor my sister Everett my best thanks for staying soe kindly with you, and hope she will not leave you tell I come. And so with my prayers for your health I comitt you to the almighty's protection

Your most respective daughter to command

Judith Barrington

Tuesday, Whitsunweek[4]

A neighbour of mine in Hertfordsheer, one Mrs Kimpton, of some 800[li] a year her husband's estate, sufred a great estate [*sic*] disgrace some fortnight agone in Hide Park, whear the queen, as she thought,

[1] See letter 237, n.l.

[2] John Lambe, astrologer and protegé of Buckingham, had been fatally injured by a London mob in 1628. *D.N.B.*; Birch, i. 363-4.

[3] Perhaps Sir Edward Alston and Simeon Foxe.

[4] Whit Sunday was 20 May.

espyed one of her gounes that she had lately lost on Mrs Kimpton's back and so sent to her to kno whear she had itt. She being out of countenance at such a speach would not answear, which made it the more suspitious, so that at last she was sent to a justice of peace whear she answered also crossly. But at last the truth was knowen. The kinge cryed her pardon, would have her brought to kiss the queen's hands, but she would not. He offred to knight her husband but she refused that also, but parted [*f. 31*] fairly, a poor recompence for so publike a disgrace; yet the kinge did nobly in itt.

I hope I shall beg your favour that if my sonnes follow not thear bookes well and carry them selves not well in my absence to you, or others that you will please to use your authority to chide them. I heer they goe much abroad to neighbours houses to fishing; I should be sorry if the eagernes of that sport should make them the less minde thear bookes, which must not be neglected.

Endorsed (*f. 31b*): To my much honored mother the lady Barrington at Hatfeeld this

248 *Sir Thomas Barrington, 25 May 1632* (*2646, f. 34*)

Madam   Your affectionate expressions in your letters doe much animate me in my suffrings and putt a stronger armor upon me, able to resist troubles with patience, for next under God's love to me nothing doth so much affect me as the vew of freinds respect towards me and myne, and the neear the relations are the more the comfort to me, I thanke my God. My daughter is much better then she was I prayse God, and I hope he will be pleased to hear yours and owr prayers for the graunting her former health by his blessing. The rest of us are all as yet resonable well in health, I prayse God, and haste downe unto yow that we may the better preserve owr healthes by the blessing of God as much as we can for owr busines, which my Lord of Holland indevors in a verie freindly way to settle on my part; but I cannot yet give yow any perticular or perfect account, so soone as I can I will. The corant of London runs so contrarye and diverse courses as that we know not which way to fasten on certaine truthes. Now at my Lord of Holland's the overthrow (which all the best reporters in London were possessed with all) is supprest, and the settled report only come to theise perticular truthes: the burning of som 80 villages in Bavaria and the king's march to Passau, in hope to take the passage, and the Duke of Bavaria makes like hast to prevent him. Papenhaim is now sayd to be broken forth of Stode with som 14 horss, and he so escaped but his army cutt in peices, and he is reported to be made the generall of the Bavarian's armye.[1] The king of Sweden is sayed by som to have an inflamation in his legg caused by the heate of his bodye distempred by the verye ayre of the greate shott which killed his horss under him, but this is not yet assured. Letters are dayly expected, and then yow shall heear more, God willing, meane while, the French king is assuredly gone to Loraine whare Mounsieur and the [*f. 34b*] Duke of Loraine are ready of meet him with a greate army, and Mounsieur le Force is by the king commaunded to beleaguer som of the duke's tounes; meane while, the ambassador com to owr king from Fraunce, Mourseiur St Choumont[2] (a greate man), hath now deleverd his message consisting of 3 perticulars:

1. The one is to give satisfaction to owr king for the late beheading Moanilhiac the marishall of Fraunce (in which daunger is the governor of Callis now comitted for offring the toune by intelligence to Mounsieur, the king's brother)
2. The 2cond is to satisfye the reson of his bringing an armye into Piccardy and neear Callis
3. The 3d to desyre the assistance of som of owr king's shipping for som designe by sea.

Owr king hath given way to the rayseing of 12 men for the assistance of the emperor of Russia, who rayses a greate armye for to side with the king of Sweden, which my lord Goearing tould me this day he had much adoe to procure by reson of the strong opposition of the Spanish partye. Colonell Fleetwood,[3] being in raiseing allso a regement for the king of Sweden, heard that there was one who had raysed som forces for the Archdutches who were on shippboord, whereupon fearing that his company would fall [*f. 35*] short he procured warrant from the lords of the councell and so gott all the Archdutches' men away to his regiment, which wondrously pleases in the toune. My cosen Cromwell condemned is reprived and generally reputed a guiltless poore youth, and this evening my Lord of Holland endevors his farther reprive and pardon, when God bless him.[4] My cozen Dunche's sister Ann she hath now maryed an apothecarye's sonn who hath but 700[ls] per annum assured him. Thus humblye desyring yowr prayers for my daughter Lucye and us all, with harty and obliged thankes for your love expressed so much to my selfe and all myne, I comitt us all to God and am ever (praying for owr comfortable meeting with yow)

Your most obedient and loving sonn   Thomas Barrington

[1] See letter 246, n. 2.
[2] The Marquis de St Chaumont. Gardiner, vii. 198-9.
[3] George Fleetwood first took a regiment to Gustav Adolf in 1630. *D.N.B.*
[4] See letters 237, n.l., and 247.

Holborn, London, May 25, 1632

[*No endorsement*]

249   *Thomas Saunders*[1] *to Lady Judith Barrington, August 1632*

(*2646, f. 38*)

Maddam   That your ladishipp may have mee related from mine
owne mouth and perceive (if I have not already made demonstration
sufficient) of my desire to peace, bee pleased to know that I refuse to
subscribe to none of the propositions I made to yow at London if yett
yow will accept of them, namely 28^{li} per annum to plough what I lust
for 6 yeares, or 24^{li} (I meane both wayes for privi tiths and all) to
plough but 80 acres at most, or if I plough above to pay for more at 2
and 4, howsoever to pay for soe much though I plowed less, as I
praesume your ladishipp doth well remember. But wheras Mr Kendall
your servant would now have it supposed that yow offred and I
refused my tiths for yeares at 2 and 4, yow may remember that I offred
to bee your tenaunt upon those tearmes, and if that bee now your
mind I am still in the same, which by these lines I assure yow, and wee
shall need noe farther care (for for my selfe I avowe it). I never did
nor will goe from my word (howsoever I have been dealt with that
way) and if there shall follow any inconvenience or less profitt to yow
in your tithing herafter, I protest that I am innocent and have persued
all the waies to peace I know, as the world may witness. And thus
with my humble service to Sir Thomas Barrington and your selfe I
subscribe mee
             Yours to bee commaunded   Thomas Saunders

Your ladishipp may bee pleased to lett mee know with speed whether
I shall bee your tenant, or else it wil bee time to looke after your tiths,
for harvest is at hand.

[*f. 38b*] Maddam   Since this letter was sealed I had the occasion
to breake it up and add this postill at the perswasion of Mr Cotton,
which I leave to the relation of your servant at large, that if your
ladishipp would bee pleased to graunt mee a lease of all tiths, that is
to saye of corne, grass and all other privie tithes of my grounds for 21
yeares at the rate of 28^{li} per annum, that then I will be content to
graunt yow (or your assigns) a waye over my grounds during the
remainder of your lease to your owne content, or if I shall not performe

---

[1] See letter 158.

the covenants and paye the rent aforsaid, or my assignes on my part,
that then it may bee in your power to use the way soe graunted at any
time during the tearme of 21 yeares also. And if it bee farther desired
that, upon your (or your heires) taking a new lease from the colledge,
the same way should continue to your use, I will graunt it if I may, or
my heires or assignes may have a new lease also of the like continuance
and upon the same tearmes I offer for this and upon the same covenants. And this I doe always except, that nothing I have written herein
shall bee any wayes binding to mee or mine or herafter bee pleaded in
law against mee if I did acknowledge it to bee due, but as meerly
gratuitous, unless your ladishipp bee pleased to admitt of this my offer
(in praesent and in future) who have ever unfeinedly desired to doe to
Sir Thomas Barrington and your selfe all the respects due to yow from
　　　Your humble servant　　　Thomas Saunders

Endorsed (f. 39b): To the right worshipfill the Ladie Judith Barrington
this with all due respect give at Hatfeild Broad Oake
[*In hand of Lady Judith Barrington:*] Mr Thomas Sanders to hire the
tythe of Beechewood, August 1632.

250　[*Lady Judith Barrington to Thomas Saunders,*] *12 August, 1632*
　　　　　　　　　　　　　　　　　　　　　　　(2646, f. 40)

Sir　　　I have receaved your letter and take itt kindly, and shall be
ready on my part to meet you halfe waye in all reasonable wayes of
neighbourhood and frendship, and I doe much forgett my selfe if I
have either in word or deed shewed the contrary. My onely aime is to
setle my sonne's estate soe as I may give him an other day a good
account, for the effecting wherof in your tythes I am to regard 2 things,
first the gaininge of a lawfull wave, by right and not upon curtesie,
and next if I lett a lease of itt for 21 years I doe stand upon 30¹ rent
yearly, and I think if this wear your owen case you would wonder that
any body should take exception at you to make the best of your owen
[much more to cross you in itt *struck through*]. I did think I had made
you soe reasonable an offer at our last parlying aboute this in London
that if you had had any inclination to have been teneant for itt you
would never have broake of for not having liberty to plow 10 akers
more then we agreed for and more then you wear to pay for. But I
love not to repeate any thing that may cause new disputes. The time
of harvest is now so instantly at hande that [now as farr as I see it's to
late to do anythinge *struck through*] I can doe no other but setle now to
the coorse of inning of this tyth my selfe, although I finde I am putt
upon by many streites and inconveniencies unexpectedly. Mr Plum-

tree's barne I was suer of and had hyred it of his brother, but I perceave he his sencible of the ill will of a neighbour, he fears some actions may for my sake be served against him, and God forbid I should buy my advantages by my frends' loss. Mr Fookes [*f. 40b*] would willingly, and another of Market Street, have erned some mony of me with thear carts, but at last I finde they dare not for your ill will. The usuall waye that hath ever been knowen for carrying in and out from your grounds is now ditched up[1] and I can heer of none but upon curtesie and you know how [dangerous a coorse this *struck through*] much it concerns mee to stande upon this in respect of all the tythes of Flamsteed, that would be but in an ill condition by this example, soe that what I am putt upon now is upon necessity. But I could have wished I might have mett with more assurances that your deeds had tended to a more curteous waye with mee [they would worke more *struck through*]. But heatherto I am willing to make the best of all [what I shall do heer after I know not *struck through*], onely thus much, I could wish I might finde encouragement now for dealinge with you heerafter, but I assuer you it will never be the way [to pull me upon you *struck through*] by necessitatinge me to charges and trouble. And thus with all good wishes and kinde sallutations to you and your wife, I rest

> Your respective frend

Hatfeeld, August 12, 1632

Endorsed (*f. 41b*): My answeer of Mr Thomas Sanders letter of August 1632 to have a lawful way allowed me by diew and not curtesy.

251   *Sir Gilbert Gerard, 28 September 1632*   (*2646, f. 42*)

Good madam   You kind letter I resceived this night, and doe acknowledge my selfe exceedingly bound unto you for your love, both in your willingnesse to accept of such poore entertainment as my house can afford you as in your care of my daughter. For your coming, as no thing can bee more comfortable unto me then the enjoying your good company, so it would be as grievouse unto mee that you should hazard your heelth in adventuring to come hither when you are not able, therefore although the weather fall out very seasonable for you, yet

---

[1] The tithe wheat was collected in 1632, with a continuing saga during August of ditches filled in and re-dug, fences thrown down and pigs turned loose into the corn. The dispute broke out again in an even more violent form the next year. E.R.O., D/DBa E60.

dare not I advise you what to doe, but will pray to God to direct you to doe what may be best for your health. And for my daughter, the estate you wright of is fare beyond what I must expect, therfore I cannot except unto it, but what the man is I desire to know, which is first to be considered of, for if he bee one that favors God, and one that can like of my daughter, although his estate be fare short of what you wright of I shalbe redie to streine my selfe beyond my abilitie for my daughter's advancment. And I beseech you to give my sister thankes for her love herein. So wishing you all hapines I rest

    Your dutifull sonne   G. Gerard

Flambards, 28 September, 1632

Endorsed (*f. 43b*): To my honorable mother the Lady Jone Barrington at Hatfeild be thaese given

252 *Lady Judith Barrington to John Kendal, 25 October 1632 (2646, f. 46)*

John Kendall   Guessing your master wilbe in London the later end of this week I have sent him all the papers I have of his Caresbrook Park[1] busines tyed up togeather, but I doubt the cheefe noate that he made for my lord Treasurer is lost, for I rem[ember] he read to me a perticular that was more meth[odical] then any of thease. Gett him quickly to peru[se] [*torn*] wherin he findes anything failinge he may [*torn*] he hath leasure make all thinges exact and [*torn*] of great consequence, and therfore will require consideration over and over againe, and your master had need be importunately putt in minde of itt. If your urdgeinge doth noe good, gett Sir John Bowcer[2] to call on him, for though your master chides us all, yet his good and creditt lyes soe much at stake in this that those that loves him must not care for his anger. I doubt he wilbe slow in goeing to my lord Treasurer and my Lord of Holland. I would not have him complement awaye his 300[1] charges that he hath been att over and above the 2500[1] for the purchase. We have noe reason to be looser 300[1]; it was soe much our charges at Easter last, and now being halfe a year more we are by interest out more mony. I see no reason but why it should be considered off, for it's at least a 100[1] more now, besides the loss of our

---

[1] Sir Thomas Barrington had spent some time in London earlier in the year extricating himself from the unfortunate purchase of Carisbrooke Park, made in 1631. The business was finally cleared up in Dec. 1632. Introduction, 4, 5.

conveniency if we part from that park. For this time I committ you to God.

October 25, 1632

Your loving mist[ress]   Judith Barring[ton]

Remember often to put your master in minde that he must be carefull of those businesses my Lady Devonsheer trusteth him withall. I have had a letter last week to call upon him from Mrs Nicolls.[1]

Heer is a patern of a good colerd cloth and lace for a suite for Jack Barrington. My French taylor last week tooke heer measure of him, and I hope it will fitt him better then Pickering did; worss hee cannot. 3 laces in a seame I heer now is the best fashion, except we would bestow all lace, which wee will not, and besides that is to costly. Thear needs no buttons on the armes or back for this winter, and the sooner he hath itt the better, for you know his need.

[f. 47b] It seemes Smyth spake to Natt Lytton to enquire if Sir Thomas Walsingham's cooke went awaye, therfore now tell Natt he need not saye any thinge, for that party is provided. Aboute Natt's binding prentice, Smyth spake it seems to his brother Jonathan to see it done, but I heer nothing, therfore delay itt no longer but see itt done, and pay the mony being 5[l] and if you can gett him to be soe bound as at the end of his years he may be a free man of London, it would do well. They will not care how longe he is unbound, being to thear advantage. John, except thear be sume more need then I see to have Smyth come to London, I should be glad to keep him at home to keep accounts, therfore if your master should talke of sending for him, you may do well [torn] him off. And keep noe more horses in London then needs [torn] its chargeable.

I hope Mr Pickering hath fitted your master somewhear with a lodgeing, to whome I writt [torn] that he should send you word to Harrow, whear [torn]

Heer is the key to your master's trunk, which comes to London by the first next week to Mr Pickering's house. In it is his cyzers and curling iron, and all that George Kinge could think off usefull. Hear is Rowland's come case to fitt with a glass, combe and combe brush and a pair of sicers.[2]

For John Kendall this

---

[1] Bourchier.
[2] Eg. 2646, ff. 44–5 contain an extensive list in Lady Judith Barrington's hand of other such matters to be attended to in London during the Michaelmas term.

BIOGRAPHICAL APPENDIX

In most instances a brief outline only is given for those who are the subject of an entry in either *D.N.B.* or Keeler. Separate entries for wives are given to record details of a previous marriage. The writers of only a small number of letters are identified in a note to the earliest of their letters.

John Barrington

Youngest son of Sir Francis and Lady Joan Barrington. In April 1621 he wrote from La Rochelle asking his father's permission to marry Marie Pinaule, a protestant woman of 'meanes and parentadg'. By 1624 they were married and John was a merchant there. A debt contracted by John in La Rochelle was discharged by Sir Francis in October 1626, only a few days before his imprisonment on the charges arising from the forced loan. John Barrington took part in the abortive mission to relieve the besieged protestants of La Rochelle in the late summer of 1628. On his return he sought further military employment and eventually secured a commission in Lord Vere's army for the Netherlands. He died there early in 1631. His wife is not mentioned in the correspondence at this time, but she subsequently lived in London and Essex on good terms with the Barringtons. When she died in 1681 she left money in France and in England.

Table 3; Eg. 2644, ff. 194, 274; E.R.O., D/DBa L15 and A15, ff. 15–18, 44b, 57b; Eg. 2646, f. 86; P.R.O., P.C.C., will of Mary Barrington, 1681 f. 22.

Lady Judith Barrington

Second wife of Sir Thomas Barrington (see below). Daughter of Sir Rowland Lytton of Knebworth, Hertfordshire. Married in 1612 to George Smith (knighted 1616) of Hertfordshire, by whom she had two sons. Smith died in debt in 1620, leaving Lady Judith to administer the estate and the wardship of their sons. Her marriage to Sir Thomas Barrington in 1624 was 'a very fit match for yeares, bloud estate, conformite of studies (somewhat poeticall) ...' There was an unfounded rumour that she was to marry the poet Thomas Carew. In the 1630s she supported the work of the poet Francis Quarles. Sir Dudley Carleton, Lord Dorchester, was her cousin, an older man with whom she appears to have been something of a favourite as a child. She died in 1657.

The Letters of John Chamberlain, ed. E. N. McLure (Philadelphia, 1939), ii. *passim*; A. Searle, *Stuart Essex* (Chelmsford, 1974); P.R.O., P.C.C. wills, 1657 f. 362.

Robert Barrington

Second son of Sir Francis and Lady Joan Barrington. Lived at Hatfield Bury in Hatfield Broad Oak. Married to Dorothy, daughter of Sir Thomas and Lady Mary Eden of Ballingdon Hall in Sudbury, on the Essex-Suffolk border. M.P. with Sir Thomas Barrington, for New-town, Isle of Wight, 1628–9. Supported puritan clergy and invested money in projects in New England. Died late 1641 or early 1642.

Letter 6; Eg. 2646, ff. 163, 169, 182, and 2650, f. 354.

Sir Thomas Barrington

Eldest son of Sir Francis and Lady Joan Barrington. Knighted in his father's lifetime, probably before 1621; succeded to the baronetcy at his father's death in July 1628. Married first Frances, daughter of John Gobert of Northamptonshire, 1611; second, Judith, widow of Sir George Smith of Hertfordshire, 1624. All his children were by his first marriage.

Sir Thomas first became a J.P. in June 1624, was put out of the commission on the loan issue in 1626, reinstated in 1628 and remained on the bench until his death in September 1644. From at least 1634 he was also a justice for the borough of Saffron Walden. He probably first became a deputy lieutenant in the year following his father's death; by 1635 he was the senior D.L. in the county. This role in county affairs led directly to his leadership and co-ordination of the county committee during the civil war. Sir Thomas was admitted as a member of the Providence Island company in 1631.

Sir Thomas was an active M.P. (and a prolific parliamentary diarist). He may first have sat in the Commons in 1614 and was certainly a member of every subsequent parliament during his lifetime.

Sir Thomas was on occasion slow to act, but he devoted immense, if sporadic, energy to his work in the Commons and Essex in the years immediately before his death. He showed considerable courage in the face of a Colchester mob in 1642, when their zeal against the royalist Sir John Lucas threatened to get out of hand. He was a busy committee man in the Long Parliament, a frequent messenger from Commons to Lords, presented his county's desires to the house in the form of petitions, and was at times sent down into Essex expressly to explain parliament's needs. He was also a lay member of the Westminster Assembly, although one of those who delayed before taking the Covenant.

By his own confession Sir Thomas was inclined to melancholy and the letters reveal lengthy spells of illness. His temperament had its artistic side. He was already interested in music when at Cambridge in 1601. Some of his verses have survived. His bookseller's bill, besides religious tracts and law books, includes works of history, travel and literature. He was one of the supporters of the educationalist Samuel Hartlib. The almost distracted depths of his feelings for his second wife are clear from his letters to his parents; he was reported 'so inamored of her and her virtues that she may make her own conditions'.

Keeler (Mrs Keeler's suggestion that in 1628 Sir Thomas contemplated going abroad as a soldier arises from letter 14 being ascribed in H.M.C., 7th *Report* to Sir Thomas rather than to John Barrington.); G.E.C., *Baronetage*; B.L., Harl. 5190, ff. 109, 111b; E.R.O., D/DHt T126/40; McLure, ii. 587; P.R.O., Index 4211, f. 168v; E.R.O., T/A 401/2, p. 269; Quintrell, 126; E.R.O., T/B 211/1, Q/SBa 2/28 and Q/SR *passim* (I am indebted to Dr Quintrell for these references and the discussion of their significance); *Commons Journals, 1640-4, passim*; A. Searle, 'Sir Thomas Barrington in London, 1640-44', *Essex Journal*, ii (1967), 35-41, 63-70; Bodl., MS. Eng. Misc. e. 262; M. E. Bohannon, 'A London Bookseller's Bill: 1635-1639', *The Library*, ser. iv, xviii (1938); G. H. Turnbull, *Hartlib, Dury and Comenius* (Liverpool, 1947), 27, 77; Eg. 2644, ff. 16, 209-220; McLure, ii. 572; Smith, 67.

Sir John Bourchier

Regicide, son of Sir William Bourchier of Benningbrough Hall, Yorkshire, and Katherine Barrington, sister of Sir Francis. William Bourchier had been declared insane at his father's death in 1598, leading Francis Barrington to petition Burghley and the Court of Wards about his sister's jointure.

Table 1; *D.N.B.*; V.C.H., *Yorkshire*, ii. 162-3; E.R.O., D/DBa F12.

William Chantrell

Rector of the Barrington living of Walkington in Yorkshire from 1616 to 1643. While there he had occasional minor brushes with the ecclesiastical authorities, suggesting the puritanism to be expected of a Barrington appointment. His earlier career is not entirely clear. He was at Trinity and Emmanuel Colleges, Cambridge, and proceded M.A. in 1598. He may have been vicar of Cardington, Bedfordshire 1610-1614, and of Offley, Hertfordshire, 1614-1616, but his relationship with Lady Joan Barrington suggests that he was at some time at Hatfield as chaplain.

Marchant, 238; Venn; Introduction, 13, 14.

Sir Richard Everard

Son of Hugh Everard, of Langleys in Great Waltham, Essex. Married to Joan, second daughter of Sir Francis and Lady Joan Barrington. Everard was created baronet in January, 1629, during his father's life-time. Unlike the other Barrington sons-in-law, he did not sit in parliament and appears not to have been a J.P. until the civil war. He was sheriff of Essex 1644-5 and is named in committee ordinances throughout the Interregnum from 1643 onwards. He died *c.* 1680.

Table 3; letter 31; G.E.C., *Baronetage*; C. H. Firth and R. S. Rait, *Acts and Ordinances of the Interregnum* (1911); E.R.O., D/AER 23/352.

Sir Gilbert Gerard

Of Flambards, Harrow-on-the-Hill, Middlesex, baronet, J.P., M.P., husband of Sir Francis and Lady Joan Barrington's daughter Mary. Lady Joan stayed with the Gerards at Harrow from June 1629 to July 1630 and Sir Gilbert helped sort out her affairs after the death of Sir Francis. Gerard was an active opponent of the crown during the 1620s and 1630s.

Keeler.

Sir Francis Harris

Son of Edward Harris of Southminster, Essex, knighted in 1608. His mother was half-sister to Sir Francis Barrington. He was a regular pensioner of Lady Joan and his letters express by turns his financial plight and a desire to use his many connexions to help the Barringtons.

Table 1; Introduction, 20; Shaw, ii. 145.

James Harrison

Lecturer at Hatfield Broad Oak from 1626 until his death in 1642 or 1643. Harrison was a Yorkshireman who went from Sedburgh School to St John's College, Cambridge in 1588. (His son later attended the same college.) He was curate of the Essex parish of Layer de la Hay, probably from as early as 1611. Although his function at Hatfield was to be as 'town' lecturer, the Barringtons were chiefly responsible for choosing him and his relationship with the family became close; for a time at least he acted as their chaplain as well and when Lady Joan was away at Christmas 1628 he and his wife took care of her favourite niece Joan Gerard. His relations with the vicar of Hatfield were occasionally strained and he was in trouble with the ecclesiastical authorities on at least one occasion, but there was no interruption to his activities as lecturer.

Introduction, 13, 20; *Sedburgh School Register, 1546–1909* (1909), 87;
J. E. B. Mayor, *Admissions to the College of St. John Cambridge* (1882),
78 and T. Baker, *History of the College of St. John Cambridge*, ed. Mayor
(1896), 432; E.R.O., D/ACV 4, where 'Harris' appears as
incumbent of the donative curacy of Layer de la Hay, and D/DBa
A15, f. 2; Eg. 2644, f. 230.

Sir William Masham

Of Otes in High Laver, Essex, baronet, J.P., M.P., second husband
of Sir Francis and Lady Joan Barrington's daughter Elizabeth.
Masham resisted the forced loan and was imprisoned in the Fleet in
1626 at the same time as his father-in-law was held in the
Marshalsea.

Table 3; Keeler; P. Laslett, 'Masham of Otes', *History Today*, iii
(1953), 535–43.

Lady Elizabeth Masham

Wife of the above. First married to Sir James Altham of Mark Hall,
Essex (died 1610), by whom she had a daughter, Joan, who
subsequently married Oliver St. John.

Table 3.

Sir William Meux

Son of Sir John Meux of Kingston, Isle of Wight. Knighted in 1607.
Married to Winifred, eldest daughter of Sir Francis and Lady Joan.
A William Masham was M.P. for the borough of Newtown in the
island, where one seat was normally held by a Barrington candidate,
in 1603–4. In 1628, the year before his father died, Meux was
offered, but refused, a commission as deputy lieutenant. In the 1630s
he acted with the leading gentry of the island on a number of issues;
Sir John Oglander thought him 'as well qualified a gentleman as any
our county bred, but of no spirit – a very coward'. He died in 1638.
His son John sat as a member for Newtown in the Long Parliament,
but, after being created a baronet in 1641, was disabled in 1644 and
sat in the assembly at Oxford.

Keeler; Table 3; Shaw, ii. 142; *M. of P.*, i. 445; V.C.H., *Hampshire*,
v. 148, 250; Bamford, 31, 54, 67, 160.

Ezekiel Rogers

Rector of the Barrington living of Rowley in Yorkshire from 1621
until his suspension for non-conformity by Richard Neile,
archbishop of York, in 1636. In 1638 he resigned the living and went

to New England, where he was one of the founders of Rowley, Massachusetts. He was the son of Richard Rogers, lecturer at Wethersfield in Essex, and was at Christ's College, Cambridge, whence he was made M.A. in 1608. He became chaplain to the Barrington family almost immediately, for, by his own account, he held that position for twelve years. The strongest relationship he formed then was with Lady Joan. But he was also in close sympathy with Sir Thomas Barrington's first wife and was later to remind Sir Thomas that he had been of considerable service to him as well – 'witnesse at my first coming my watching with you in the time of your melancholy, and risings at midnight to cherish and comfort you'. But Sir Thomas and Rogers later became estranged, so that although Neile allowed Rogers to keep the income from his benefice while he was suspended, Sir Thomas was anxious to use the opportunity to give the living to the current chaplain at Hatfield, Thomas White. White was presented when Rogers eventually resigned, but the exact terms continued to be a subject of acrimonious dispute between Sir Thomas and Rogers. Roger's subsequent career in America is well documented; he died in 1661.

D.N.B.; Venn; Introduction, 13; Eg. 2644, f. 196 and 2646, f. 104; Mather, *Magnalia*, 408–413; Marchant, 96–102; E. A. E. and E. M. A. Jewett, *Rowley, Massachusetts ..., 1639–1850* (Rowley, Mass., 1946), 30, 31.

INDEX

Figures in *italics* refer to the numbers of the letters, those in roman to page numbers.